JACK DEVINE is a thirty-two-year veteran of the Central Intelligence Agency who served at the pinnacle of his career as the CIA's top spymaster—head of the CIA's operations outside the United States, in which capacity he had supervisory authority over thousands of CIA employees involved in sensitive missions throughout the world. He is also a founding partner and the president of The Arkin Group, an international risk consulting and intelligence firm. He lives in New York City with his wife, Pat.

GOOD HUNTING

GOOD HUNTING

An American Spymaster's Story

JACK DEVINE

with Vernon Loeb

PICADOR

A Sarah Crichton Book   Farrar, Straus and Giroux   New York

GOOD HUNTING. Copyright © 2014 by Jack Devine. All rights reserved. Printed in the United States of America. For information, address Picador, 175 Fifth Avenue, New York, N.Y. 10010.

www.picadorusa.com
www.twitter.com/picadorusa • www.facebook.com/picadorusa
picadorbookroom.tumblr.com

Picador® is a U.S. registered trademark and is used by Farrar, Straus and Giroux under license from Pan Books Limited.

For book club information, please visit www.facebook.com/picadorbookclub or e-mail marketing @picadorusa.com.

Designed by Jonathan D. Lippincott

The Library of Congress has cataloged the Farrar, Straus and Giroux edition as follows:

Devine, Jack, 1940–
     Good hunting : an American spymaster's story / Jack Devine with Vernon Loeb.
        p. cm.
     ISBN 978-0-374-13032-9 (hardcover)
     ISBN 978-1-4299-4417-5 (e-book)
     1. Devine, Jack, 1940–   2. United States. Central Intelligence Agency—Officials and employees—Biography.   3. Spies—United States—Biography.   4. Intelligence officers—United States—Biography.   5. United States. Central Intelligence Agency—History—20th century.   6. Espionage, American—History—20th century.   7. United States—Foreign relations—1945–1989.   8. United States—Foreign relations—1989–   I. Loeb, Vernon. II. Title.
     JK468.I6 D48 2014
     327.12730092—dc23
     [B]

                                                                                              2014001349

Picador Paperback ISBN 978-1-250-06963-4

Picador books may be purchased for educational, business, or promotional use. For information on bulk purchases, please contact the Macmillan Corporate and Premium Sales Department at 1-800-221-7945, extension 5442, or write to specialmarkets@macmillan.com.

First published in the United States by Farrar, Straus and Giroux

First Picador Edition: May 2015

10   9   8   7   6   5   4   3   2   1

For Pat, without whom this story would not have been possible

and

for all the CIA personnel who have served their country gallantly

Contents

GOOD HUNTING

Introduction

There's a model truck on the windowsill of my office overlooking Central Park that takes me back to the border towns in Pakistan with just a glimpse. Very few of my clients ever comment on it. They come to my firm in Midtown in New York City with all sorts of thorny problems and ask for help figuring out exactly what is going on. They're usually doing business in an environment, or with people, they don't fully understand, and they want to know the risks involved and how best to proceed. The truck, in fact, symbolizes a life in the intelligence world, and in turn the reason they have come to my office in the first place. Charlie Wilson gave it to me as a reminder of the guns and ammunition we moved across the border into Afghanistan. Charlie was a Democratic congressman from Texas who developed an intense interest in the Afghan mujahideen and their determined opposition to the Soviet Union's occupation of their country in the 1980s. I ran the last, and largest, covert operation of the Cold War as head of the Central Intelligence Agency's Afghan Task Force.

Afghanistan will always loom large in my mind as the crowning accomplishment of my past work as an intelligence officer—and one of the greatest challenges ahead for the CIA and the American intelligence community. I'm in the corporate intelligence business now, commanding a distributed network of hundreds of contacts who in turn have hundreds of sources they can tap into around the world. It's fair to say that I can put a tail on someone just about anywhere in the world faster than most spy agencies. I've assessed the risk of a chem-bio attack at Madison

Square Garden, vetted the prospective owner of an NBA franchise, foiled a cyberthief in China, and freed trucks in Moscow belonging to one of the world's great magicians. My work obviously colors the way I think about the future of U.S. intelligence, where I still occasionally serve in an advisory capacity, having kept my clearances active. Of course, it's my thirty-two-year career at the CIA that has made me the intelligence professional I am, even though I scrupulously avoid contact with former agents, sources, or foreign intelligence officers I knew on the job.

When I walked away from the CIA in 1998 with nothing but a government pension, I thought I had my feelings under control. I thought I was done. But over the years, I've never quite been able to let go. This book is my best shot at sorting out my complex emotions and experiences. I served during the middle years of the CIA—from Nixon to Clinton—and know that period of CIA history intimately. I lived it, I breathed it, and I loved it. During those times, we ended many of our cables with the phrase "GOOD HUNTING," which referred to the covert, relentless pursuit of our enemies and sources of intelligence. And so it has been the "hunting" conducted by U.S. intelligence officers and their diplomatic and military brethren that led us to victory in the Cold War, as well as to the dismantling of al-Qaeda. Yet I still feel the Central Intelligence Agency, caricatured and lionized by Hollywood, remains one of the least-understood instruments of the U.S. government. Agency critics tend to focus on failed operations that are exposed or compromised, either by screwups in execution, leaks in Washington, or the release or declassification of once-secret cables. But these accounts typically shed little light on either the CIA's internal culture and discipline or the professionalism among its officers. I don't want to hide behind the cliché often cited by those who've run the CIA that our relatively few failures become public while our many successes remain secret. But there is more than a little truth to that. In over thirty years, I never saw or participated in a "rogue operation"—something the CIA executed on its own without explicit approval from the White House. My seven overseas postings, interspersed with headquarters assignments, also made me understand how valuable it is that the CIA plants its flag in almost every country. The president and other members of the U.S. national security community cannot know when a country will suddenly take on strategic importance. Grounding in foreign capitals, and an ability to influence events through covert means, is critical for Washington. No one can provide those things better than the CIA.

I want to set the record straight, to the best of my ability, for history's sake, about the Agency's essential intelligence contributions to national security. And I want to talk about the future of the CIA post-Iraq and -Afghanistan, with the nation fatigued by large ground wars but still in need of protection against an array of enemies, from al-Qaeda to the Mexican drug cartels, from Iran to North Korea. Like it or not, a powerful intelligence service capable of stealing secrets from our adversaries and mounting effective covert operations is, for the United States, an imperative of modern statecraft. I hope, after many years of war, we do not come to resemble those whom T. S. Eliot wrote about at the end of World War I in his poem "The Hollow Men." In it, he describes leaders as "shape without form, shade without color, paralyzed force, gesture without motion." I saw few such people in the CIA. The model truck on my windowsill speaks to my belief in the efficacy of covert action. It is true that the CIA's biggest mistakes involved covert action. But it is also true that these mistakes, without exception, also involved operations carried out at the behest of presidents pursuing flawed policies. And for every covert action that failed spectacularly, there have been others that enabled presidents and policy makers to achieve ends in the nation's interest with an unseen hand, which is almost always preferable to a heavy footprint. Through hard experience, including running all CIA operations in the mid-1990s, I understand the difference between good covert action that is effective and representative of the best of American values, and bad covert action that is poorly conceived and destined to fail. I have developed over the years a set of principles designed to ensure the former and prevent the latter. It's time that the policy makers and Congress conduct a comprehensive review of covert action, its appropriate use, and general principles of operation so we can come to a better appreciation of what the CIA can do for the nation at this complex moment in our history. Needless to say, this can't become a public debate about ongoing operations that would jeopardize our people, allies, and national interests. Such a discussion can more appropriately be handled through the existing oversight process. But it is nevertheless imperative.

I have been engaged in all aspects of the spy business. I've written in invisible ink and run black bag jobs. I have argued against flawed coup plots and directed the largest covert action of the Cold War. I spoke out inside the CIA against the operation in the mid-1980s to send missiles to Iran (to no avail) and ran the clandestine service during the drawdown after the Cold War and the aftermath of two devastating betrayals, one by the CIA mole Aldrich Ames, and the other by the FBI turncoat Robert Hanssen. I am writing this memoir now to demonstrate the necessity of using the CIA and covert action to their fullest potential at this critical period of history. If not, we will have lost the opportunity to exploit these important tools of statecraft, with potentially grave consequences. After spending billions on intelligence since the 9/11 terror attacks, I still believe we're underinvesting in spies: instead we have been militarizing intelligence in a way that ultimately will detract from our ability to engage in espionage and conduct covert action. I'm not an apologist for the CIA, and I have publicly criticized certain of its practices. Thomas Polgar, the legendary CIA station chief in Saigon, was a straight shooter and never afraid to speak up on matters of principle. His assessments in Vietnam—what was known and not known during the war—were hugely controversial. I asked him once why he was willing to take on such issues. "When you get to the level I'm at, you have an obligation to stand up for what you believe," he said. When I was deputy director of operations, I passed his remark on to departing station chiefs before they took up their new assignments abroad, because I do believe it's true. This was a trait that was encouraged and fostered by many others as well, in the formative years of my career at the CIA. I hope this trait has continued to be emphasized to this day.

In this vein, I was troubled by torture and waterboarding and other extrajudicial tactics that became part of the Agency's operational program in the years after 9/11, and made my view clear to the CIA leadership and to the media without compromising any sources or methods. I should note that I am fiercely nonpartisan—as were most of those I worked with at Langley. It is essential to maintain balance and objectivity in the intelligence business. Objectivity's value to the system is often not fully appreciated. Likewise, I found the attempt to politicize intelligence on weapons of mass destruction in Iraq deeply disturbing.

The most glaring example was related to a questionable source known as "Curveball." The CIA had given this oddly apt code name to a young Iraqi chemical engineer named Ahmed Hassan Mohammed, according to *Curveball: Spies, Lies, and the Con Man Who Caused a War*, by Bob Drogin, a veteran reporter for the *Los Angeles Times*. Curveball surfaced in Munich in 1999 seeking asylum, and fed German intelligence a fabricated story about Saddam Hussein's secret network of biological weapons factories, which could be moved from place to place on trailer trucks. This unverified information was sent to the White House, despite concerns about Curveball's reliability voiced by a cadre of experienced Agency officers. Curveball's bogus story ended up in President Bush's 2003 State of the Union address, two months before America invaded Iraq, and in Secretary of State Colin Powell's dramatic presentation to the UN Security Council on February 5, 2003, making the case for military action against Saddam. The CIA finally pressured German intelligence to arrange a debriefing of Curveball in March 2004, a year after the invasion of Iraq. The veteran CIA operations officer who interviewed him concluded that Curveball was a liar, and the Agency put out a worldwide notice: "Key Mobile BW Source Deemed Unreliable."[2] This episode did incalculable damage to the CIA's credibility.

In the wake of the weapons of mass destruction scandal, I decided despite my nonpartisan politics to serve on Barack Obama's intelligence committee in his first campaign. There I had a single focus: to try to protect the historically independent role of intelligence and to resist the use of its capabilities in wrongheaded actions in the war in Iraq or "nation building" in Afghanistan. That said, during Obama's first term, I publicly and privately challenged the administration for not keeping enough heat on Osama bin Laden and for pursuing a doomed, Soviet-like military strategy in Afghanistan to the chagrin of many in the CIA. I wasn't surprised when the CIA and U.S. Special Forces finally tracked Bin Laden down and killed him in Pakistan in May 2011, not far from where we might have killed him a decade earlier. I had wrongly assumed that this would have happened in the months immediately following 9/11.

Intrigue drew me to Langley as a young man, and I came across plenty of it, beginning with my first assignment in the basement at headquarters, analyzing cables as I awaited training as a clandestine operations officer. One of my fellow analysts, Rick Ames, would go down a dark and treacherous path that haunted me many years later when we found ourselves together in the Rome station. Training prepared me for a range of missions, but not betrayal by one of our own.

I served under eleven CIA directors. Through all the leadership changes, my colleagues and I remained apolitical and disciplined. We prided ourselves on telling it like it was, not like the White House wanted it to be, and so did our counterparts on the analytic side of the administration. While CIA officers are a microcosm of American politics, fairly evenly split between Republicans and Democrats, we all checked our politics at the door and took great pride in our public service. I took quite seriously the words from scripture chiseled in marble in the CIA's lobby: AND YE SHALL KNOW THE TRUTH AND THE TRUTH SHALL MAKE YOU FREE.

Throughout my career, I always felt I could speak truth to power, inside and outside the Agency. I tried always to do this to the best of my ability, and I was never punished for doing so. My first chief in Central America had a plaque over his door, adorned with two mud-stained pigs and a saying that went something like "If you wrestle with pigs, you'll end up with mud on you." He wanted us to know: if you start dealing with unsavory people, or conduct unsavory operations, you should expect to get stained in the process. Back then, I thought it was a rather inelegant way to describe our business, especially by a senior officer. Over time, however, I've come to truly value the import of that observation, having wrestled with unsavory characters throughout my career—and ending up in the mud on occasion. Over the years that expression became more and more relevant for me, and I quote it even today.

Ian Fleming's *Casino Royale* introduced the world in 1953 to the indomitable 007, James Bond, a man dedicated to covert action. But when I think of the top intelligence officers I've read about, John le Carré's greatest character, George Smiley, more often comes to mind. He is cunning but restrained, charming but deeply analytic, and ruthless when need be. He is also patriotic, and loyal to what Le Carré calls the "Circus." Many of the actual CIA legends I encountered over the years would have felt right at home in Le Carré's fictional world: Tom Polgar; the "Blond Ghost," Ted Shackley; Dewey Clarridge, the Latin America chief who once showed up in Venezuela pushing a covert action coup in

Suriname; Nestor D. Sanchez, the operative who handled the Cuban point man in the CIA's plot to assassinate Castro; Milt Bearden, the highly effective and flamboyant chief in Islamabad who was so funny, he could have done stand-up comedy; Clair George, the clandestine chief who blanched at the plan to sell missiles to Iran but still got indicted (and then pardoned) in Iran-Contra; David Spedding, head of the British Secret Intelligence Service, MI6, who was otherwise known as C, for "Chief"; as well as most of the CIA leaders who I got to know very well indeed over the past fifty years.

My very first station chief, Ray Warren, remains the CIA operator I look up to most. He taught me the importance of tradecraft, and paying attention to the smallest of details, so operations would not be compromised. More important, he stressed maintaining the integrity of our reporting and staying within the lines of established U.S. policy. While simply stated, this is not always easy to accomplish in a very street-tough business where you have to deal with some of the world's more disreputable characters. We live to recruit, which is a sanitized way of saying we live to convince people to commit treason on our behalf by selling us the secrets of their homelands. This is difficult to do even when an asset has been alienated by his country's antidemocratic system. But we sign up to this mission because we are deeply committed to protecting America's national interest and our way of life. To accomplish this, all CIA operatives must become hunters.

ONE

Inside the Invisible Government

The Farm, 1969

It never occurred to me growing up that I would someday join the Central Intelligence Agency. I was the son of an Irish-Catholic heating contractor. My forebears were weavers and farmers who immigrated to the United States in the wake of the potato famine of 1846, settling in South Philadelphia and joining the building trades and the police department. But somehow covert action was in my DNA, a fact I came to understand in 1966 when my wife, Pat, gave me a book for my twenty-sixth birthday.

The Invisible Government, by David Wise and Thomas B. Ross, was intended as an exposé. The reader was supposed to be shocked and outraged by its revelations of a vast and secret intelligence bureaucracy, a CIA that had become so powerful that it threatened the very democracy it had been created to preserve. But a careful reading belied the book's argument. In fact, rather than an out-of-control intelligence community engaged in clandestine operations that endangered the nation, the book revealed a system of safeguards put in place by President Dwight D. Eisenhower. Reading it, I was struck by the sense of mission and vitality of the Agency, and I was so intrigued and energized by the covert operations described in its pages—not to mention the presumed adventure of living and working with foreigners in exotic places—that as soon as I finished the book, I sent off a letter to the Agency seeking employment.

At the time, I was a high school social studies teacher in suburban Philadelphia, and the CIA was the furthest thing from my mind. I supplemented teaching with summertime work loading and unloading trucks at a food distribution center in South Philly, where I got closer to the rock and rumble of life in dangerous foreign settings. I had to join the Teamsters union to work there, and heard Teamsters boss Jimmy Hoffa speak at the Philadelphia Convention Hall. He reminded me of Castro as he rambled on nonstop for over an hour, but his charisma was undeniable. The Teamsters were a tough lot. Once, I was let off work early to attend the wake of a coworker. When I asked what had happened, I was told in hushed tones that the man had organized a dissident labor group and ended up in a fight that included baseball bats.

This was far from my rather parochial upbringing. My sisters, Anna Mae and Mary Lou, and I grew up in an *Ozzie and Harriet* world. After World War II, our parents moved to the suburbs in Delaware County. Ours was a blue-collar family, and wonderfully loving and secure. I naïvely felt that nearly everyone in America shared this experience.

I met my future wife, Pat, on the beach in North Wildwood, New Jersey, when she and her friend Nancy Paul strolled past my lifeguard stand. After my career in intelligence, that was the best job I ever had. I still spend my summers and weekends at a shore home in nearby Ocean City, and recently I represented the Ocean City Beach Patrol Alumni in the National Lifeguard Rowing Championships with my former CIA colleague Jim Campbell. With the support of fellow guards Joe Grimes and Jack Brooks, we survived the competition. In 2012 I won the championship in the over-seventy age group with the Ocean City legend Joe Schmitt. Pat and I didn't hit it off at first, but when I removed a splinter from her friend's foot, she was taken with this act of gallantry. We were married at Good Shepherd Church in Philadelphia in November 1962. From the moment we met, Pat knew me better than I thought anyone could. It is not surprising that four years later she would give me the book that would change our lives.

Some time passed before I received a response to my handwritten letter to the CIA, directing me to an office in Center City Philadelphia for an interview. I was impressed with the Ivy League–looking CIA officer with excellent diction in a tweed suit and wing-tip shoes. Truth be told, the Agency was always more egalitarian than its high-profile cadre of Yale and Princeton men led many to believe. Still, I was relieved when the interview went well, and I was given an entry examination that measured intelligence, writing skills, and psychological stability. This was followed weeks later by much more comprehensive testing in Washington, D.C., including a polygraph examination and extensive interviews. Drugs were not an issue among middle-class America in the early 1960s. Instead, the polygrapher seemed to have a special interest in how much beer I had drunk as a college student and lifeguard. After two grueling days trying to convince the CIA that I was right for them, I returned to teaching. Finally, weeks later, I received a letter inviting me to return to Washington on February 7, 1967, to become a member of the Central Intelligence Agency.

My first assignment was to the Clandestine Service's Records Integration Office, to become a "documents analyst," until it was time for me to be sent off to the "Farm" for training as a clandestine operator. In the windowless basement vault of CIA headquarters, I reviewed cables for retrievable data sent back to Langley, Virginia, from officers in Eastern Europe, while ten feet away, my new colleague did the same for those from the Soviet Union. His name was Aldrich Ames. He would go on to become one of the greatest traitors in CIA history.

While I couldn't believe I was now working inside the invisible government, my colleague was blasé about it. He had followed a different path to the secret vaulted room. Rick, as we called him, was a CIA brat. He'd spent his early teens hanging around a proper British yacht club in Rangoon, Burma, where his father worked from 1953 to 1955 as a CIA operative undercover. After flunking out of the University of Chicago and setting off on his own as a theater hand in the Windy City, Rick had come back home to McLean, in Northern Virginia. His father, Carleton Ames, then holding down a desk job after his foreign assignment, immediately helped his son land a position at the Agency.

When I met him in the fall of 1967, Ames was just finishing up his degree as a night student at George Washington University. My colleague lacked the savoir faire I associated with spies. He was unkempt, with stringy dark hair and bad teeth stained by the Camels he practically chain-smoked, and his clothes could have been charitably described as thrift shop specials. Still, he was arguably the best-read among us on intelligence, and had already cultivated an abiding interest in Soviet operations and counterintelligence.

In the claustrophobic, fluorescent-lit basement of CIA headquarters, my worldly, cynical office mate and I spent hours in earnest debate over the great issues of our time. Our conversations were worthy of graduate school dialectics. The more I talked on about covert action and Agency derring-do, the harder Ames would shake his head and flash a wry smile. "Jack, the core of the business is counterintelligence," he said. How ironic.

Ames was several months ahead of me in pre-career training, but we became friendly, finding common ground living on our meager GS-8 salaries. One evening, Pat and I met Ames's girlfriend, Nancy Sege-barth, a pleasant, intelligent young woman working on the analytical side of the Agency, the Directorate of Intelligence, and in May 1969 we attended their wedding, at a Unitarian church in Northern Virginia. There I met Ames's father, Carleton, who was just retiring after spending fifteen years with the CIA. I could sense that there was some distance between him and his son, which Ames had spoken about in the past. In any case, Ames was about to depart for his first assignment as a case officer in Ankara, Turkey, working for the Soviet/Eastern Europe (SE) Division.

Before he left, and we went our separate ways, we exchanged books. Ames gave me *A Coffin for Dimitrios*, a spy novel by Eric Ambler whose narrator, a mystery writer, descends into a netherworld of double agents and espionage and becomes indistinguishable from the subjects of his fiction. I gave him *Psychopathology and Politics* by Harold Lass-well, about how political behavior is basically predetermined by our Freudian nature. I got the book back many years later. I was surprised Ames remembered who gave it to him, and now wonder how much it applied to him.

Years later, I raised this with Sandy Grimes shortly after her book on Ames, *Circle of Treason: A CIA Account of Traitor Aldrich Ames and the Men He Betrayed*, was published in mid-November 2012. She and I met for breakfast at the Palace Hotel in New York and spent an hour over tea puzzling over him. Sandy had spent her career supporting the Agency's recruited Soviet assets. She joined her coauthor and counter-intelligence officer, the late Jeanne Vertefeuille, on the Ames mole hunt team in 1991. They were the two officers most responsible for finally unmasking Ames in 1994, nine years after he began spying for the Soviet Union. He gave the Soviets the names of our best Russian agents, all of whom were executed after Ames's betrayal. In *Circle of Treason*,

Sandy describes how Ames came into her office as she was beginning the investigation that would ultimately lead to his capture and lectured her on counterintelligence. She and I spent our breakfast that day trying to figure out why he'd done that.

We talked about the impact his second wife, María del Rosario Casas Dupuy, had had on his behavior. She was high-maintenance and clearly liked to present a *bella figura*, requiring that Ames support her in high style. She had come from a family of some standing and wealth in Colombia. Apparently, the family's net worth had diminished substantially over the years, but Rosario's self-image had not. Interestingly enough, the initial investigation into Ames erroneously concluded that Rosario came from money and therefore this provided the explanation for Rick's expenditures. Sandy and I also talked about how Ames had attempted to mask the millions the Russians paid him by buying a used Jaguar, only to pay cash when he bought his home. This would have been a red flag if CIA investigators had been allowed to look more carefully at his personal finances. This limitation has been lifted since then.

In the end, Sandy and I shared the view, over the last sip of tea, that Ames had been the perfect storm waiting to happen: family issues, financial pressure, excessive drinking, underperformance at work, and an inflated ego accompanied by a gravely exaggerated evaluation of his superior intellect. Still, he might not have volunteered himself to the Russians if his job had not provided a pretext for regular contact with them. To their credit, they played him like a violin and appealed to his psychic needs.

•

As you enter CIA headquarters at Langley, there are two statues, each commemorating spies. One, outdoors, is a fairly inconspicuous tribute to Nathan Hale, the first American spy to give up his life for his country, during the American Revolution. (We shouldn't dwell on the fact that he met this fate due to poor preparation and shoddy tradecraft.) The other, depicting General William J. "Wild Bill" Donovan, looms large in the lobby, and large in CIA history. When World War II broke out, the U.S. government decided it needed a professional intelligence service, which became known as the OSS, the Office of Strategic Services. It was led by Donovan, a Wall Street lawyer whom the journalist Thomas

Powers has described as "a man of enormous crude energy and the open, adventurous mind which was to characterize American intelligence until the Bay of Pigs."[1] Donovan is still held in great esteem by the employees of the CIA.

Across the lobby, also etched in marble, are stars representing CIA officers who have fallen in the line of duty. Sadly, I have watched these stars increase in number each year. Many remain anonymous because of their covert status.

Because secrecy is so critical to everything the CIA does, the people who work there become obsessed with betrayal. At its worst, this obsession can lead to paranoia, like that demonstrated by the Agency's legendary spy hunter James Jesus Angleton, who came to believe that nearly all our agents were "moles" penetrating the CIA. Angleton himself had fallen victim to betrayal by the infamous British defector Kim Philby. The two had worked and lived together in Italy and had shared many confidences through the years. Philby's defection to the Russians hit Angleton hard and probably distorted his view of mankind and the intelligence business.

Hunting for moles is a staple of the business, and the counterintelligence staff has to be directed at carefully observing where cases go wrong. However, you can't allow this to paralyze your initiative. As with many aspects of spying, you need to keep at least two compartmentalized disciplines in your mind simultaneously, operations and counterintelligence. To emphasize only counterintelligence can lead to a form of paranoia that can be very debilitating to an aggressive intelligence service such as the CIA. We spend a great deal of time training at the knee of experienced officers, learning the proper balance between valuing our agents and command alertness when looking at issues of betrayal.

•

My early training was a mix of classroom study and fieldwork. It lasted nine months and was split between spying and paramilitary instruction. It included agent targeting and recruiting, surveillance, technical operations, clandestine meeting preparation, and communications programs. In the second half, we underwent paramilitary training in arms use, jungle survival, jump training, and demolitions. While the training was rigorous, it had its comic moments.

One of the more embarrassing occurred when I was attempting to make a brush pass, which is handing over a document to an agent in an undercover manner, a quick walk-by scenario. From my perspective, I had selected a particularly clever spot for the pass, which involved brushing past the agent as he entered a revolving door in a downtown hotel near the training center. It would have been virtually impossible to see the handoff from any angle. I executed it without a flaw, but the agent, one of our instructors, refused to put out his hand to complete the pass, which meant that I would have to repeat the exercise at a different time and location. In my annoyance, when I reached the bottom of the steps outside the hotel, I turned and directed an obscene hand gesture toward the instructor's back.

That night back at camp, the trainees were assembled for a critique of the day's performance. The commentator announced that they had a special treat for us: they had secretly videotaped selected meetings throughout the day, a viewing of which would prove entertaining and instructive to the entire class. We were all caught off guard. This was the early days of clandestine video; we had not been exposed to it before. My graphic gesture was first on the docket, and it looked even worse than I remembered. The room howled—at my expense. I learned an unforgettable lesson that night: all my operational activities in the future could be videotaped. And I learned this, too: if you're trying to go unnoticed and maintain your cool, obscene gestures in public won't cut it.

The operational aspects of the clandestine training course finished up with a field exercise designed to bring together all we had learned. The class was divided into several teams, each sent to a different location in a major northeastern city. My team ended up at one of the most prestigious hotels in town. I assume our CIA instructors had chosen it because the Agency had ties to the hotel's security office and would be able to ensure that none of us would be scooped up by the police if our strange behavior were reported. My team passed with flying colors its debriefing and surveillance exercises against multiple targets, role-played by our instructors. The rub came when we had to surreptitiously place an audio device in a hotel room. The placement went well enough, and our team transcribers diligently waited for the surveillance team to report the arrival of the target. The large reel-to-reels were running; earphones were on. Everything was going smoothly—until a maid walked in without knocking to turn down the bed. The transcriber had forgotten to lock the door! The maid, startled, beat a hasty retreat to the security office. The room was soon visited by hotel security—and our instructors. The embarrassing lesson was etched in my memory forever: when performing a clandestine act, lock the door behind you.

Finally, after working for months on tradecraft, we headed off to a special, still-secret facility for paramilitary training and courses on explosives and bomb making. (You can't do this work in just any neighborhood without upsetting the locals.) The program began with a briefing by an instructor straight out of Central Casting. When he took to the podium, we held back a collective gasp. A jagged V-shaped scar covered a good part of his forehead. If that wasn't enough, he was missing a couple of fingers. He extolled the excitement of working with explosives. He also stressed the need for caution when handling such materials. Looking at him, I didn't need convincing. After that presentation, I was determined to leave the course with head and fingers intact.

One of the exercises involved blowing up telephone poles. Half a dozen students would line up, and each would walk slowly to his individual pole, where he would plant an explosive, ignite the charge (which burned at a specific rate per second), and walk briskly back to the starting position. You were told not to run, because if you ran, there was a chance you'd fall and get hit by the detonation. While that sounded reasonable enough, I decided I wouldn't take any chances and added several extra inches of detonating cord for each of my charges, which allowed me more time to return to my starting spot. The explosives should have detonated sequentially. But because I'd lengthened my detonating cord, my telephone pole was the last to fall. My instructors didn't see the humor or the wisdom in what I'd done. I received my lowest grade in this course, and a not-so-gentle note for my file suggesting that I "not be allowed to handle explosives." The irony is that, in the mid-1980s, I probably handled more explosives than any other CIA officer in history.

Next we headed to Panama for a weeklong jungle survival course that included rappelling down waterfall cliffs and rafting across alligator-infested rivers. It was the rainy season, and we were perpetually drenched. When our team was able to carve out a clearing to camp for the night, we divided up the work assignments: hanging hammocks, collecting firewood, locating water. I volunteered to do the cooking, given that I had a modicum of experience. The instructors provided the food: a bag of rice and a small alligator. I didn't have the foggiest idea how to cook the alligator, so I cut it up, threw it into boiling water, and, near the end, added rice. When chow time came, everyone was starving and eagerly scooped the gruel into their mess kits. But when I checked the kits later, it was clear that nobody had eaten more than a few mouthfuls, despite their hunger. It was a dreadful concoction.

Early in the course, I learned a lesson that stuck with me ever after: you can't tell a survivor by his looks. Back at camp, embarking on our mission, I spotted a very self-confident colleague who looked like a former Green Beret and was dressed like Jungle Jim, with a feather tucked in his Indiana Jones hat. I figured his was the team to be on, so I positioned myself accordingly. I noticed he wasn't paying any attention whatsoever to the way we had been instructed to carry a machete into the swamps.

"Why should he?" I thought. "He's an experienced warrior."

We were no more than a hundred yards into the jungle when he tripped and slid down on his machete. He let out a shriek and began bleeding so profusely that he had to be evacuated to the medical facility. As the hardships mounted, I realized it was some of the least likely officers who performed best under stress. From then on, I kept this in mind whenever I needed to assemble a team: look beyond the obvious.

The final task in the program was jump training, in which we would be expected to make five parachute jumps from a cargo plane. This was optional, but if you opted out, you were given two weeks of administrative leave. That sounded good to me. By that time, I was weary of training in general. Then, as we neared the decision date, Pat urged me to sign up anyway. She felt I would miss out on the camaraderie and fun involved in jumping from an airplane at fifteen hundred feet. She may have been right, but she wasn't persuasive enough. The next person who urged me to jump was the commander, an ex-paratrooper colonel. Jumping, he said, is "better than sex." That got my attention, but I quickly concluded he was missing a bolt or two. By then I'd made up my mind: it made no sense to me to voluntarily jump out of an airplane. Had it been mandatory, I would have done it. But volunteer to do it?

As luck would have it, we had arrived at the point where you selected, or were selected for, a specific line division or staff. I was a little uncertain how covert action programs were organized within the Clandestine Service, so I asked to join the Covert Action staff, a unit within the service that ran political, economic, and covert propaganda operations. Shortly thereafter, I had an interview with its chief, Hugh Tovar. Tovar was a legend. He'd served as station chief in Laos. He was also an accomplished parachutist; his office was strewn with jumping memorabilia.

I walked through his door for the interview. He looked up and said, "Have you jumped yet? It's the greatest thing a man can do."

Without missing a beat, I said, "No. But I'm really looking forward to it."

Off to jump training I went.

•

Once I had a better understanding of the difference between the Covert Action staff and the ongoing activities of the Agency's primary operating units, I switched my interest to the Soviet Division. Near the end of the operation training course, I had a private chat at the base club with Rocky Stone, then chief of that division, during which he encouraged me to sign up with them. Stone was a legend, too. A very charismatic senior official, he suffered from profound hearing loss and relied on a hearing aid, which he supplemented with lipreading and focusing on facial expressions. He had been one of the key players in bringing the Shah of Iran to power in 1953.

My career counselor, a man who had played an important role in the Bay of Pigs operation under the alias Tom Bender, was not encouraging. "You're too tall for Soviet operations," he said, chewing on his cigar.

I failed to see the connection between spying and height. The trick was to do everything with sleight of hand in a natural setting, not hiding behind bushes. In any case, Bender was a Latin Americanist and he was recruiting for the Latin America Division. He took me to see William V. Broe, yet another legendary officer, who had joined the CIA in 1948 and served as chief of the Western Hemisphere Division (later renamed the Latin America Division) from 1965 to 1972. I remember

Bender telling Broe, "This guy belongs in LA Division"—and hardly because of my height. Theirs was a division that was heavily invested in covert action and therefore just the right spot for me. Not long after, I'd get my first overseas assignment: Chile.

By the time I had completed training as a clandestine officer and joined the Latin America Division in late 1969, the CIA was, by historical standards, still a fledgling agency—just twenty-two years old. We would go through middle age together: I wouldn't retire until after its fiftieth anniversary in 1997. But at the time of my first posting, it had already matured greatly since its overthrow of Mohammad Mossadegh's government in Iran in 1953 and the Bay of Pigs invasion in 1961. And by my time, it was already an established arm of the U.S. government— and a lightning rod for criticism, particularly from those on the left concerned about the "invisible government." This was well understood within the upper reaches of the government and the intelligence community, where the pluses and minuses of espionage and covert action were being critically reviewed.

As I prepared to enter clandestine training, a committee of academics and former intelligence professionals convened by CIA director Richard Helms and called the Covert Operations Study Group submitted its report on "Covert Operations of the United States Government." It was December 1, 1968, and though they presented it to President-elect Richard M. Nixon,[2] I wouldn't be able to read the document until it became public decades later.

Even then, the intelligence community's thinking on covert action was nuanced. In a cover letter accompanying the report, Franklin A. Lindsay, an OSS operative and close associate of Frank Wisner, the man who founded the CIA's Clandestine Service, stated that the "CIA has not been a political organization. Its people have served successive administrations with equal loyalty." It's a point worth repeating, because it is as true now as it was then, even as critics on the left and right demonize the Agency. The report made clear that the CIA had been, and should remain, squarely under the president's control. "Covert operations are an instrument; their only legitimate objective is to serve the foreign policy of the president," the document stated. "They are not an independent aspect of U.S. foreign policy, but simply one way of furthering that policy. The expertise of the clandestine service is secrecy. Covert operations should be called upon only when something should be done in a secret manner—and only when secrecy is possible. It is up to the President to determine what he wants done and whether it should be done secretly or openly. A covert capability is like a military capability. Its use is a presidential prerogative. As with the military service, the clandestine service should not be pursuing any projects, much less self-generated ones, except by presidential decision."

The Lindsay panel described covert action—appropriately, in my judgment—as a useful tool for the president, enabling him to engage in "forms of conflict" while avoiding open hostilities. Clandestine operations allow the CIA to maintain important relationships in foreign countries and support causes without the need to give all countries in a region "equal treatment." And they "permit the Government to act quickly, by-passing domestic U.S. political, bureaucratic, and budgetary controls." But the panel was also sanguine about the limitations of covert operations, which, they said, "rarely achieve an important objective alone" and often "cannot be kept secret . . . At best, a successful covert operation can win time, forestall a coup, or otherwise create favorable conditions which will make it possible to use covert means to finally achieve an important objective." At the same time, there are grave risks involved with covert action, as the report spelled out clearly. "Our credibility and our effectiveness" as advocates for the rule of law around the globe, it stated, are "necessarily damaged" when our covert activities in foreign countries are revealed.

Much has changed since the panel made its report. Indeed, some of its recommendations seem almost quaint with the perspective of more than forty years. But the panel was dead-on in concluding that covert action was an indispensable foreign policy tool because there will always be times when the president has to make things happen in secret. And secrecy is the CIA's "expertise." I do not deny that secrecy can be corrosive, but it can also be a powerful enabler. In *Safe for Democracy: The Secret Wars of the CIA*, published in 2006, John Prados concludes that for sixty years presidents have "continually harnessed" CIA covert action to meet foreign policy goals, and in the end concludes that covert operations have been a "negative factor" in the pursuit of U.S. foreign policy objectives. This is where Prados and I part company. I believe such operations have worked far more often than Prados or anyone on the outside will ever fully understand. Like it or not, covert action is a very powerful arrow in the quiver of a robust intelligence service, an imperative of modern statecraft.

That said, I agree that there have been good covert operations and bad covert operations, and I spent my career examining the difference between the two. In the course of this book, I will describe both. Perhaps because of what is going on in the world right now, at the top of my list of some basic lessons we have learned over the years is this: in order to best utilize the CIA and its assets, the White House must avoid dangerous "dabbling" based on the myth that "all it takes is a spark." I can't count the number of times over the years I have been approached to support a regime change because the local circumstances were considered so propitious that all it would take was "a little spark." Those who say this usually have greatly inflated views of the opposition strength and no idea how much real thought, hard work, and generous resources have to go into any program to bring about significant political change abroad. They generally don't want to do what is needed themselves and hope that the United States gets involved. I usually showed such people the door.

Additionally, covert action is bound to fail when the following criteria are not present:

- **Viable partners in place.** The United States must have partners within a host nation who truly share U.S. goals and objectives and are willing to fight and die for their cause. Relying on exiles is a recipe for miscommunication, blunders, and often disaster. A base of operations contiguous to your target is often critical.
- **Real-time, accurate information.** Foreign agents directed by CIA officers must be capable of collecting real-time information. When we rely solely on spy satellites, communications intercepts, and other technical means of collecting intelligence, we run the risk of missing key contextual details that could make or break an operation.
- **Adequate resources.** "Dabbling" with small sums of money and limited capability is at best ineffective and at worst dangerous. When policy makers direct the CIA to conduct covert action, they must equip the Agency to succeed, in terms both of money and of personnel.

- **Bipartisan political support.** Covert action, like war, should reflect, in general terms, the wishes of the American people, even if they don't know it's happening. If your planned action has significant detractors on either side of the aisle in Congress, you're probably planning on doing something unwise.
- **A direct threat to U.S. security.** To garner support domestically and internationally, the White House must demonstrate that its adversary poses a real threat and needs to be eliminated.
- **Proportionality.** The desired outcome must be relatively commensurate with the cost and the collateral damage, particularly with regard to civilian casualties. The CIA or the Pentagon can't kill thirty thousand people to save five thousand or it will never have the political support or moral high ground required to succeed.
- **A reasonable prospect for success.** Before an operation is launched, policy makers have to possess a clear objective and believe—based on fact, not desire—that accomplishing the operation is possible.

It is the responsibility of policy makers in the White House to make sure these conditions are met before directing the CIA to initiate a covert action campaign. In Afghanistan in the 1980s, they did just that. Since the 9/11 terrorist attacks on New York and Washington, Afghanistan has loomed large in the nation's global war against Islamist terrorism. But the antecedents to 9/11 lead back to Afghanistan, "graveyard of empires," to when the Soviets occupied the country and Islamic fighters from across the Middle East flocked to the Afghan border to fight against the Soviets alongside the Afghan mujahideen. One of those was Osama bin Laden.

TWO

Mules, Pickup Trucks, and Stinger Missiles

Afghanistan, 1986

After he gave me the model truck that I keep on my windowsill, Charlie Wilson told me I wasn't going to like the movie *Charlie Wilson's War*. He was right. I prefer the real story.

That story began for me in early 1986, after five tours overseas, three as chief of station. Everybody knew there was an office at CIA headquarters supporting the mujahideen fighters struggling against the Russians in Afghanistan. But exactly what went on behind a locked door on the sixth floor at headquarters remained largely a mystery. The CIA had been funneling hundreds of millions of dollars of weapons to these Afghan "holy warriors" since President Carter first authorized the covert war in late 1979 after the Soviets had invaded Afghanistan, concerned about the loyalty of the United States' client regime in Kabul. President Reagan reauthorized the covert war in 1981, as the first .303-caliber Lee-Enfield rifles purchased with U.S. tax dollars gave way to AK-47s, rockets, and mortars. Secret congressional appropriations grew from $30 million in 1981 to $200 million in 1984, and thanks to an agreement secured by the Agency, the Saudis were matching American appropriations dollar for dollar.

Support for the mujahideen was stoked on Capitol Hill by U.S. representative Charlie Wilson, a Texas Democrat who had come to passionately support the anticommunist crusade.[1]

By late 1984, the return on investment was enormous. Our initial goal had simply been harassment and costly damage to the Soviet military: we wanted to make the Soviets pay as high a price as possible for

their occupying Afghanistan. But when it became clear that the mujahideen could fight and that the Soviets were mortal—the mujahideen,
by now well armed, had killed thousands of Soviet soldiers and controlled much of the country—Director William Casey ordered a review
and reevaluation of the effort. And with Charlie Wilson adding even
more funding to the mix, Casey started to believe that the Soviets
might actually be defeated. In league with him were other hard-liners
at the National Security Council and Defense Department, and the
result was National Security Decision Directive 166, a plan for ramping
up the CIA's covert war in Afghanistan. Signed by President Reagan in
March 1985, it authorized the CIA to prosecute the war.

The planning was well under way when Tom Twetten, deputy chief
of the Near East Division, called me to his office on the sixth floor and
said he wanted me to lead what was now likely to become a full-blown
task force on Afghanistan. I had a very good relationship with Twetten
and his boss, Near East Division chief Bert Dunn, both of whom knew
that I had been an outspoken critic of arms dealer Manucher Ghorbanifar before the Iran-Contra scandal erupted. I didn't need much convincing that running the Afghan Task Force was something I wanted to do.
This is why I had joined the Agency in the first place. I had had my first
big taste of covert action in Chile in 1973, and now I was being given an
opportunity to run a major covert operation.

The compartmented program that I would be taking over had for
two years been the personal domain of Gust Avrakotos, chief of the
South Asia Operations Group. His close relationship with Wilson became the basis for George Crile's 2003 book, *Charlie Wilson's War*, and
the movie Wilson would come to warn me about years later.[2] After the
president signed NSDD 166 and the decision was made to up the ante
in Afghanistan, Casey and his deputies on the seventh floor thought
Avrakotos too combative and difficult to manage the escalation, and
transferred him to a job in the Africa Division. His counterpart in the
field, a Russian specialist serving as chief in Islamabad, who was seen
as too cautious and pessimistic about the prospects for success in Afghanistan, was also reassigned.

As I took over the reins for the Afghanistan issue, I was stunned to
learn just how large this "little" program was, and realized only much
later that Twetten had put me in charge of running the last, and largest,
CIA covert operation of the Cold War. One day early on, I found myself

sitting on the sofa in Director Casey's seventh-floor office, explaining how I planned to turn Avrakotos's crew of about a dozen operations officers and analysts into an organization capable of acquiring enough Soviet Bloc weaponry to arm 120,000 insurgents and move millions of tons of ammunition and matériel a month through Afghanistan's treacherous mountain passes.

I had, by then, dealt with Casey on several occasions. As a station chief in Latin America, I brought the head of my host country's intelligence service to see him at CIA headquarters. I hadn't gotten off on a very good foot with this foreign official. He was a talented intelligence operator but somewhat arrogant and hard to deal with. I inherited a grudge he had against the Agency, through no fault of my own, but then I unintentionally made it worse. A few years before my arrival, his political party had been voted out of office and he had called the station to ask for help in obtaining a U.S. visa, which he should have been given as a matter of professional courtesy. Instead, he was told with a flash of petulance to take his place "in line outside the embassy just like everyone else." I'm sure a fed-up case officer thought he was bringing the official down a peg by denying him the favor, but the satisfaction the case officer would have felt from such an action is almost always ephemeral and sets up a disastrous second act should your target ever return to power—as he did a few years later. By that time the case officer was gone and I was just arriving. Almost immediately, I paid a call on the foreign official. He told me he wanted to conduct a joint mail-interception operation. I told him that with new rules and regulations flowing from the Church Committee investigation—a congressional committee that had looked into illegal intelligence gathering by the Agency, the NSA, and the FBI—I wasn't sure how much help we could be, but that I would check. This was my mistake. "Just tell me whom I need to talk to, who has the authority to do it, and I will deal with them," the official said. I clearly should have given him a more deft, Latin answer, something like, "Sure, sounds like a good idea; I'll look into it," then moved on to another subject and let the topic die a slow death from neglect. Lack of follow-through would have been a more sophisticated response, which he would have understood without losing face or being given an opportunity to challenge my authority.

Shortly thereafter, we made the liaison visit together to Langley, which gave me the chance to start mending our relationship. I am used to large egos; his was huge. By the time he told me he was the equivalent of the CIA director, I had learned my lesson and let that claim sit unchallenged.

When I brought him in to see Casey after lunch, I ended up translating, even though my guest spoke fairly good English, because of Casey's tendency to mumble. This official liked to pontificate—and Casey fell asleep. I started interpreting louder and louder. Eventually, Casey woke up. I was never quite sure whether it was fatigue or a strategic ploy by Casey to take the air out of his visitor's puffery. I had heard from others that they had had similar experiences in meetings with the director. Nevertheless, when our meeting was over and the official and I walked out of Casey's office, neither of us said anything, but we both knew that the foreign spy chief had just been insulted. It gave me some psychological leverage over him, given our unspoken agreement that we were going to keep this between us. We never discussed it again, but our relationship improved after Casey fell asleep on him.

Casey reveled in running the CIA. When I served as station chief in Argentina in the early 1980s, I learned at one point that he wanted to come for a visit after the country's disastrous war against the British over the Falkland Islands, a war that led to the toppling of Argentina's military junta. The Argentines weren't happy about the director's planned visit, but I told them he was determined to come, and they reluctantly acquiesced—on the condition that he fly into a clandestine airport, keep a low profile, and use a false passport. I sent a cable back to Washington telling headquarters as much. In response, I was told by one of the director's aides, "Casey is going to fly in on a C-130 with his wife, doctor, and a team of advisers, as well as his dog and kids. He's not flying into a half-assed airport. He's flying into the main airport in Buenos Aires, and he wants a band playing"—an exaggeration for effect, I'm sure.

I went back to the Argentines and told them, in less vivid language, of Casey's plans, and they flatly turned him down. They were fearful of the potential damaging publicity that might jeopardize their position in the delicate transfer of power to civilian rule. Before I could get a cable back to Washington telling the director of central intelligence (DCI) the Argentines' response, the trip was canceled. Another Latin American country chief of station had beaten us to the punch with a similar rejection of Casey's proposed visit. I was relieved on several levels.

Around the same time, I attended a CIA conference with Casey in Panama. It was a logistical nightmare for CIA officials, who had to coordinate not only the director's visit but also the visits of other Agency officials from around the hemisphere. I was impressed by their organization, but they were thrown off course when Casey asked if everyone could stay an extra night for a breakfast meeting the next morning. He added, "We will keep it simple. Coffee and donuts." They hustled about to make the necessary travel arrangements, but procuring U.S.-style donuts was impossible in Panama in those days. Every five minutes during the breakfast, Casey would bellow in obvious annoyance, "Where are the donuts?" Of course, they never appeared, and in a thank-you cable to the chiefs following the conference, Casey signed off with "NEXT TIME, YOU WILL GET DONUTS."

I was spared having to host Casey in any of my foreign postings. He never ended up coming to visit me, and I could not help but think that the Argentine officials had had a point in their refusal to meet Casey's demands: the director of the CIA should come into a country with a very low profile and without an entourage. Before Casey, directors did not travel often, for security reasons. Today, the director travels with the fanfare of most cabinet-level dignitaries, as Casey had demanded. I have always been opposed to this type of director travel. But I should give Casey his due: in all his grandiosity, he reenergized the Agency after the Carter doldrums, and he was a covert operator at heart, going all the way back to his OSS days. He also had excellent access to President Reagan while at the same time genuinely valuing the role of the Agency. He didn't tamper with its culture, which involved calling things as we saw them and not as the president might have wanted them to be.

That said, I had reservations about Casey. Perhaps I caught him too late in his tenure as DCI, when he might have been beyond his prime. It certainly made me uncomfortable that he, an avowed archconservative, wasn't averse to using the CIA to advance a political agenda—for example, supporting the Contras in Central America and, by extension, the Iran-Contra affair.

Still, my personal relationship with Casey was friendly if formal. I wasn't in awe of him. Rather, I was guarded, both because he could be hard to read and, as I've said, difficult to understand.

There's one moment when I understood his words—but failed to understand the wisdom in them. It was unwise of me. I was meeting with him about Afghanistan, and I finished by saying I thought I needed a staff of about six dozen for the Afghan Task Force. He looked at me quizzically.

"Jack, are you sure this is right? Are you sure you've got enough?" he asked.

"Yes, I am," I said.

He was right to question my manpower estimate. In retrospect, I should have told him flat out that I needed more than one hundred people. (We eventually went to well over 120.) But this was the biggest responsibility I had been given at the Agency up to that point, and I was trying to calibrate how much staff I could suck out of the far reaches of the CIA structure while keeping everybody supportive of what we were doing.

Once the Afghan Task Force got rolling, there was no micromanaging from Casey. He didn't get involved, and neither did anybody else on the seventh floor. I felt they all understood that this was the only way it would work. You had to trust the person in charge, and if things weren't working, you needed to remove that person immediately. There's no way I could have briefed Casey or anyone else often enough about the fast-moving situation and still have done my job.

With authorization to use "any means necessary" to expel the Soviets from Afghanistan, the Reagan administration had to decide if this would include the U.S.-made Stinger, a lethal shoulder-fired antiaircraft missile with an infrared seeker that can lock onto the heat emitted by an aircraft's engine at a range of up to fifteen thousand feet. Despite all the pain the mujahideen had inflicted on the Soviets, the Soviets had managed to stop our supply lines through the mountain passes. All the matériel we had been shipping through for years had made the war so deadly for Moscow that the Politburo had responded by deploying fierce Mi-24D Hind helicopter gunships and the USSR's special forces, Spetsnaz, to close the mountain passes. Now our guns weren't flowing. Convoys of pickup trucks and mules laden with guns and crates of ammunition were no match for the Hinds, which flew in low and rained down barrages of missile and machine-gun fire. And the mujahideen lacked an effective antiaircraft weapon that could turn them back or shoot them down.

What if we armed the mujahideen with Stingers and trained them to line up the gunships in their sights and fire? There was some concern about the Stinger's effectiveness. In fact, the manufacturer, General Dynamics, estimated only a 25 percent success rate. The Soviet analysts, who historically tended to overrate the Russian capability, also argued that the Stinger could be jammed by high-tech Russian equipment, but we tested the Russian jammer and established that it was totally ineffective against the Stinger. Still, a much bigger strategic issue had to be resolved before the Stingers would find their way to eastern Afghanistan. My predecessor, Gust Avrakotos, had always adhered to classic CIA doctrine, which called for arming insurgents with the same weapons as the army they were fighting, so that the insurgents would already be trained to use any arms they captured from the other side. He also shared the belief, expressed most forcefully in this case by John McMahon, the CIA's former deputy director—he retired just as I assumed my position—that introducing weapons that were easily traceable to the United States, as the Stinger was, could provoke the Soviets and lead to a larger conflict. (Interestingly, McMahon was a lightning rod for conservative critics, who thought he personified an overly cautious CIA.) The two men had a point, but I put the higher priority on pushing the Russians out of Afghanistan. I was less concerned about the likelihood of an expansion of the conflict, which seemed very remote to me. There were limits, but we were in a covert war that could be recalibrated if need be. A similar debate raged within the CIA's analytic ranks, with Soviet specialists—who tended to see the Soviets as larger-than-life—arguing that the Russians were winning. Even our officers in the region seemed to support this view, based on the great difficulty they were having moving arms and supplies into Afghanistan. Analysts from the Near East Division countered that the Soviets were vulnerable and that the mujahideen were doing better than most people thought, even with their fire-and-run approach—that is, firing from a long distance.

Not long after my meeting with Casey, I represented the Agency at a meeting in the White House Situation Room, located in the basement of the West Wing, where we debated the Stinger issue one final time. A dozen of us from across the executive branch settled into the thick leather armchairs and listened to a Pentagon staffer explain this missile's particular lethality. A brief testing range video shown at the meeting resolved any lingering doubts I had when the missile literally made a right-hand turn in midair and scored a direct hit on the test aircraft. "Okay. It's clear we need to use it," I said to those around the table. Everyone else had the same reaction. Our consensus was passed to the president. Almost immediately, Reagan signed an order authorizing the Stinger's use in the covert war.

Up until then we had been playing a covert chess game with the Russians. They invaded, and we sent some weapons in. They brought in more troops, and we countered with more sophisticated weapons. They deployed the Hind helicopter gunships and the Spetsnaz special forces, and now it was our move. We hoped the Stinger would open up the mountain passes. Time would tell.

Several days later, I went over to the Pentagon to meet with an army three-star general to find out when the Department of Defense could make the delivery.

"The White House has approved it, and we need the Stingers as soon as possible," I said.

"Jack, I understand," the lieutenant general said, "but this is the latest system, it's coming off the assembly line, and it's going to the frontline troops."

"General," I said, "we've got the only fighting war in town, I really have to have them."

"I understand your position," he said. "I just can't do it. It was nice meeting you. Godspeed."

He was gracious and, frankly, he took the position I would have taken had I been in his shoes. He wanted to give the Stinger to U.S. troops first.

I went back and brought the bad news to the White House. "The DOD refuses to part with the Stingers," I said.

My contact on the National Security Council staff promised to call me back, which he did a short time later. A call had been made to the lieutenant general, and a second meeting was set up for the next day. By then, he had a better understanding of who was behind my request. Now it was practically a pro forma discussion.

"How many do you need?" he asked.

When I told him, he barely concealed his displeasure. "You're taking nearly my entire inventory," he said.

"That's what's needed."

Compared to my meetings with the lieutenant general, my first meeting with Charlie Wilson went off without a hitch—thanks to Gust Avrakotos. Among the many problems with the movie *Charlie Wilson's War* is its depiction of my predecessor, played by the late Philip Seymour Hoffman. There is no arguing that Avrakotos, the son of Greek immigrants from Aliquippa, Pennsylvania, could be difficult to deal with at times—even Wilson told me that Avrakotos was "the most difficult man [he'd] ever met"—but he was nowhere near the maverick the movie made him out to be. When Avrakotos told Wilson that I was replacing him, he said I was a "good guy." That seemed to be enough of a recommendation. Wilson was important to the program, the key congressman on Capitol Hill, someone deeply committed and paying careful enough attention to Afghanistan. He alone was responsible for hundreds of millions of dollars of needed funding. When Avrakotos exited the program, he left quietly. He did not try to pull an end run around me. And he unplugged his phone with Charlie Wilson; he didn't take any more calls from him. He was told not to deal with Wilson again, and he didn't. That's a disciplined officer, not a rogue on the loose, as depicted in the movie.

The task force's expanded offices were on the fourth floor, by a set of red elevators, in the same space where Avrakotos had had his. We had a suite of vaulted cubicles and open desks, not executive offices with doors. There was a large, formal wooden desk in my office when I arrived, but I had it immediately replaced with an oval conference table as a sign that we were going to do this more collegially by opening up the discussion. It took months, given the almost military chain of command that existed inside the Agency, before I was able to bring people around to where they could challenge my views without hesitation. I wanted to encourage people to come in and say, "You've got it wrong and this is what you ought to do." I recognized that I had a lot of learning to do, and I had to rely heavily on good people to fill in the gaps in my understanding of weaponry and the battlefield. I spent weeks adding staff, arranging space, building capability, developing strategy.

I was also responsible for overseeing the field operations conducted by the new chief in Islamabad, Milt Bearden. Bearden could have been a stand-up comic; he was that funny. He was also a very talented operations officer, having recently led a covert operation in which he rescued five hundred Ethiopian Jews from the Sudanese desert. For the Afghanistan program, he and his officers were managing the mujahideen's needs through Pakistani intelligence. I had to manage relations with Congress, as well, and brief the intelligence committees, the other agencies, and the White House—all while keeping Charlie Wilson in the loop. The more we kept everyone informed, the less they got in our hair.

Since the task force resided within the Near East Division of the Directorate of Operations, the operations officers detailed to me tended to be first-rate, thanks in part to my close relationship to Tom Twetten. The analysts from the Directorate of Intelligence (DI) were sometimes a problem, however. Their uneven quality complicated my life, but analytic support from the DI was critically important. Papers and briefing books had to be written for Congress, the White House, and the policy people on the CIA's seventh floor. Cables were constantly going back and forth between headquarters and the field.

Michael Barry, a Middle East analyst who led the analytical charge on mujahideen operations, got it right. He understood just how much damage the mujahideen were inflicting on the Russians and what they were capable of if armed with the latest weapons. The analysts from the DI's Office of Soviet Analysis were less optimistic, tending to see the Soviet army as invincible. SOVA, as that office was known, apparently reserved its top people for other tasks, such as analyzing Soviet missile silos, wheat harvests, and industrial production. I couldn't help thinking, "Okay, we're kicking the hell out of them and you don't want to be a key part of it?" I, therefore, increasingly relied on analysts from the DI's Office of Analysis for Near East and South Asian Studies. My successor on the task force, Frank Anderson, encountered the same analytical rifts. The SOVA analysts "missed the indicators that the Russians were being defeated," Anderson said. "It was very shortly after I joined the task force that I was persuaded that the Russians were losing badly . . . It is true that the analytical community, all of academia, and most of the 'experts' were just unable to get their heads around the idea that the Red Army could be defeated."[3] But we felt strongly that our best analysts on the task force were right. Our Soviet military analyst Bob Williams was particularly strong. He once helped us parse an intercepted Soviet field communication, called a morning report, that showed a shocking number of Soviet troops were unable to fight because of illness. Williams, a retired infantry officer and Russia specialist with combat experience in Vietnam and Korea, often disagreed with the SOVA analysts because he relied on his own tactical information. He understood from personal experience what the Russian troops were actually going through on the ground. "You needed to know what it was like to hold back forces in a gully . . ." he said. "It made a big difference to have had personal combat experience to understand what the Soviet soldier was experiencing. Something that the SOVA analysts seemingly did not have."[4]

I didn't feel overwhelmed running the program, but I probably should have. There weren't many people in the Agency who knew much about weaponry other than specialists in the Special Activities Division, the paramilitary unit in the Directorate of Operations. Avrakotos was fortunate enough to have found Michael Vickers, a very smart former Green Beret who had been detailed to the Agency, and who now serves in the Obama administration as under secretary of defense for intelligence. In addition to Williams, we were fortunate to have an A-plus weapons expert, a former Marine captain named Clifton Dempsey.[5] Dempsey looked more like a young professor than a five-year veteran of the Marines. An expert in mortar fire, shortly after my arrival on the Afghan account, he started modeling the next year's weapons requirements for a mujahideen army of 120,000 fighters. Before I could go out later in August 1986 and negotiate with the Egyptian and Chinese suppliers, Dempsey and I, along with Tim Burton, our highly skilled logistics chief, needed to figure out what kind of weapons the mujahideen would require beyond the Stingers, how much ammunition they were likely to expend, and what other kinds of matériel they would need to fight through the winter.

Vickers had worked up a smart, detailed formula for determining the military supplies necessary for the mujahideen, one based on an old World War II formula. Burton took Vickers's calculations and did his best to fit them into the current political reality. At this time, we had already shifted away from the .303 Lee-Enfield rifles to the greater fire-power of the AK-47, the Russian-designed assault rifle. (At that point, the formal decision to deploy the lethal Stinger had not yet been made.)

Dempsey and others on the task force worked hard to find an effective antiaircraft missile that would neutralize the devastating helicopter attacks. The British-designed Blowpipe had been tested and rejected because it was too complicated for the mujahideen to handle. The Brits also wanted to sell us the Javelin, an upgraded version of the Blowpipe, but for the same reason we said no. Dempsey recalls that we needed a "fire and forget" missile equipped with an internal guidance system that could lock on to an aircraft, and that nothing else would be viable. The SA-7 antiaircraft missile was ubiquitous worldwide, and it would have been easy to flood the field with it, but our research showed that it was not very effective and had been a failure in trying to knock down U.S. aircraft during the Vietnam War. The Swedish had the RB-70, which was exceptionally effective, but we doubted we would get Swedish approval to deploy it in combat. So in the end we turned to the lethal Stinger.

At the same time, we were also looking for a higher-caliber round that could penetrate the armor of the Hind helicopter. Dempsey recalls finding a Chinese antiarmor tungsten round that was not as good as the higher-velocity SLAP (saboted light-armor penetrator) round, but it was cheaper at just a dollar a round rather than $15 to $20. This was a significant difference when we needed to supply approximately 120,000 fighters. So we married the tungsten round to the 12.7-millimeter machine gun, which is very similar to the U.S.-manufactured .50-caliber. It worked well but not great. Still, it got the job done and helped knock out Soviet aircraft.

The procurement of weapons came through a somewhat complicated budgeting device known as end-of-year supplemental funding—that is, whatever the Department of Defense hadn't managed to spend by the last day of the fiscal year, September 30. Covert action is often paid for with end-of-year funds. Weeks ahead of time we would get a report that read, "The Department of Defense is going to have this amount, and it looks like we'll get this much." That meant we had to have cables with all our field stations and suppliers around the world ready to go, with someone on the other end agreeing to the order. If you were a day late, the money would be gone. There were some discretionary funds that didn't have to be committed in this way, but they amounted to peanuts when compared to the end-of-year Pentagon funds. And we never knew exactly how much we were going to get. Congress did not want a line item.

Every year that I was there, DOD always had a large surplus. For the Pentagon, $1 billion is a relatively small number, but there were other high-cost technical programs, such as satellites, that had to be funded. The Stingers were different—a direct purchase from the Pentagon. They weren't too expensive—at around $60,000 each—so a few million dollars got you a lot of these lethal weapons. Still, it remained to be seen whether the mujahideen could be trained to fire them effectively at the Hinds, and whether the Stinger's guidance system was superior to the Soviet's antimissile technology, despite our field testing.

The entire time I was running the task force, the only calls I ever received from the White House were requests for a surge prompted by a news story—"Can you ramp up operations in the field as fast as possible?" But given our funding system, a surge was impossible, since virtually all major purchases were made on the last day of the fiscal year, and there was nothing left to surge with after that: the piggy bank was empty. Likewise, the weapon assembly lines around the world took months to crank up; there were no shelf items to draw upon. This was not an ideal way to run a war, but somehow it worked.

In the summer of 1986 we knew we would be getting a huge amount of money in addition to the end-of-year surplus, thanks largely to items Charlie Wilson was inserting into appropriations legislation. Instead of getting $200 million, we received $350 million, not counting matching funds from the Saudis.

When Tim Burton and I traveled abroad that August to make sure we had everything in place for the end of the fiscal year, our first stop was Egypt. There was an arms factory there built with U.S. tax dollars that was two blocks long. For the Egyptians, our orders represented a huge infusion of cash, which helped them build up their arms industry. Wilson had particularly close relations with the Egyptians. Consequently, we were buying about 60 percent of our weapons from Egypt and 40 percent from China. One of the most important things we did was to change the equation to 60 percent Chinese and 40 percent Egyptian. This was critically important—both in terms of cost savings and quality. The Chinese-made weapons were cheaper and more reliable. Why use *both* the Chinese and the Egyptian? If an incident such as that which occurred in 1989 in Tiananmen Square had happened in either country during our Afghanistan tenure, we would not have wanted to be solely reliant on one country. So we had to have at least two suppliers, and sometimes you paid a higher price in order to keep two suppliers going.

I enjoyed negotiating these deals. Sometimes on these trips, I would wonder if I had missed my true calling. Still, negotiating with the Egyptians over arms pricing wasn't easy, and sometimes the bartering lasted several days. On one trip to Cairo, we ran into stiff opposition over the price to be paid for an AK-47, which practically every Afghan fighter carried into the battlefield. As I recall, the Egyptians were demanding $165 per weapon, and we were holding firm at $145. Fortunately, when the negotiation reached an impasse, we enjoyed an extended interruption in the bartering, because our guests had programmed a visit for us to Mount Sinai and Saint Catherine's fourth-century active monastery. It was a fascinating trip by helicopter. We flew fast and low across the Sinai Desert. At that time, this historic site had few roads to it and was virtually devoid of tourists.

The chief Egyptian negotiator came along for the trip. When we arrived at Mount Sinai, he personally walked me to the biblical "burning bush," through which, in Exodus 3:2–8, God is said to have told Moses to save the Hebrews. After a few minutes of reflection, he reverently asked me what I thought about visiting this sacred site. Without hesitation, I remarked that it was an amazing experience, adding in a hushed and grave tone that the burning bush had spoken to me. I paused for effect, then added: "It said, 'The price is one forty-five.'" Apparently, our host had a good sense of humor, and everyone found time for a deep laugh of relief. We settled at $145 without any further negotiation. The Egyptians were careful, however, not to bring me back to the bush on future trips when we were negotiating arms prices.

I drove the same kind of tough bargain with a Greek shipowner we met with after leaving Egypt. I spent two days negotiating a lease for his ship and whittled him down to the last dollar. The ship would take the weapons from Cairo to Karachi, in Pakistan. Then they would be shipped by train up to the Afghan border, where they would be loaded on trucks. (We were probably one of the largest owners of Toyota pickup trucks in the world at that time, because those were the trucks best suited for use on the border.) Once the trucks had gone as far as they could, the weapons would be loaded onto mules for the final leg of the trip, through Afghanistan's treacherous mountain passes.

One year, we bought nine thousand mules from the Chinese, and the Chinese supplier drove them, as in an old-fashioned Western cattle drive, across China and into Pakistan. At one point, someone suggested we go to Nigeria to buy inexpensive mules, which we did. What did I know about mules? I grew up in Philadelphia. But I quickly learned that we needed special mules, ones acclimated to high altitude. We couldn't take a Nigerian or Tennessee mule to Afghanistan. "Using a Tennessee mule that hasn't ever been above a thousand feet in the mountains of Afghanistan wouldn't work," Burton said.[6] Bert Dunn, then the associate deputy director of operations, made the same point, drawing upon his West Virginia roots. Needless to say, the Nigerian mules didn't work out, and the Afghans probably used them for field food rations instead. Burton remembers procuring mules from China, then herding and trucking them to the Afghan border to turn them over to the mujahideen. He recalls that it was "an extraordinarily successful operation," particularly considering the parties involved. I would agree that it was, indeed, one of the most complicated parts of the whole operation.

There was an art to dealing with the Chinese, for mules and, far more important, for weapons. Socializing was important for building rapport and trust, and our meetings were all very structured. The first half hour would be devoted to testimonials. I would begin, "We trust you. Friendship is important. We're here not because we're looking for weapons but because it's our mutual destiny." This would be translated. Then we'd take a break. They would come back and give me the same speech. Later in the day, we would go out to dinner. Then, the next day, we would finally get down to business.

"Okay, this is what I'm looking for," I'd say. "What are the best prices you can give us? Because we are friends, good friends. And we are in this together, and we have a common enemy, the Russians."

I was, of course, negotiating with representatives of the People's Liberation Army. They would go away to consider what we had offered, and then they would come back with their prices. I'd look at my price sheet, prepared by Burton and Dempsey, and because we'd decided ahead of time what we were prepared to pay, we would start the haggling. The Chinese knew exactly where the weapons were going, and one of the reasons I got a good price with a minimum of haggling was they wanted to be helpful in the fight against the Russians.

The only inappropriate weapon that almost got into the Afghan inventory was the Swiss-made twenty-millimeter Oerlikon cannon, which fired large and very expensive cartridges. It wasn't called a cannon by accident. It was way too large and cumbersome for an insurgency force and would have required tremendous logistical support to position it in the field. Also, the cost of feeding this cannon an ample supply of shells at three hundred rounds per minute would have been extremely high and would have cut into the purchase of other, more valuable weapon systems.

My assumption is that prior to my forming the task force, Wilson and Avrakotos had settled on the Oerlikon out of desperation, because up until then all other efforts to deter the menacing Russian Mi-24 helicopter had failed. The Redeye, SAM7, and Blowpipe had all come up short. Still, until we neutralized the Soviet helicopters, our arms supply train would be badly debilitated. Wilson tried to force-feed the Oerlikon to the task force, and in the end Avrakotos apparently acquiesced and bought a few of them, partly to keep Wilson happy and supporting funding for the program, but as I recall, they never made it into combat. The chief of the Near East Division, Tom Twetten, remembers Wilson's insistence on using the Swiss weapons as well.[7]

When I took over as chief of the task force, I was briefed about the Oerlikon with great skepticism by the staff, especially Dempsey and Burton. Fortunately, before we got too far down the road with the Swiss arms company on a new and major contract, the Stinger emerged as a more viable option, and I canceled any further acquisitions of the Oerlikon gun and replacement ammunition.

While we factored in the inevitable slippage of weapons we shipped into Afghanistan, we worked hard to make sure only a small percentage "fell off the back of the truck," as it were. The Stingers were different;

we carefully controlled all of them. Each one had a serial number. A mujahideen commander would not get a new one, via our go-betweens in Pakistani intelligence, until he had given back the expended tube after an attack, and the Stingers went only to the mujahideen leaders considered most reliable. Those who got them were specially trained and monitored, and when I visited the facilities to look at where the weapons were being kept and logged in, I was always impressed with the thoroughness of the mujahideen's efforts. There was a great deal of management oversight. One of the things our case officers did in Pakistan was regularly go through the gun markets in the North West Frontier and elsewhere to determine how many of our weapons found their way into the market, and I was consistently surprised that almost nothing, and certainly no Stingers, showed up there.

In 1986, great anticipation greeted the arrival of the Stingers in theater. Even though we had seen the tests and knew how deadly these missiles were, firing them required certain skill and precision. A PhD wasn't necessary, but a certain facility with technology was helpful. Could this ragtag group of mujahideen fighters be trained to handle a sophisticated weapon? I never had any doubt that they could.

THREE

"Your Friend Called from the Airport"

Chile, 1971–74

As I look back on it now, Santiago was an indescribably exotic first for-eign assignment. It was September 1973, and rumors of a military coup against President Salvador Allende had been swirling for months. There had already been one attempt. Street protests by Allende opponents made Santiago chaotic. Strikes and economic disarray made basic ne-cessities difficult to find. Occasional bomb explosions rocked the capi-tal. The whole country seemed exhausted, waiting.

I was at Da Carla, a noisy Italian restaurant in downtown Santiago, for lunch on September 9, when a colleague joined my table and whis-pered in my ear: "Call home immediately; it's urgent." I ducked out as discreetly as I could, to get back to the station to call from a secure line. I thought I knew what my wife would tell me. Amid all the chaos, Pat, who had never been outside the United States and Bermuda before we came to Chile, was raising five young children. She could have been calling me about any number of urgent matters. But my instincts were right. "Your friend called from the airport," she told me. "He's leaving the country. He told me to tell you, 'The military has decided to move. It's going to happen on September eleventh. The navy will lead it off.'"

It was the first indication received by any member of the CIA sta-tion in Santiago that the coup had been set in motion. A second source later called the station; we agreed to meet at his house just after dark. He confirmed the earlier report and added one key detail, the time the coup would begin: 7:00 a.m. With two sources, I sent CIA headquarters in Langley a top secret cable—a CRITIC, which overrides all other traffic worldwide and goes to the highest levels of government. Markings on the document, declassified in redacted form in 2000, indicate that it was distributed to President Nixon and other top U.S. policy makers the following day.[1] The source's name has been blacked out—and I am not at liberty to divulge it now—but his message bears an unadorned sense of urgency: "A COUP ATTEMPT WILL BE INITIATED ON 11 SEPTEMBER. ALL THREE BRANCHES OF THE ARMED FORCES AND THE CARABINEROS ARE INVOLVED IN THIS ACTION. A DECLARATION WILL BE READ ON RADIO AGRICULTURA AT 7 A.M. ON SEPT. 11 . . . THE CARABINEROS HAVE THE RESPONSIBILITY FOR SEIZING PRESIDENT SALVADOR ALLENDE."[2]

This is how the U.S. government learned of the coup. That may be hard for many Americans to believe, given a central conclusion reached in 1975 by the Senate Intelligence Committee, headed by Frank Church: "There is no doubt that the U.S. government sought a military coup in Chile" in 1970.[3] But I can say with conviction, flat out: the CIA did not plot with the military to overthrow Allende in 1973. It's important to get this straight for the sake of history: the CIA should not be blamed for things it did not do.

As mentioned in Chapter 1, the Agency has been involved in misguided covert actions, driven by presidential authorization, most of which are well-known by now. But the 1973 overthrow of Allende wasn't one of them.

"We helped to keep the opposition in Chile alive, but we did not promote the military coup that overthrew President Salvador Allende in 1973," said Ed Boring, a longtime Latin America hand and colleague who was in Chile with me at the time.

A highly respected former State Department official and later an ambassador, Jeffrey Davidow, who was a junior political officer with the State Department in Chile in 1973, noted that the work the U.S. government did was designed to bolster the opposition against Allende so the opposition could hang on until the next elections, but those efforts also, to some degree, had "the effect of roiling the waters" and contributed to the military stepping in. This is a far cry from orchestrating a military coup.

Even the Church Committee reported, "There is no hard evidence of direct U.S. assistance to the coup, despite frequent allegations of such aid."[4]

Nevertheless, the impression persists that the CIA sponsored the coup that toppled Allende. The confusion arises, I believe, because of one of those misguided covert actions I spoke of. In September 1970, after Allende finished first in a three-way presidential election, President Nixon summoned CIA director Richard Helms to the White House and told him in no uncertain terms to foment a coup.[5] Despite the Agency's assessment that it could not be done, especially with such a short time line, Nixon believed it was essential to U.S. interests in all of Central and South America to keep Allende from taking office. This coup attempt, which Nixon ordered the CIA to conceal from the U.S. ambassador and other American officials in Chile, came to be known as the highly secretive Track II—a secret complement to Track I, the political and propaganda efforts that had been mounted to keep Allende from being elected in the first place.

Track II meets my definition of "bad covert action," for a number of reasons. Conditions were simply not ripe for military action. The Chilean military was standing behind the constitution and wanted no part of a coup after the election. Likewise, the Chilean people were not supportive of blocking Allende. He had been democratically elected, even if his margin of victory was small. Later, his government's mishandling of the economy would galvanize the people and the military, but as Allende had not yet taken office, there was not even a pretext for action. Not only were the conditions not conducive to lethal action, the cost of military intervention—as Augusto Pinochet's actions demonstrated years later—was excessive in terms of loss of life and the violation of human rights and democratic freedom. From a policy perspective, and with the advantage of hindsight, I see that the Nixon administration should have heeded the CIA's advice and limited its efforts to supporting the political opposition and letting the democratic process play out until it was clearer that Allende was in fact pulling Chile into the Soviet orbit.

Before being assigned to Chile, I had worked the night shift for the Chile Task Force at Langley, synthesizing cables from Santiago into a morning intelligence report for the bosses. It was my first assignment after covert training at the Farm. The station chief in Santiago did not hide his doubts about a coup: "PARAMETER OF ACTION IS EXCEEDINGLY NARROW AND AVAILABLE OPTIONS ARE QUITE LIMITED," read one cable. "[DO] NOT CONVEY IMPRESSION THAT STATION HAS SUREFIRE METHOD

FOR HALTING, LET ALONE TRIGGERING COUP ATTEMPTS," read another.[6] His concerns proved to be well-founded. However, the chief of Latin American covert action at the time recalls that there was a great deal of pressure on him to push hard for a coup. In fact, the headquarter's covert action chief was sent by DCI Richard Helms to Santiago to explicitly tell the station chief that if he wasn't prepared to press for a coup, he could return to Washington that day and the covert action chief would take command of the station. The station chief said he would do the best he could, but he remained pessimistic about the likelihood of success.

On October 22, 1970, a small group of bungling retired military officers and members of the right-wing Patria y Libertad organization attempted to initiate a coup by kidnapping General René Schneider, the commander in chief, who was a staunch opponent of military intervention in Chilean politics.[7] Schneider was killed, and the event had the effect of rallying the country around Allende, who was inaugurated two days later. At that point, all coup plotting ended. In fact, Nixon drastically altered his policy. The new goal was to avoid giving Allende any excuse to use the United States as a target to rally domestic loyalty and international support.[8] Nixon appointed an ambassador, Nathaniel Davis, who liked Allende personally and who had an intellectual curiosity to see whether the transformation from a capitalist to a Marxist economy could be accomplished peacefully—what Allende called "the Chilean path to socialism."

There are many reasons that CIA officers have rocky relationships with ambassadors. Most have to do with the conflicting cultures and power struggles between the CIA and the State Department. This is a tension that dates back to the creation of the Agency, and became so bad by the mid-1970s in many stations (including Chile) that the two sides agreed to formal ground rules establishing the ambassador as the head of the country team at any foreign post, though the CIA worked some strong footnotes into the rules about protecting methods and sources.

On the ground, relations between ambassadors and station chiefs often became strained over the high level of political access a chief can enjoy as a result of our covert actions and the substantial support the host country's intelligence service received. Being plugged into a host nation's intelligence service gave us special access to the country's governmental system, access the State Department did not always have. In politically turbulent countries, the embassy could deal only with the party in power or else risk the wrath of the government, whereas the CIA could operate below the radar across the entire political spectrum. We could support an array of political, media, military, police, and intelligence leaders, some of whom would eventually become heads of state or cabinet-level officials. This gave the CIA a significant leg up when the opposition returned to power. People don't forget the support they got on their way up.

Our ability to pay sources for information and access was also always a bone of contention with State, which thought it gave us an unfair advantage in gaining political access and influence. CIA recruitment is based largely on the American capitalist system: namely, buying sources' cooperation. It has been my experience that the taking of money, often because of an urgent financial need, makes sources more reliable and responsive. Once on the payroll, they are compromised and cannot divulge the relationship without hurting themselves. This is a very important factor in controlling an asset's potential negative behavior. Still, money doesn't guarantee reliability, and all information has to be vetted independently. Wherever possible, the Agency tries to get confirmatory sources and independent data, and it tracks agents over a long period of time to determine their reliability, accuracy, and consistency. (To the CIA, "agents" are not employees but individuals—typically foreigners—who are paid to steal secrets, provide intelligence, and broker access. The CIA equivalent of an FBI agent is called a "case officer.")

I do not believe that paying agents and other sources of information corrupts the intelligence-gathering process. As a general operating principle, we select targets who have known access to information we want. Hence, we start from a very strong position, because the source does not have to invent information to get paid. He or she already has the access. Furthermore, a high percentage of our recruitments begin with ideological identification with the United States. Many of them either don't identify with the political systems in their countries or have been harmed by them. The money is a reinforcing inducement, not the be-all and end-all in a source's productivity. Plus, there is a work ethic among most agents. They respond to financial incentives and try to collect good information to continue earning them.

The issue of false or corrupted information comes into play when you have a walk-in (someone who appears at an embassy and volunteers his services) or a double agent. Nearly as troubling is the fabricator who tends to be creative and substantively smart, albeit without real access. Guarding against these impostors is where tradecraft kicks in. Beyond polygraphs, background checks, and surveillance, the most effective way to evaluate sources' reliability is to vet their information. Even with very good fabricators, their information doesn't hold up under routine professional questioning in a debriefing, which is what most asset meetings are. Over time, a phony source will show himself to be inconsistent when his or her information is compared to that from other, reliable reporting.

During my first tour, the CIA resumed its strategy of opposing Allende by supporting his political opponents in Chile and making sure he did not dismantle the institutions of democracy—the media, political parties, and labor organizations—that kept the opposition robust. We were under strict orders that all military contacts we made should be for the purposes of gathering intelligence, not fomenting coups. But we also understood that Allende did not represent the majority of Chileans. Under the terms of the Chilean constitution, his Unity Party had been elected with just over 36 percent of the vote. The opposition was, in fact, the majority.

At this point, readers who are wondering why the CIA continued to act against Allende at all are surely too young to remember the proxy war between the democratic West and the Communist Eastern Bloc waged by the United States and the Soviet Union during the Cold War. We believed that the fate of the democratic world was at stake. When a country went Communist, it was a victory for the Soviet Union. Dictatorship inevitably replaced democracy, and U.S. interests were defeated. That's what had happened in Cuba, and the United States was bound and determined to keep communism from spreading in our own hemisphere, even as the Soviets were working hard to promote it in the region. To the United States, Allende represented a dangerous new front for the Soviets in the Cold War. In his 1977 interview with David Frost, Richard Nixon recalled being warned that, with Castro in Cuba and Allende in Chile, Latin America was a "red sandwich" that would eventually be all red in between.[9] We were no longer under orders to topple Allende, but we certainly wanted, and were willing to assist in, his political defeat.

It was into this atmosphere that I arrived in Santiago in August of 1971, with my wife and five children between the ages of two and seven. There were no direct flights, so we had flown first to Buenos Aires—after an emergency layover in Paraguay for a repair—and then to Santiago, an eighteen-hour trip that frazzled all of us. We got to our temporary quarters—a rather drab three-bedroom apartment—around dinnertime and discovered that the only thing available to eat was a can of Dinty Moore beef stew. Our six-year-old son burst into tears. Perhaps I should have been overwhelmed at that moment—at the audacity of our mission, the odds against success, and the sheer culture shock I was putting my family through—but I was not. Quite the opposite. I was supremely confident in the correctness of our cause, the power of our tools, and the resilience of my family. I was also elated at my good fortune: a junior officer on his first foreign assignment landing in Chile, the focal point, at that moment, of the Agency's Western Hemisphere Division. I was exactly where I wanted to be.

Recruiting—asking a foreign national to betray his country and work for Uncle Sam—is one of the most difficult tasks for a spy to pull off. There are many people who are very good at developing relationships, but few who have the instinct to close a deal. Timing is crucial. If you wait too long to make your pitch to an asset, when your relationship has become too close, you end up seeming manipulative and to be betraying a friendship. If you pop the question too soon, you run the risk of rejection and of causing a political flap if the potential asset reports the recruitment attempt to the authorities. Some people come by recruitment naturally, others need to be prodded, and everyone gets better with experience. Nailing down your first recruitment is a milestone in any case officer's career.

Truth be told, recruiting did not come naturally to me. As a young officer, I was by nature reserved, if not socially awkward, and (I came to realize) rather intimidating-looking. I'm six foot five and tend not to smile in business settings, so my natural demeanor appears stern. I wasn't aware of the impression I was giving until my boss told the

ambassador he wanted me in on a sensitive meeting, and the ambassador replied, "You mean the big, sinister-looking guy?" Up until then, I
had never quite looked at myself that way. Years later, a foreign intelligence service gave me the nickname Easter Island Man because of my
supposed resemblance to the famous statues there. I actually was grateful for this rather gentle description, especially since one of my predecessors abroad had been called the Poison Dwarf! I got off lightly. Still,
it did reinforce a growing perception that I hadn't fully appreciated: to
recruit, I would need a whole new skill set.

Once more, and not for the last time, the highly social Pat became
my most valuable asset. She is as diminutive as I am tall and as outgo-
ing as I was seemingly introverted back then. She would literally lead
the way, walking in front of me at parties, engaging the guests, and asking them, "You know Jack, don't you?" In time, her sociability rubbed
off on me, and eventually I moved rather easily through the social banter at cocktail parties and the disco parties we threw at our home, hoping to recruit Soviet agents. A dance called the Hustle was all the rage
at that time, and I couldn't help but think how appropriate it was when
our house was packed with prospective foreign targets dancing the
night away.

•

As I settled into my assignment in Santiago, I was mixing it up well
with many of the locals, but I was having difficulty positioning myself
for a recruitment. Fred Latrash, the deputy station chief, sensed my
hesitation and he appropriately leaned on me. The spy business is a
trade, and the process of spying is often referred to by insiders as
tradecraft. In its ideal form, tradecraft is learned at the knee of a master
journeyman. While much can be taught in the classroom and in training exercises, there is no substitute for working in the field under the
leadership of an experienced professional. I was most fortunate in my
early career to work for such a master journeyman. Fred was a flamboyant, experienced operations officer with extensive experience in
covert operations in the Middle East and Africa. The word was that
he had been sent to Chile to take more aggressive action than the
more cerebral chief Ray Warren, whom I looked up to and tried to emulate in managerial and operational style. They made a good team. It was

better that Ray was calling the political shots, but I also valued what Fred taught me about recruitment. He suggested that I recruit a senior Communist Party official whom the station had had periodic contact with for a number of years but had not put on the payroll. Our "cutout," or go-between, with this official was a local businessman, who agreed to set up a lunch at his home for me and the official so I could make the pitch.

I was apprehensive, but our host tried to put me at ease. He graciously served us a local delicacy, a deep dish of *erizos*, raw sea urchins. I can handle just about any exotic dish, but this was tough to get down. Fortunately, he accompanied the *erizos* with an excellent bottle of Santa Rita 120 white wine. After every spoonful of *erizos*, I had a big gulp of wine. Before too long the *erizos* started to taste better and the target seemed more amenable to cooperation. Nevertheless, I was taking too long to get to the point for our host, who finally blurted out, in so many words, "How much money are you going to give this Communist for his cooperation." I immediately suggested a thousand dollars per month, he accepted, and my first recruitment was behind me. In retrospect, I'm convinced that it was somewhat of a setup by Fred to get me over the hump of making a recruitment pitch. It is much easier to make the second pitch, even if the first one is a cakewalk. This is a classic example of the journeyman-apprentice relationship when it works well.

I wish I could say the road was smooth from there on out, but the learning curve was steep. During one of my very first meetings with an asset, I climbed into his car and we drove slowly around a small city park. Unexpectedly, the asset handed me a sheaf of documents. I had to decide whether to take them, knowing that my cover could be blown if I were caught with them on the street. But this was a onetime offer, and my car was parked nearby, so I grabbed the papers and cut through the park on foot—only to find myself chased by five wild dogs. Imagine the scene: a very tall CIA spy, secret documents in hand, running from a pack of snarling canines. As I turned a corner, I remembered that one of my colleagues lived nearby, and I headed straight for his front door. By then the dogs had decided to rest, but when my colleague and I drove back to my car, there they were, waiting like sentries. They looked incredibly ferocious, but when my colleague approached one of the four-legged assailants and held out his hand, the dog started licking it. "I bet you have cats," he said to me. It took me a while to live that one down.

Several weeks later, I handed over a substantial amount of cash to another asset—this time a man from a Chilean newspaper opposed to Allende. Since the CIA is, first and foremost, a large bureaucracy, I needed a receipt to send back to Langley at the end of the month. And since I was just out of spy school and wanted to try some of the high-tech gear I had been exposed to in training, I wrote out the receipt and had the asset sign it in invisible ink, which had been touted in training as a means to protect an agent's identity if a document fell into unfriendly hands. The asset was, needless to say, impressed by such tradecraft. I then went back to the station and applied the magic chemical meant to expose the ink. Everything worked perfectly. There was only one problem: when I went to file the asset's expense account several weeks later, I discovered that the invisible ink had eaten through the paper. I had to go back to my source and beg for a new receipt, this time signed with a Bic pen.

Still, I would become a fervent believer in putting gadgets to work in the field. One of my favorite devices was SRAC, or short-range agent communications. I installed in my personal vehicle, and in the vehicle of one of my top assets, a very low-powered SRAC device that allowed us to communicate while driving around town in relatively close proximity. There were no visible signs of connectivity between us—the perfect cover.

Fred Latrash was even more enthusiastic about technology. He was continually sending messages to the tech staff at headquarters, pointing out some device he had seen in *Popular Mechanics* that could be deployed operationally or was less costly than a similar device in our inventory.

For a time, if we wanted to talk to Fred in his office, we had to use one of his pet gadgets, a Hush-a-Phone. This was basically an upscale variation on the old Boy Scout soup-can-and-string device that kids used to use to talk to each other over a very short distance. The device had a miniature microphone attached to a headset, which in turn was attached to a similar set that Fred wore. Users had to sit ten feet apart and speak to each other in hushed voices, a guaranteed impediment to the free flow of discussion. This was Fred's solution to the security implications of office conversations, which were indeed vulnerable to audio eavesdropping. The Soviets were always finding creative ways to plant bugs, and we did our share of bugging them as well.

National security officials attempted to solve the bug problem by placing a soundproof plastic room, called a bubble, in virtually every U.S. facility around the world. These were generally located in an inconvenient spot. There simply wasn't enough time in the day for officers to check into the bubble every time they needed to talk about an operations matter. Fred's solution, though, turned out to be just as impractical. For weeks on end, we all vigorously avoided conversations with him in his office so we wouldn't have to use the ludicrous-looking Hush-a-Phone. Eventually, Fred gave up and hung the Hush-a-Phone on his wall—a symbol, he said, of case officer obstinacy in the face of advances in technology.

The truth is that, at least during my tenure, relatively few case officers liked new technology, even though it played an important role in Agency history and is part of the romance of the job—the hidden microphone, the spring-loaded secret compartment, the camera camouflaged in a commonplace object. The very popular spy museum in Washington, D.C., was founded on the public's enduring fascination with such things. But they truly are just adjuncts to our trade.

The most powerful tools I used in Chile remain the most powerful the CIA has: money and relationships. They were at the heart of my most important responsibility, which was the media account. *El Mercurio* was one of the oldest newspapers in Chile, serving, with the other publications in its chain, more than half the country's reading public. As a profitable enterprise dedicated to free expression, it was a natural ally in our quest to keep the Allende government from establishing a Marxist regime. The owner legitimately feared that such a government might expropriate its papers and put the media under government control. Our chief of station, Ray Warren, brought me to meetings with his key contacts, and I gradually took over more of the account. It was a first-rate learning experience on how to manage top-level covert action assets.

I hasten to clarify that the CIA had no role in what was printed in *El Mercurio*. The notion persists that the paper was an organ of the

Agency. I can state categorically that this is not true. In fact, the editor did not take kindly to outside influence on the paper editorially. We did give them money that enabled them to continue publishing, but we met only with folks on the business side of the paper. Fred Latrash was always harping on the contention that *El Mercurio* needed to be more strident in its attacks on Allende, but Ray and I disagreed; I thought its stance was just right. The paper never used propaganda to deliberately mislead readers about the Allende government's economic policies, but it did emphasize such issues as the seizure of private property, the illegal and violent actions of certain segments of the ruling coalition, and the specter of economic disaster. It managed to keep its credibility even as it became increasingly antigovernment.

Our involvement in *El Mercurio* was this: we gave the paper roughly $2 million, but our purpose was the opposite of co-opting it. What we wanted was to ensure continued press freedom. True, there was no official censorship by the Allende government; half a dozen dailies in Santiago represented the full spectrum of political opinion, and each operated independently. However, shortly after my arrival, the government blocked *El Mercurio*'s access to newsprint. This, along with cutbacks in advertising and labor unrest, threatened to shut it down, and that would have been a tremendous loss.

One of my first cables from the field was a request for $1 million to keep the paper afloat. A declassified memorandum[10] shows that the request was the subject of a lively discussion in the 40 Committee, the covert action subcommittee of the National Security Council. I knew nothing of this at the time. I knew only that I received an okay to provide *El Mercurio* with an initial sum of $700,000, but it had to be orchestrated through a very complex funding mechanism. It was a valuable education for me in high finance and clandestine funding mechanisms.

We also had sources inside the Chilean military. But the Church Committee overestimated our military ties, which were not nearly as numerous or important as our assets in the media and political parties. We weren't getting regular information from flag-rank officers, and we didn't have close ties to any of the decision makers—though not for lack of trying. Fred Latrash had, as his top priority, making friends and recruiting sources in the military. To help with this effort, he joined the military riding club, which was an important social milieu, and even bought an "operational horse" with headquarters' approval. The horse was named Bismarck. One afternoon, I could hear the normally soft-spoken station chief vigorously dressing down Fred. Though his voice was raised, I couldn't tell what the issue was, but I noticed on the table outside Ray's office, where the day's cables were displayed, a memo explaining that Bismarck had died from lack of use and requesting that headquarters write the animal off as a loss on our books. I surmised the absurdity of writing off an "ops horse" must have driven Ray up the wall.

Fred, nonetheless, was very effective in meeting a wide range of army officers. But, to the best of my knowledge, none of them ended up in the recruitment column. One of his most memorable contacts was General Augusto Pinochet, who would also become one of Fred's most memorable misjudgments. Fred was unimpressed with him, feeling he was too weak ever to lead a coup. In the end, we had no meaningful relationship with Pinochet before the coup. We did, however, have good insight into the Allende government through our contacts in the Communist Party. Its members turned out to be keen analysts and worthy assets. At one point, they secured for me a typewriter and blank Communist Party letterhead. I never did make use of these things. As it turns out, that was for the best.

•

When we arrived in Santiago, Pat located a lovely house for us three blocks from the Russian embassy. After we moved in, I was struck by how many cats there were in the neighborhood. I mentioned this to one of the old-timers in the office. He laughed and told me an operational secret: several months earlier one of our officers decided to tweak the Russians by placing an ad in the local press that said that anyone who delivered a cat to the front door of their embassy would receive a handful of escudos, the local currency. Dozens of people showed up with stray cats, demanding payment. When the embassy refused to compensate them for the cats, the visitors left the cats and walked away, thus infesting the neighborhood with strays.

The Russians were mightily annoyed and reciprocated with a similar operation. Unfortunately, this type of tit-for-tat harassment was carried on throughout the Cold War. It was humorous but mindless—the wrong way to approach psychological operations. Covert operations should be based on solid objective evidence with important national security benefits. They never should be used for amusement.

Pat soon felt at home in Santiago but realized she needed to learn how to drive to get around town on her own. Being a city girl, she had no license and had never really driven a car. I gave her a quick driving lesson, which left her feeling confident—and me uneasy. An embassy employee helped her get a license, which was secured, after all the paperwork was completed, with a bottle of scotch. Pat's first test was to drive to an embassy function at the ambassador's residence. When it came time to leave, Pat graciously offered to give a close friend, Terry Svat, a lift without revealing that she had just learned to drive. I heard from several sources that the trip was not uneventful. Apparently, approaching the entrance gate, Pat went for the brake but hit the gas pedal instead, jumping the curb and proceeding at a relatively high speed in the direction of the guardhouse, barely missing it and the armed guards. Today, any car jumping a curb in front of an embassy or ambassador's residence should expect to be fired upon. Fortunately, this took place long before our embassies became modern-day fortresses.

While I was out meeting contacts and supporting the opposition media, Pat was coping with running a household for a family of seven in a country that was slowly falling apart. It is, in part, her experience in Santiago that convinces me still that Allende would not have lasted long whether the CIA had been there or not. Too many people were being hurt by his economic policies—not just the moneyed but the middle and working classes, too. Allende, perhaps fearing that his narrow margin of victory gave him a short time line to pursue his vision of a Socialist Chile, rushed into a multipronged program of land reform, nationalizing industry, and government spending to stimulate the economy. Initially, his program seemed to be working. In the government's first year, GDP grew by 7.7 percent, production increased by 13.7 percent, and consumption levels rose by 11.6 percent.[11] But by the time I arrived with my family, those economic policies had come back to bite him. Inflation was over 45 percent and climbing.[12] Landlords were reluctant to spend money to maintain property that might be seized at any moment; business owners who could were leaving, taking their capital and entrepreneurial know-how with them; and there were massive consumer shortages.

Pat spent a good portion of her day hunting for basic household items on the black market. Flour could be obtained at one location, soap at another. She had a network of contacts and secret codes to rival my own. Hers were aimed at locating particularly scarce products. She would be told, for example, to go to a garage or building and "knock on the green door" to find black-market oil and toilet paper, which were in very scarce supply in Santiago. Butter was so scarce that some of the embassy wives made their own. Pat was raised in a row house in Philadelphia; she had no desire to learn how to churn butter. So we did without a lot of things. Beef was one of the things we gave up; it was nearly impossible to find. We switched to fish, chicken, and pork. One day, a colleague told me that he had found a black-market butcher who could provide steak. I got him to take me there, and I felt like a hero coming home with a bagful of supposed "quality" beef. It did look odd, with a yellowish tint to its fat. Pat was a little skeptical, but she prepared it. One taste and we knew we'd been had. It was horsemeat! We fed it to our dogs, who seemed to enjoy it well enough.

These deprivations were much worse for Chileans—who, after all, were not on temporary assignment—and contributed to growing unrest. Allende had his political problems as well domestic ones. The moderate Christian Democrats, alarmed by the brisk pace at which they thought he was nationalizing industries, moved to oppose him legislatively,[13] while the left in his own coalition thought he should be moving faster. Their impatience gave rise to the Revolutionary Left Movement, known as MIR, which sponsored ad hoc seizures of land in the countryside, often by violent means, creating a climate of fear and worsening food shortages.

Far from being humbled by this turmoil, Allende took the provocative step of inviting Fidel Castro to Chile in November 1971, further inflaming fears that he intended to take Chile down the same road as Cuba. My colleagues and I were kept busy following the Cuban president's travels through the country. We were eager to stay on top of what formal or informal cooperation the leaders might be agreeing to, but we soon concluded that, rather than an official state visit, Castro was enjoying a wonderful vacation. He waded in streams; took day trips to remote areas such as Caletones, where he toured the recently nationalized El Teniente copper mine; and did a lot of public speaking. His one-week visit turned into two weeks, then three; then December came, and he was still there. We found that moderate and conservative Chileans resented having Castro around. The high times he was enjoying seemed an insulting contrast to the shortages and inflation making their lives so difficult.

This is when I learned, almost by accident, that a little bit of money can go a long way in covert action, and sometimes your greatest successes come from your most unexpected assets. Among my pool of assets was an elderly middle-class woman—a grandmotherly type. She was a civil activist but had not proved a valuable source of intelligence, and because every meeting posed a risk, we met with her infrequently. She suggested raising the voice of the opposition with a march of women, who would carry pots and pans along with banners protesting the scarcity of basic food supplies and household goods. It sounded like a good idea and worth a small investment to help her get it organized. I gave her several hundred dollars but had low expectations, and after days passed with no march materializing, I wrote it off as a bad call on my part.

So I was stunned a few weeks later when I was walking near a park not far from the embassy and heard the thunder of thousands of women parading enthusiastically and boldly down the street, pounding pots and pans. And there was my asset, among those directing the marchers toward La Moneda, the presidential palace. I watched with pride, feeling that the mission had been completed—but it was only just beginning. Early that evening, I went to the Carerra Hotel for dinner. It had a very plush, upscale rooftop restaurant overlooking La Moneda. Halfway through dinner, the restaurant patrons pressed against the wide windows to watch what was taking place below. Buses had pulled up in front of the presidential palace, where the women were still demonstrating. Suddenly, students with bandanas pulled up over their faces surged out, clashing violently with the women. Images of Chilean housewives being set upon by leftist youths flashed around the world, creating a publicity nightmare for the government and a rallying point for the opposition.

Watching this unfold from the luxury of the Hotel Carrera rooftop was surreal for me. I felt I should be in the fray with my asset, but of course that would have been impossible. Such marches became known as *cacerolas*, and this particular one as the "March of the Empty Pots," an emblem of popular opposition to Allende. It emboldened other segments of the Chilean middle class as it galvanized women to speak out against the president's economic policies. As former ambassador Davis put it, "Together with Castro's visit, the march . . . brought a change in Chilean politics, from the relative normality and social accommodation that had prevailed in preceding weeks to a greater spirit of confrontation."[14]

Allende tried to mitigate the damage by suggesting the United States was behind the *cacerolas*.[15] After the failed coup attempt, blaming the United States was usually a good strategy, but it brought him limited success this time. From that small initial investment, a movement grew that would have a profound impact on the events that followed. More marches took place, under the banner of *poder femenino*, "woman power."[16] Consumer shortages were no longer people's only complaint; they feared the instability in the countryside and the threat of violence from the left. They increasingly aimed their protests at the military, asking it to act against Allende. In one particularly memorable protest, the women threw chicken feed at soldiers, suggesting they were too timid to oppose the president. As events would show, the military was not immune to this kind of persuasion.

Women were not the only ones putting pressure on the government. In October of 1972, the truckers' federation went on strike, touching off a wave of shutdowns. Truckers were the lifeblood of Chile. There were limited railroads and air transport; most things were carried by trucks owned by small mom-and-pop companies operating close to the bone with just one or two trucks. The truckers' grievances had been building. Spare parts to make repairs had to be imported and were difficult, if not impossible, to get. The truckers felt squeezed and worried that theirs was another industry Allende was planning to nationalize. When the president announced plans for a mixed government-private transport operation in Aisén, the truckers walked off the job. Shop owners closed their doors, partly in sympathy, partly because there were no goods without the truckers working. Within two weeks, bus and taxi drivers had joined in, and the next thing we knew, professionals—engineers, health care workers, pilots—joined in as well. A *Time* article from October 30 describes a "pall of tear gas" hanging over Santiago, with half the city seemingly out on strike.[17]

Another part of the mythology of U.S. involvement in Chile is that the United States paid the truckers to go on strike. This is not true. They did ask us for support, and the station chief thought it was a good idea, but Ambassador Davis was against it. Davis did not dismiss it out of hand, however. He tried to maintain an open relationship with Ray Warren because he always feared the station might take drastic action behind his back, as it had done to his predecessor during Track II. So he sent the truckers' request to Washington, and it was the White House that rejected it.[18]

As the economy spiraled downward and street demonstrations became routine, rumors of an imminent coup were pervasive. Indiscriminate bombings started to rock the town. Late one night we were awakened by a loud noise that shook the house. We thought it was an earthquake—a regular occurrence in Chile—and went back to sleep. The next morning, I was surprised to see a huge crater in our yard and much of the plaster siding blown off part of our house. The tremor we'd felt had been a bomb. It was at this point that I began to consider the physical risks to my family if the internal strife grew. I had been given a shotgun by a friend as he was departing Santiago, and one afternoon shortly after the bombing, I showed Pat how to use it if the house were raided while I wasn't home. We slid the table about ten feet from the front door, and she practiced crouching behind it and aiming the shotgun at imaginary intruders.

She stowed the gun, along with some nonperishable food, in our tiny attic, in a "special basket." The plan was that, should worst come to worst, she would boost the children into the attic, then climb in herself and wait out any trouble. Both of us treated the plan as perfectly natural, but in retrospect, it seems exceedingly foolhardy. When you need to instruct your wife on how to gun down intruders, it's time to send your family to a safe haven. What was I thinking? Living in a dangerous environment is like exposing yourself to the cold. It does its damage as you adjust to it. I had grown numb to the risks we faced. I have always considered it one of my worst judgment calls, and the family's wellbeing became a terrifying distraction when the coup finally came.

The station dutifully reported to Langley the coup talk we were hearing. The Directorate of Intelligence analysts were skeptical. They did not believe the military would subvert the constitution, but we were not immune to false alarms. Early in 1973, an asset called his case officer and reported, "My aunt is sick and may not live to recover." The authentic agreed-upon phase between the asset and the case officer to indicate that a coup was under way was somewhat different—"My aunt has died." This communication technique was to be used in an emergency, when the asset could not meet his case officer. This somewhat ambiguous call, coupled with collateral chatter about a possible coup and the Argentine military mobilization exercises along with the border with Chile, led the station management to believe that a coup had indeed started. Consequently, a CRITIC cable was sent to Washington indicating that a coup was imminent. The next morning, when nothing happened, the station ended up with egg on its face. This false alarm lowered the headquarters analysts' willingness in the future to act on coup reporting from the field.

These incidents of garbled CRITIC communications became part of the Santiago station folklore, and after that I made it a policy never to have officers working with me use code phrases as indicators for action. The message has to be unambiguous, or a meeting must be made to confirm its meaning before it can be reported.

This misstep notwithstanding, an actual coup attempt did come, in June of 1973. A small group of about eighty soldiers, who had been drinking heavily the night before, decided it was time to act to free an officer who had been arrested for making seditious statements calling for a coup against Allende. They obtained his release from the Ministry of Defense and drove a column of sixteen armored vehicles from the Second Armored Battalion in Santiago to La Moneda and the Ministry of Defense, convinced that they would provide the spark that would ignite the entire armed forces. But the army's commander in chief, Carlos Prats, determined to secure the military's nonintervention tradition, personally went to La Moneda to stop them. One of our embassy's political officers, Jeff Davidow, was on the street watching events unfold. Davidow, who went on to become ambassador in several countries and one of the most senior diplomats at the Department of State in the 1990s, recalls the scene: "Prats and the High Command strolled right out to the tanks and told the soldiers inside to turn them around and take them back to their barracks. 'We're in charge,' he told them. It was extraordinarily dramatic . . . Of course, as events unfolded it was clear that the events of the day stimulated the generals to take action themselves rather than leaving it in the hands of their subordinates."[19] The soldiers returned to their base with little resistance. This attempt, known as the *tancazo*, or "tank putsch," was over by 11:30 a.m. After that, we believed there never would be a military coup against Allende, and we directed all our activity to the next election, to help the moderate Christian Democrats, the strongest opposition party, mount a credible challenge in 1976.

We did not know, at that point, that senior officers in the military were seriously rattled by the challenge to their authority in the *tancazo* and gravely concerned that the breakdown in discipline would spread. They believed, we learned, that the younger officers would press for a coup, and senior officials such as Pinochet worried that if they didn't join forces with the upstarts, they would be swept away by them. Far from the end of coup plotting, the *tancazo* was when it began in earnest. In the street, strikes and protests continued apace. After a protest by military wives, in August, General Prats resigned, General Augusto Pinochet became commander in chief, and less than three weeks later, I got my coup alert message while having lunch at the restaurant Da Carla.

There were people in our own embassy in Santiago who did not believe our information about the impending coup. When I hinted at it to a friend in the political section, he scoffed: "You issue a memo like that every Friday." It's true that we had been hearing and reporting coup rumors for weeks, but we had never before had the solid information we now had, and from such reliable sources: information we'd confirmed four times over, with increasing levels of detail, by the morning of September 11, 1973—even more if you count the almost humorous string of calls we'd received the night before.

A skeleton crew, including the station chief and me, had stayed in the station that Monday night, September 10, so we could be ready to take reports from observation posts set up at key places—including directly across the street from La Moneda—the minute the action began. We were excited, on edge. The phone rang. "The baby will be delivered tomorrow," a voice said, then hung up. I had no idea what this meant, but I sensed someone was trying to tell us something. Then the phone rang again. "Uncle Jonas will be in town tomorrow" was the message this time. There were more calls through the night. Bemused, I can still only guess that some case officer in the past had given these unknown assets code phrases to use if they ever learned of a coup. In any event, the messages were utterly useless because they didn't match any known codes.

As the station chief recalls that night, there was competition between the station and the military attachés, who stayed in the embassy overnight to see who would call the coup first and advise Washington. "I received a call from the attachés near dawn," the station chief said. "They had a report of gunfire at a military base outside of Santiago. Did we know anything? I didn't."

At 7:00 a.m. on September 11 we were on tenterhooks, waiting to see if our more reliable sources were correct. Time passed with no word. We feared we had another false alarm on our hands and that our credibility might be permanently compromised. Then, at 8:00 a.m., we got the report—exactly as one of our assets had told us. The navy had started the coup with an uprising in Valparaiso. The asset had been just an hour off.

Some months later I was told in some detail by my primary source how the coup came about. He knew the principals well, but I have never been able to verify his account. Former ambassador Nathaniel Davis, though, has a similar account in his book.[20] My source told me that navy vice admiral José Merino had forced the army into action by drafting a note saying he would initiate the coup and asking each of the other military service commanders to sign on to the note confirming that they were prepared to support him. Merino supposedly gave this handwritten note to Rear Admiral Sergio Huidobro and Captain Ariel González to take to the commander of the air force, Gustavo Leigh. Leigh signed up quickly, the story goes, and sent the note on to the director of the Carabineros, who also signed. With the three signatures in place, Pinochet was left with virtually no alternative but to sign it and act. As an aside, the ensign who was delivering the note to the military chiefs was so nervous that he forgot his ID and had to do an about-face and return halfway between Valparaiso and Santiago to retrieve his wallet.

By 9:00 a.m., September 11, the armed forces were in control of all of Chile except for the center of Santiago. When informed of the coup, Allende had gone directly to the presidential palace and refused to resign. Troops filled the streets downtown. Skirmishes and sporadic firefights erupted. Barricades went up around the U.S. embassy, and traffic ground to a halt. Shortly before noon, Hawker Hunter jets from the Chilean air force screamed across downtown Santiago and began firing rockets into La Moneda. The whole city erupted in gunfire.

At the station, we dove for cover as stray bullets shattered windows, and we ended up taking refuge in "the vault," the steel-enclosed chamber where we kept our classified documents.

Around two o'clock that afternoon, Chilean troops stormed the presidential palace. Allende was protected by a special force—his "group of personal friends," or Grupo de Amigos Personales, called the GAP. Some were former members of Chilean Special Forces, but some had been imported from Cuba, because Allende never completely trusted the military and wanted bodyguards of whose loyalty he could be assured. They, indeed, defended him to the death that day, as the military, which had found the GAP an insult and an irritant, showed no mercy in getting to Allende. As for the president himself, our intelligence found that the military planned only to capture him, not to execute him. However, he took his own life rather than become a prisoner of the junta. By 2:30 p.m., the seventeen-year rule of Augusto Pinochet had essentially begun.

That evening, the military imposed an ironclad curfew across Santiago. My colleagues and I were trapped inside the station. We had a limited ability to track what was happening in the streets in the coup's aftermath but were following sporadic reports of "cleanup operations."

One of these reports stopped me cold. The military was about to launch a large raid at a house in my neighborhood—next door to my home, where Pat was trying to maintain a veneer of calm for the sake of our children. What if the soldiers went to the wrong house? I got on a station radio network with Pat and my colleague Jerry, who lived a few blocks away. The military had declared a short break in the curfew so people could take care of basic necessities, and there were about ten minutes left in which Pat could get out safely before the raid. I told her to get the children and stand near the front door to wait for Jerry. Jerry came on the radio and said, "I'm on my way." He had a very small car and was concerned about how to fit Pat and our five children into it, but somehow he managed, and they sped off to the relative safety of his nearby home, a military helicopter filled with trigger-happy soldiers hovering menacingly overhead.

Back in Washington, the fall of Allende was greeted as a major victory. President Nixon was pleased, and his secretary of state, Henry Kissinger, was very satisfied. Against all odds, the station had helped create a climate for the coup without taking actions that might taint the effort. We were bathed in the glow of success. That glow, of course, would quickly dim when, during a meeting with a longtime asset, I got a glimpse of what the new Pinochet government was capable of. A high-value penetration of the extremist wing of the Socialist Party, this asset had been arrested in a post-coup military roundup and tortured. When he was finally released, he triggered the emergency meeting with us. Since his former case officer had departed the country, I was selected to meet with him. We were concerned that he might have cracked under pressure and divulged his ties to us, so we approached the meeting with caution. He was a tough guy. Fortunately, the military had no inkling of his affiliation with us and didn't ask about CIA ties. If he had been compromised, he could have been run against us, blowing our officers' cover and feeding us false information about the Pinochet government.

As part of the arrangements, the asset had been instructed to meet his new handler at a predetermined time and place. The site had been well selected so that we could smoke out possible hostile surveillance. To make sure he was clean, a four-person surveillance team monitored his movements approaching the site and then while he waited for us. Today it would be much harder to feel comfortable. The use of drones and satellites and global positioning system devices would have made it easy for the Chileans to stand off and monitor his movements electronically from the sky without detection by our surveillance. Absent such technology, we were convinced the asset was clean. But before we could approach him, he walked right up to one of our team members and asked in Spanish, "Are you my new case officer?" His move was so sudden that our officer became rattled, and instead of ignoring the inquiry, he blurted out, "Not me, him," and pointed to me. It wasn't our finest operational moment, but even well-trained operators can be caught off guard and react inappropriately. This was a point I would repeatedly drive home with surveillance teams: be ready, not only physically, but mentally, for the unexpected.

We met inside an Agency-controlled car owned by a local asset. He described his torture in graphic detail. He was still very angry about the treatment he had received at the hands of the military, who believed he might be a leftist extremist. Despite the torture and beatings, he stuck to his story and eventually convinced his jailers that he was not affiliated with a far-left element within the Socialist Party. The asset may have detected a bit of suspicion on my part—was his story incomplete? Was he exaggerating his abuse? In order to prove his point, he rolled up his pant legs to reveal the ugly scars and black-and-blue marks from the abuse he'd suffered after being shackled and yanked around by his captors. Whatever reservations I might have had disappeared when I looked at the physical damage to his legs.

That memory has stayed with me. It has helped to reinforce my belief that torture is an unacceptable policy and inconsistent with our best traditions—the end does not justify the means. Unlike some of the experts, I don't argue that torture is ineffective or that the same results can be obtained through psychological manipulation and time. It's just wrong, and not consistent with American values. In the case of our Chilean asset, it didn't work because his torturers didn't ask the right question. If they had, it is very likely he would have compromised our relationship.

Within a year, newspaper reports about CIA actions, including Track II, would lead to the formation of the Church Committee and put our operation in Chile under a cloud. By that time, General Pinochet's human rights violations and imposition of martial law had cast doubt on the wisdom of U.S. policy in Chile. But in the heady days immediately following the coup, we could take unvarnished pride in how well we had defended the democratic institutions that we believed would soon resume governing Chile. The junta had promised to hold elections in sixty to ninety days, and that is what we expected to happen.

Still, in my enthusiasm, I almost made a major blunder. Our government contacts were looking for ways to strengthen their case against Allende. One of my sources mentioned that the Chilean foreign minister, Ismael Huerta, was going to the United Nations to give a speech explaining the rationale behind the coup. I suddenly remembered the typewriter and letterhead my Communist Party asset had given me. In a moment of faulty inspiration, I suggested we use them to fake evidence that Allende himself had intended to initiate his own coup just before the military intervened. My source thought it was a great idea and was going to bounce it off Huerta. Fortunately, before I went any further with this, I consulted the station chief, to share my plan with him. He was rightfully livid, pointing out that we had no policy authority for such an initiative. He made it clear that I needed to cap it off immediately. It was instantly obvious that he was right, and I sheepishly returned to tell my asset that the plan was a "no-go." Never again in my career would I entertain an action initiative without considering the need for appropriate authorization and reflecting on its impact on history. It was an invaluable lesson that would serve me well in the years ahead.

However, I was not the only one with such a "brilliant" idea. The Pinochet government had its own version. It pushed the line that, days before the coup, the Allende government had developed something called Plan Z (or Plan Zeta), which called for the GAP to assassinate top military commanders and opposition leaders as part of a left-extremist seizure of power, an *autogolpe*, or "self-coup."

Years later I would be reminded of this episode when I ran into former secretary of state Henry Kissinger at the Four Seasons restaurant in New York City. I spotted him across the room and reintroduced myself, noting our mutual experience in Chile. He politely said we should have lunch and talk about it. While I agreed, I didn't expect to hear from him and was very surprised when I returned to my office to find that there was already a note on my desk setting up a lunch with Kissinger. Over that lunch, it didn't take him long to get to his real and perhaps only interest: Hadn't Allende been planning an *autogolpe* shortly before the military ousted him? Kissinger clearly was disappointed by my response—that while that might eventually have been a possibility, at the time there was no credible reporting supporting the military's allegation. This was at odds with Kissinger's long-held views. Not surprisingly, it was the last time we had lunch together.

The station did try, after the coup, to establish closer ties with the junta, but it was a rocky road. We continued to hear disturbing reports—about mass arrests, torture, and the murder of people regarded as subversives. Many Chileans were not troubled by these actions. They had truly feared the MIR and didn't fully believe that the military would harm innocent civilians. They were wrong. In a secret memo dated September 24, 1973, less than two weeks after the coup, the station reported that "the deaths of the great majority of persons killed in cleanup operations against extremists . . . are not recorded. Only the Junta members will have a really clear idea of the correct death figures, which they will probably keep secret." On October 12, 1973, another memo quoted a source as saying that sixteen hundred civilians had been killed between September 11 and October 10.[21] Swept up in the military's wave of repression were two Americans, Frank Teruggi and Charles Horman, whose kidnapping and murder in the immediate aftermath of the coup inspired the 1982 Jack Lemmon–Sissy Spacek movie *Missing*. The movie's unfriendly presentation of the CIA has helped fuel a persistent, and bogus, theory that the CIA was somehow involved in the murders. Agency officer James E. Anderson became involved in the very emotionally disturbing search for the bodies of Horman and Teruggi. After the bodies were found, Anderson was deeply distraught about the murders for years to come.

Within two weeks of the coup, we also got our first inkling that Pinochet did not plan to hold elections. One of my colleagues had a political source who'd anticipated a role in the new government. This source had relatives in the military who must have given him the bad news; he came to my colleague chagrined. "They're not handing it back," he said, meaning the military was not handing power back to the politicians. The military was angry at the political parties we had worked so hard to defend. It felt as if the politicians' failure to defeat Allende electorally or curb him legislatively had forced the military to act in a way it hadn't wanted to. But now that it had seized power, it was not going to return it to the politicians to let them muck things up again.

If we made a mistake in Chile after the coup, it was a policy mistake. According to a longtime Agency colleague and friend who also was in Chile at the time, "We didn't put enough pressure on Pinochet to move to a civilian government." That said, no one at the station would ever have imagined that the Pinochet dictatorship would last until 1991. We still felt we'd accomplished the mission we'd been given: we had prevented the establishment of a left-wing regime aligned with Castro that could have become a Soviet asset in our hemisphere. In fact, as we climbed, over the years, to the highest levels at Langley, the case officers involved in that extraordinary operation became known around the CIA as the Chile Mafia.

We were seriously disillusioned, though, at the unforeseen consequences of the coup: the brutality and repression of the Pinochet regime. Obviously this has troubled me over the years, but it has not shaken my faith in covert action, at least not in "good" covert action. When I arrived in Santiago, every indication we had was that the Allende government had its eyes set on undermining the political opposition and threatening free media. In that environment, it was fair game to support those parties and the media in resisting. I'm convinced that if the military had not intervened in September 1973, our covert action programs would have sustained the opposition until the next election and that the Allende government would have been defeated at the ballot box. That would have been a far preferable outcome to the Pinochet regime.

•

As I was preparing to depart Santiago in 1974, I began to turn my assets over to my replacement, a newly arrived case officer. One of these assets was a Chilean politician. I made it a general policy not to use an alias with public figures, because you run a high risk of meeting them in a casual setting in the presence of others. Under these circumstances, it is quite easy to find yourself being referred to by your alias. Still, I asked the new case officer how he wanted to handle the introduction. He had had a few tours abroad, but he nonetheless decided that he wanted to use "good tradecraft" and meet the politician under an alias. Shortly thereafter, the politician invited the two of us and our wives to a dinner. The case officer's wife sat next to him. I could overhear parts of the discussion and heard her refer to her husband several times by his true name. At one point, the politician paused the discussion and said with a huge smile and for all to hear, "Don't you know your husband's name?" Flustered, his wife said she "confuses him all the time with his brother." We all laughed at her clumsy response. The jig was up.

When a new station chief arrived shortly before my departure, he asked me to write a memo about the situation in Chile. I produced a rather blunt document suggesting that the United States start using the very same covert action tactics on Pinochet that we had used against

Allende, to bring about a return of a democratic government. I doubt the station chief agreed at the time or sent my memo to Washington—if for no other reason than to protect my career, since it surely would have seemed a brash assessment by a first-tour case officer. But Chile taught me a lesson about unintended consequences that has served me well. If the coup that toppled Allende was an episode that has plagued the CIA ever since, for all the wrong reasons, my next reminder to be careful what we wished for was even more disastrous. Like the coup in Chile, it was instigated by the White House, and as in Chile we were, to a great extent, left holding the bag.

FOUR

"We Need to Polygraph Him"

Washington, 1985–86

One morning in early 2011 a story on the front page of *The New York Times* brought back a rush of memories. My former colleague Duane R. "Dewey" Clarridge was in the news again. Two decades after his indictment and pardon in Iran-Contra, he was running a private intelligence operation in Afghanistan under a multimillion-dollar Pentagon contract. I was astounded but not completely surprised, given Dewey's energy and charisma. As I read the piece, I remembered the call.

I was sitting in my Langley office in December of 1985 when Clarridge rang me out of the blue. By that point in our careers, we knew each other well, having worked together for a few years in Latin America, though we'd both moved on since then. Clarridge was chief of the Europe Division. I was head of the Near East Division's Iran branch at headquarters. He was calling to tell me to expect to hear very soon from Director Casey. "It's very urgent and extremely important," he told me. He didn't say the call would involve secret arms shipments to Iran.

Clarridge was a swashbuckling officer whose gung-ho support of the Contras, the right-wing rebel groups opposing Nicaragua's Sandinista government, made him a Casey favorite. The director had first taken a liking to Clarridge when he was serving as chief of station in Rome, then made him head of the Latin America Division, with authority for overseeing development of the Contra force, even though Clarridge couldn't speak Spanish and had no background in the region.[1] He had charisma and knew how to motivate people, and at the end of the day, running a division at the CIA was about leadership and driving the culture. We were a very top-down organization.

From his time in Rome, Clarridge dressed with Italian-style flair. He favored light suits and often had a silk handkerchief peeking out of his breast pocket, in red or blue to match his tie. Soon several of the station chiefs started sporting handkerchiefs as well. Once, when we were both back in Washington, during lunch in the Executive Dining Room, Clarridge pulled out a monocle to peer at the menu. I laughed profusely. "I might go for the handkerchief," I said, "but I'll be damned if I'm going to start using a monocle to emulate your style." He got a little testy over my remark, but to the best of my knowledge, he never wore the monocle again. I'm convinced that if he'd worn it to the chiefs of station conference, many of the chiefs would soon have been running around with monocles.

This tendency to emulate leaders can be a good thing, if it's not taken to an extreme. If you want to lead the Agency and you are trying to live by the creed on the wall in the lobby—"And Ye Shall Know the Truth and the Truth Shall Make You Free"—it's a great trait. But if you're motivated by a desire to please the president politically and the policy makers no matter what, it can lead to contaminated intelligence and unwise operational activity.

My substantive disagreement with Clarridge, if I could call it that, came in 1981, when he invited all his station chiefs back to the Washington area to talk about the Contras. The Contras were already receiving substantial support from the Reagan administration, through the CIA, but Clarridge was considering arming the groups, and he went around the table and asked each of us what we thought about it. I was one of only two who voiced a strong objection. I was, and remain, constitutionally opposed to building up exile forces as part of covert action programs. Instead, my strong inclination is to build up internal forces. I felt the main fight should have been inside Nicaragua, and I said so. If you can't move it inside, don't move it. I also thought that using other Latin Americans to train the Contras in Honduras was foolhardy, given nationalist sensitivities in the region. After I spoke up, challenging him, Clarridge walked out of the room in a huff, but he apparently didn't hold it against me.

"He was apprehensive about another potentially volatile operation and was frank in expressing his reservations," Clarridge wrote of me in his memoir, *A Spy for All Seasons.* "I appreciated his honesty," he continued. "There were some, however, who were not so kind. They saw him as someone motivated largely by a desire to advance his career."

That's nonsense. Challenging a new superior in a public forum is hardly the recommended path for career advancement. But it is quite true that speaking truth to power never hurt my career—and so it was with Clarridge. I could argue with him, and he wasn't intimidated; he held his ground, and I never felt that I was being penalized for speaking frankly to him. He was aware that I'd been around a long time by then, and that I knew the area well. I had a voice. He indicated that I was entitled to be listened to but not necessarily agreed with.

In 1982, during my tour in South America, Clarridge tried to convince me to take over the Central America Task Force, the operations group at headquarters responsible for organizing all matériel and personnel support for the Contras, despite my outspoken opposition to the Contra program. I had disagreed forcefully with those on the task force who wanted to shut down an opposition newspaper in Nicaragua, *La Prensa*, that was being menaced by the government. They thought this could be used to show how undemocratic the government was. But from my days working with the opposition media in Chile, I pressed the point that the paper could be an invaluable tool. Not to my surprise, the owners themselves wanted to keep up the fight and they stayed in business, to the chagrin of my colleagues.

I told Clarridge I wasn't the right choice for the job.

"I really don't want to do this one," I told him. "You and I have a serious difference about how to tackle the task."

"It's not a problem," he said.

"Dewey, this isn't a problem for you," I said, "but it's a problem for me. I don't agree with the Contra strategy, and if I take the job, I rightfully would be expected to carry out your plans."

Clearly, he was unhappy with my response. It took something off our relationship, which was fully understandable under the circumstances.

The next time I saw him was in 1983. As we headed toward town, he announced that he had something extremely important he wanted to discuss. I expected him to try to change my mind about the Contras and started to push back, when he interrupted me to say he wasn't there to talk about Nicaragua—"I'm here to work up an invasion of Suriname, from here," he said. I don't want to say I never get dumbfounded, but it was a stunner. Suriname, on the northeast coast of South America between Guyana to the west and French Guiana to the east, had been a Dutch colony until 1975. Both Dutch exiles and senior officials in the Reagan administration, including those in the CIA, did not want to see either the Soviet Union or Cuba expand their facilities in Suriname. The exiles, I understand, had asked the Agency for help overthrowing Suriname's Communist-leaning government.

Later that night we met at the Hilton with the commanding general of the U.S. Southern Command, Paul Gorman, and with Judge William P. Clark, Jr., the national security adviser under Reagan. I arrived late because my daughter Amy had been attacked at our front door by an armed robber who jumped out of a car and, with accomplices, tried not only to rip off her gold necklace but to force her into the car. Amy was a strong-willed and feisty teenager who somehow managed to pull herself free, and the robbers fled the scene with only the necklace. Nevertheless, the security team arrived, and a report had to be prepared for the police. I relayed the story to Clarridge, Gorman, and Clark when I arrived for our meeting, anticipating some sympathy, and was surprised at how quickly they passed over it and got down to talking about Suriname. It was a good indicator of just how serious and driven they were about the task. That said, it was one of the craziest operations I'd ever heard proposed in my career. It defied all of my basic rules for covert action and had little chance of success.

The next day, Clarridge and I had meetings with officials about developing an invasion team, with Clarridge talking about bringing in South Koreans and Gurkhas. They were incredulous, but they had a quintessential Latin response: Sure, sounds like a great idea; *we'll look into it.* Afterward, one official came to me and said, off the record, "Jack, we haven't tapped your phone, but we're going to start to tomorrow, and the reason is this is too important and we want to make sure you're playing it straight." What a unique approach to running a telephone tap operation! Since I never used the phone for operational matters, it posed no security threat. We always assume our phones are tapped.

Clarridge and his team went off to Brazil to sell the invasion plan. Brazil wanted numerous questions answered before considering it. Ultimately, the Americans were waved off, thanks to opposition in Latin America and on Capitol Hill, where people had come to their senses. One congressman went so far as to say publicly that it was the dumbest operation he had ever heard of. I continue to find it amusing for the absurdity of it and the bizarreness of that period. At that point in my career, I still had the view that you could humor bad policies because they would surely die under their own weight.

Iran-Contra changed all that. By now, Congress had passed the Boland Amendment, effectively stopping the CIA from providing support to the Contras. But officials in the executive branch were continuing to find ways to aid the cause on a covert basis.

Clarridge was circumspect when he phoned in 1985, saying only that Casey would be calling momentarily. The White House had already decided that shipping arms to Iran could gain the release of seven American hostages being held in Lebanon by Iranian-backed terrorists. Clarridge had, unwittingly, already helped facilitate a shipment of arms from Tel Aviv, through Lisbon, to Tehran, using the Israelis as middlemen. He would be indicted years later for his testimony about this, although he pleaded not guilty and consistently said he believed the flight contained parts for oil drilling. He was ultimately pardoned by President George H. W. Bush, in 1992.

As he predicted, that day in December 1985, I was summoned to the seventh floor within five minutes. Casey welcomed me into his office. He told me there was someone who had useful information about Iran, and he wanted me to meet him. His name was Manucher Ghorbanifar, a disreputable Iranian arms dealer.

I didn't even have to leave the building to check him out. We already had a thick file on him dating back to January 1980, showing a history of false leads and bad information peddled with an eye toward padding his own finances. He'd failed two polygraphs, and we'd issued what's popularly called a "burn notice" on him. These are fairly rare official statements that the subject is known to be untrustworthy. Ghorbanifar, according to his file, was to be regarded as an intelligence fabricator and a nuisance. He hadn't come to the Agency directly but, rather, through a foreign policy activist who was at the time a consultant to the NSC.

I met with the NSC consultant at his Georgetown home later that month. I used an alias because I had grave concerns about being exposed to Ghorbanifar. The consultant talked with enthusiasm about the arms dealer. He was proud of the work they were doing: they were going to free U.S. hostages held by Hezbollah in Lebanon, he told me, by arranging a sale of U.S. arms to the Iranians. I was shocked. I had never heard of such an operation, and given what I had just read about Ghorbanifar, I could hardly believe he was the middleman in such an undertaking. The NSC consultant assured me the whole thing had White House approval. Not only that, it was already under way. The release of a hostage, the Reverend Benjamin Weir, in September of that year, had been the result, he believed, of their help in shipping 96 TOW antitank missiles to Tehran. Weir, a Presbyterian missionary and teacher for almost thirty years in Lebanon, had been kidnapped sixteen months earlier from a street in Beirut by Islamic Jihad Organization, a terrorist group backed by Iran. The Iranians had then reneged on a promise to release six other hostages in exchange for another 408 TOWs in September, and they failed to release any hostages after another 18 Hawk antiaircraft missiles had been sent in November. The early arms shipments to Iran were made through the Israelis, so that the Reagan administration would not be accused of contravening its own arms embargo against Iran. Reagan approved the shipments out of concern for the hostages. But now the U.S. Marine lieutenant colonel Oliver North, from the NSC, was proposing that the United States itself sell arms to the Iranians. What wasn't clear to me or anyone else at the Agency, with the possible exception of Casey, was that proceeds from steep markups on the weapons would go to supporting the Nicaraguan Contras, in contravention of the Boland Amendment, which prohibited such assistance.

I listened patiently to the NSC consultant and agreed to meet the following day with him, Ghorbanifar, and North. Then I made a beeline for the home of Bert Dunn, who was chief of the Near East Division. A West Virginia lawyer who was also a smart, seasoned, and highly respected officer, Dunn had spent a great deal of time on the ground in the Middle East and Southeast Asia and knew it like the back of his hand. He had run into the likes of Ghorbanifar in his travels. He arranged a meeting for us with Casey and Clair George, head of the Directorate of Operations (DO), for the next day, before my rendezvous with Ghorbanifar, the NSC consultant, and North. At the appointed hour, we went to the director's office and I related what I'd been told. Clair George let out a moan and bent over like he'd been punched, his head in his hands. It appeared to me that he was hearing this for the first time. By contrast, Casey sat quietly listening and asked me to keep my appointment.

I was the first to arrive at the NSC consultant's house. North and Ghorbanifar came in shortly after me, grinning and in high spirits. I took an instant dislike to Ghorbanifar. His first gesture was to reach into his bag and take out three large cans of very expensive Iranian caviar, one for each of us. I handed mine right back to him. "I can't take that," I said. "It's against the rules." Clearly chagrined, he attempted to turn on the charm to try to win me over. I suspect he knew he wasn't making progress, but he is the type of hustler who believes that somehow, in the end, he will prevail.

The next day, I briefed Casey, Bert Dunn, and Clair George on the details of the meeting about the NSC-sponsored arms-for-hostages operation. I told them I was even more convinced that Ghorbanifar could not be trusted. To my surprise, Casey told me to keep dealing with him. I said, "If we're going to go forward with this, we need to polygraph him." I was confident of the results and thought for sure they would torpedo Ghorbanifar.

In addition to the grave policy issues, I was beginning to have career concerns. From what I was hearing, I was afraid there might be no recourse but to vote with my feet. I went home that night and in a state of agitation told my wife, "I might have to resign. I just can't do this one." Pat, not surprisingly, didn't flinch, simply saying, "Do what you have to do. We will survive."

We administered the polygraph to Ghorbanifar at a hotel in Georgetown a few days later. The polygrapher asked him about a dozen questions. The test results indicated that Ghorbanifar had lied on virtually all the relevant questions. The only things he answered truthfully, as I recall, were his name and nationality. I went straight to Bert Dunn and shared the results.

Ghorbanifar, meanwhile, apparently went straight to the NSC consultant, complaining that the polygraph test had been more expensive than he expected and that he had been physically injured by the examination techniques—a laughable claim. Nonetheless, the consultant called the CIA twenty-four-hour watch center, which handles after-duty communications. He demanded to talk to me, and reportedly threatened that he would have me fired if I didn't call him back immediately. Of course, when referring to me he used the alias I'd given him, so it took the watch officer some time to figure out whom he was talking about.

Clair called to ask about the results of the polygraph. When I told him about Ghorbanifar's rather spectacular failure, he said, "The hell with him." We were supposed to meet with Casey the next morning to brief him, but the meeting was called off for an unexplained reason. Clair told me that Ghorbanifar's lies had led everyone to the same conclusion: we wanted no part of any operation he was involved with. "The DO is out of it," he said. I was to have no more contact with Ghorbanifar or the NSC consultant.

I was satisfied. Not only did I not have to make a career-ending move, but I figured I had helped the U.S. government back off from a policy disaster. Shortly after meeting Ghorbanifar for the first time, I had written a note to senior management calling the arms-for-hostages deal with Iran "inimical to U.S. interests" and calling Ghorbanifar "a fabricator who has deliberately deceived the U.S. government concerning his information and activities." But mine was a short-lived feeling of satisfaction. What I did not count on was that Casey would simply transfer the arms-for-hostages operation to an analyst in the Directorate of Intelligence. He told Charlie Allen, our senior antiterrorism analyst and head of the Hostage Location Task Force, to meet with Ghorbanifar to take another look at him and figure out what he might be able to tell us.

Two days after Ghorbanifar failed the polygraph, and a day after Clair George declared that the Directorate of Operations would have nothing to do with him, Allen said he had spent five hours with Ghorbanifar at the NSC consultant's home.[2] Allen has said that he made pretty much the same appraisal I did: Ghorbanifar could not be trusted and was looking mostly to line his own pockets. But Allen, like Casey, held out hope that the arms dealer, whatever his motives and whatever false leads he might generate, might also provide information that would help get the American hostages back home.

The hostages were a grave concern for Reagan, and for the Agency, especially after William Buckley was seized in Beirut, where he was chief of station, in 1984. Clair George's chief of staff, Norm Gardner, had been a close friend of Buckley's, and to this day he feels unreasonably responsible for Buckley's capture. He had encouraged Buckley to go to Beirut, reasoning that, for Buckley, unmarried and childless, the post would not be as great a hardship as it would be for a family man. Only after Buckley was taken did Norm begin to berate himself for overlooking what a meticulous, organized man Buckley was, how beholden to schedules and patterns. It was Buckley's predictability that supposedly enabled Hezbollah to capture him. And they knew whom they had. The station chief was tortured mercilessly. We later learned that he died as a result of the torture, before the arms-for-hostages deal even started, but at the time, there was hope that we could get him out.

With Ghorbanifar still very much in the picture, Tom Twetten, Dunn's deputy, came to me stoically and started an ominous conversation by saying, "You're not going to like this," and indeed I did not. He said the president had signed a presidential finding (an executive directive) to trade missiles for hostages using Ghorbanifar as the middleman. Twetten asked if, under these circumstances, I would arrange the logistics and flights with retired major general Richard Secord of the Air Force, who was providing support for the operation. Knowing where I stood on Ghorbanifar, he added, "And you don't have to deal with Ghorbanifar." I agreed to help. In my mind, once the president authorized the mission, we had crossed the Rubicon. There now was no turning back. Since a decision had been made to proceed with the operation, I agreed to do what I could to make sure there were no logistical mishaps that would further increase the political risks associated with this high-stakes task. I would handle the complicated logistics and sensitive finances for the Agency, working with Secord and North. Arrangements had to be made for pallets of missiles to be loaded onto planes and paid for through the appropriate covert mechanism. I met once with Secord, in Northern Virginia, and once with North, at CIA headquarters. There were also a few meetings with North at the White House, where it was all business—no socializing or kibitzing.

On the night of the first flight, in February 1986, I went to the operations center at CIA headquarters, because it was the only place where we had special monitoring equipment for listening to the crew preparing for takeoff with the TOW missiles in the cargo hold. Since a part of me couldn't quite believe this was happening, I wanted to be there just in case something went wrong or, at a minimum, to report the plane's orderly departure. A few days later the missiles arrived in Tehran, and the compensatory funds were wired to the United States. This marked the beginning of what became the biggest scandal of the Reagan administration, one that engulfed the CIA and, at its peak, threatened to bring down the White House.

At that time, the Agency had a program focused on Iran. It included trying to locate assets and recruit sources. Cataclysmic political events, such as the Iranian Revolution, produce large communities of exiles. Many of them maintain lines of communication to, and networks of contacts in, their homeland. In the case of Iran, we spent a great deal of time meeting with such groups and trying to develop an organization that would bring them together. We helped establish an office for a political opposition group, with headquarters in Europe, but it was never very effective. Its members were a disparate bunch, ranging from leftists to royalists, and they spent a lot of time fighting among themselves and squandering money.

At one point we thought Reza Cyrus Pahlavi, the U.S.-educated son of the deposed Shah of Iran, might be a unifying force. But it would have been a very long stretch to assume that the son could play the same role his father had played decades earlier. His father had come to power in 1953 with essential CIA support. Kermit "Kim" Roosevelt, Teddy Roosevelt's grandson, along with first-tour operations officer Rocky Stone, coordinated the now well-known Operation Ajax, which ousted the Iranian prime minister Mohammad Mossadegh in an orchestrated coup d'état. (Rocky Stone, remember, was the chief of the Soviet Division who during training in 1969 urged me to join his group.) I recall how in our discussion back then, he told me that in the midst of the coup, he had had to dress the shah, who couldn't dress himself because he was too nervous. The shah remained grateful to the CIA, and to Kim Roosevelt and Rocky Stone in particular, for many years.

Nonetheless, in the mid-1980s, the son, known in our circles as "Baby Shah," had a certain following among the exiles and in the Iranian military, particularly the air force. We met with him from time to time, but I don't think he was ever deeply serious about leading a resistance movement. He had an idea that things might get so bad in Iran that there would be a popular revolt and a call for his return. In the meantime, his best play was to stay in the background and try to appear to be a forceful leader. This was frustrating, but it must be said he was still very young (in his mid-twenties) and was enjoying a safe and prosperous existence in the United States. He had a large house in McLean, Virginia. We were a little worried about his security for a while and asked the FBI to alert us to threats. Neither the best-case nor the worst-case scenario came to pass. The counterrevolution never happened, and Baby Shah settled down.

Another important exile was the former Iranian prime minister under the shah, Shapour Bakhtiar, who had a fascinating history, having fought in the Spanish Civil War against Franco and in the French Resistance against the Nazis in World War II. He was a tough and dedicated nationalist. I met him at his home in Paris and talked at some length about his past and his hopes for Iran. The house was seemingly well protected, with French police guarding the entrances. Nevertheless, I had an eerie feeling that he wasn't safe in his fortress. I couldn't put my finger on what made me so uneasy. Perhaps it was just a sense that he was challenging an Islamic fundamentalist regime that was prepared to take violent risks to remove its enemies. Perhaps it was the lingering history of exile assassinations. The Russian revolutionary Leon Trotsky was murdered in Mexico in 1940 by an ice-axe-wielding assassin, and Georgi Markov, a Bulgarian dissident writer and employee of the BBC, was done in by the Bulgarian Security Service in 1978, struck with a toxic ricin pellet fired surreptitiously from an umbrella by an assailant as Markov walked across Waterloo Bridge. Both these acts were international sensations.

Shapour Bakhtiar proved to be a steady nuisance to the Iranians, leading the National Movement of Iranian Resistance from Paris. As I feared, he barely escaped an assassination attempt in his Paris home in 1980, and his luck ran out in 1991 when he was murdered, along with his secretary, in his apartment—stabbed to death. Two of the assassins escaped to Iran, but the third, Ali Vakili Rad, was captured in Switzerland. In 1994, a French court found Rad guilty and sentenced him to life in prison; however, he was released in 2010 and returned to Iran.

Bakhtiar's meager accomplishments as an exile, and his ultimate demise, show why intelligence professionals generally put very little stock in exile reporting and activities. Exiles are rarely in a position to report reliable data or organize a meaningful opposition. Yet they often find an "in" with other branches of the U.S. government, particularly with officials who are eager to find a way to achieve their policy goals. Witness the sway that Iraqi exile Ahmad Chalabi exercised over Congress, which passed the Iraq Liberation Act in 1998, authorizing support for Chalabi's Iraqi National Congress and other exile groups; or over the Defense Department in 2002 and 2003 when the Bush administration was looking for a rationale for invading Iraq. Not only did Chalabi accommodate the United States with suspect intelligence on Saddam Hussein's supposed weapons of mass destruction, but he went so far as to claim that the Iraqi people would greet U.S. intervention forces with flowers. Neither turned out to be true.

During my tenure as chief of the Iran branch, I similarly witnessed the eagerness with which hopeful government officials could place undue stock in exile reporting. At that time, there was a keen desire at the White House to find moderate forces inside Iran whom we could work with in support of our foreign policy objectives. On one memorable occasion I was summoned to a meeting with NSC director Admiral John Poindexter and the NSC's CIA representative Gary Foster to discuss the possibility. Because it was a high-level meeting, I had the staff of the Iran branch pull together all the relevant available data and consulted with the Agency's analytic experts, whose job it is to weave together "all-source" intelligence to provide assessments. Poindexter was particularly interested in Akbar Hashemi Rafsanjani, who was then chairman of Iran's parliament. Poindexter's interest was obvious, since the arms-for-hostages deal had been Rafsanjani's brainchild, according to subsequent reporting. But there was no case to be made that Rafsanjani was a moderate. He did come from a wealthy, commercial family and supported privatization of business, but this is not to be confused with political moderation or respect for human rights. With the benefit of hindsight, we can see that during his presidency, from 1989 to 1997, he presided over the execution of hundreds of dissidents and made no significant gesture toward normalizing relations with the United States.

At that meeting, I told Poindexter that our information consistently showed there were no meaningful moderate forces inside the Tehran power structure, including Rafsanjani. Poindexter seemed to accept our analysis, and I left the meeting feeling we had put the idea to rest. Clearly I had overestimated the power of facts and logic. The NSC continued to run the arms-for-hostages program and, unfortunately, continued to involve the CIA.

At the same time that the Iran-Contra scandal was unfolding, the Agency was starting to lose its best agents inside Soviet intelligence, one by one. Senior officials inside the CIA's Soviet/Eastern Europe Division and their counterparts in the Counterintelligence Division came to the realization that their agents may have been betrayed by a mole within the CIA who knew their identities and had alerted the KGB. Burton Lee Gerber, head of SE; Milt Bearden, his deputy; and Clair George briefed Casey. As the Agency's Soviet operations officers began comparing notes with the sleuths in counterintelligence, Casey ordered an internal investigation of his own. It would be eight long years before the Agency connected all the dots and determined who was responsible: my debating partner from our days as career trainees, Aldrich Ames, had walked into the Soviet embassy in Washington on April 16, 1985, with a letter that contained the names of intelligence agents and a $50,000 demand. Thus began his career as the Agency's greatest traitor.[3]

Meanwhile, the Agency's involvement in the NSC's arms-for-hostages operation remained fragmented, and most of those involved were never told the whole story—that proceeds from the sale of arms at severely inflated prices were being diverted by Ollie North to fund the Nicaraguan Contras in violation of the Boland Amendment.

Charlie Allen continued to deal with Ghorbanifar for months, even though he did not trust him, and in fact Ghorbanifar's promises that hostages would be released in exchange for the arms we were sending continually proved empty or, at the very least, overstated. As mentioned earlier, we did get Reverend Benjamin Weir back, after the first arms shipment in 1985. A year later, Hezbollah released Father Lawrence Jenco, an American priest who headed Catholic Relief Services in

Beirut, and later, in 1986, David Jacobsen, director of Beirut's American University Hospital. But William Buckley was dead, the other hostages remained in captivity, and three new hostages, Frank Reed, Joseph Ciccipio, and Edward Tracy, had been kidnapped by a separate terrorist group and would be held for years. Reed was director of the Lebanese International School, Ciccipio was acting comptroller of the American University of Beirut, and Tracy was an American writer.

Allen did believe Ghorbanifar was telling the truth about one critical thing. In the summer of 1986, the arms dealer began to complain about the huge markup the United States was charging the Iranians for the missiles. One evening in August, he provided Allen with price lists and figures showing that the Iranians were being charged double the normal rate for these arms. As Allen studied the documents, his suspicions were aroused by the fact that two men who had replaced Ghorbanifar in channeling arms to Iran, the Iranian businessman Albert Hakim and the retired air force officer Richard Secord, were also involved in private efforts to aid the Contras. He didn't know for certain but suspected that the markup must have been a way to get around the Boland Amendment, which prohibited giving money to the Contras. He spent the next month gathering information about it, and in October he wrote a seven-page memo to Casey outlining his concern that money from the arms sales had been diverted to "other projects," and that the entire operation was a disaster, in danger of spinning out of control.[4] This was the first warning to Casey about a possible diversion to the Contras of profits from the Iranian arms deal.[5]

In short order, the White House operation came unglued. A plane carrying military supplies was shot down in Nicaragua in early October. The lone survivor, an American named Eugene Hasenfus, was immediately identified by his wife as working for the CIA. Despite Allen's memo, both Casey and the White House denied involvement. Then, in early November 1986, *Ash-Shiraa*, a pro-Syrian magazine in Lebanon, reported that the United States had been secretly selling arms to Iran. Soon the artifice collapsed. President Reagan at first refused to discuss the arms sales, but by mid-November, with the U.S. media now digging into the story, he acknowledged that "defensive weapons and spare parts" had been sold to Iran to improve relations. The Justice Department launched a probe and found that Oliver North had shredded sensitive documents in his NSC office, where investigators found a memo describing the diversion of $12 million from Iran arms sales to the Contras. Finally, at a televised news conference on November 25, Reagan stunned the country by saying that he had not been fully informed about the arm sales to Iran, and that up to $30 million had been secretly diverted to the Contras. This was the first time I learned of the diversion and the enormity of this fiasco. The president said North and Poindexter had stepped down from their positions. His White House was in disarray. The biggest scandal of his six-year-old presidency was about to unfold.

By this time, in late November, I was running the Afghan Task Force. One day I was called to a meeting in Casey's office with Bob Gates, deputy director CIA; Clair George; and a few staff members. "Boys," Casey said to us, "this will blow over in a few days, right?" I was incredulous, thinking, "You've got to be kidding! This will be on the front pages for months to come." But to my astonishment, as I looked around the room, everyone was nodding in agreement. I wondered if maybe I was missing something the others were seeing. I decided that no one actually believed it was going to blow over, but the situation was so bad that it served no purpose to disagree with the director.

The fallout began immediately. The next day, President Reagan commissioned former senator John Tower of Texas to investigate the matter, and Attorney General Edwin Meese turned the Justice Department's investigation over to the Criminal Division, with the FBI assisting. Within a month, Lawrence Walsh was named as independent counsel on the matter. Congressional hearings started in January 1987. Anyone involved in the matter had a very full dance card. That included me.

My first taste of the process was being called to the Office of the General Counsel to answer questions from the Justice Department. An Agency lawyer went with me, giving me, temporarily, a false sense of security. Just before we entered the debriefing room, he pulled me aside. "Jack, remember," he said, "I'm the Agency's lawyer. You are on your own. I will step in only when the conversation infringes on the Agency's interests." What an eye-opener! Thankfully, I was comfortable with all I had done and didn't fear talking to Justice, but his words had a significant impact on me. Shortly thereafter, I signed up for legal insurance, which I hold to this day. It provides peace of mind; you can never be sure how your actions might be misinterpreted or misrepresented in a lawsuit.

A short time later, Walsh's team deposed me. Again, the note takers were from the FBI, but one of their transcripts from the deposition was badly flawed. I corrected a number of factual mistakes when I reviewed it. The various committees and commissions called dozens of witnesses, but they were never able to resolve a central question about Iran-Contra: What was Bill Casey's role? Casey suffered a stroke in his office on December 15, 1986, the result of a brain tumor, which left him unable to talk and caused his death a short time later. There has been much conjecture over the years about whether he helped the NSC orchestrate the operation. Lieutenant Colonel Oliver North implicated Casey in the scheme. Bob Woodward, the *Washington Post* investigative reporter who broke the Watergate story, wrote in his book *Veil: The Secret Wars of the CIA, 1981–1987* that he sneaked into Casey's hospital room just before the director died to ask if he had known about the diversion of funds and that Casey had nodded yes.

Perhaps it was frustration over the enduring mystery around Casey's role or over Congress granting immunity to North and Poindexter early on, making it impossible for them to prosecute successfully, but Walsh made life very difficult for a number of my colleagues. These were men who had spent their entire lives in service to their country. Many of them knew that the arms-for-hostages scheme was ill-conceived, but none of them had thought it was illegal. In fact, that is what got some of them in trouble. Clair George appeared before Congress without immunity because, I believe, he was actually trying to help in the fact-finding process. But when he gave an incorrect answer, he was slapped with a perjury charge. He was finally convicted in December 1992 on one count of making a false statement to Congress in denying CIA involvement in the Hasenfus supply flight, and one perjury count for denying knowledge of Secord's role in the provision of arms to Iran and the Contras. His conviction on what were essentially technicalities—George had not approved of, or participated in, arms sales to Iran or the Contras—said more about the excessive and overreaching prosecution of independent counsel than it did about moral turpitude at the CIA.

Walsh's six-year investigation cost $33 million, and George's legal bills alone exceeded $1 million, threatening to bankrupt him. He was the highest-ranking CIA officer convicted for official acts after only Richard M. Helms, the former CIA director who pleaded no contest in 1977 to withholding information about CIA involvement in Chile around the time of the Allende coup.

Even lower-level officers were targeted and had to hire attorneys, an expense they never could have managed on Agency salaries. A fund was set up to help defray their legal expenses, and the hat was passed to raise money. Several lawyers offered their services for little or no payment. This is how I came to know Stanley Arkin, who was to become my friend and business partner. Stanley represented Alan Fiers, who had been chief of the Central America Task Force. When the scandal broke, Casey told Fiers he'd need a lawyer and called his friend J. Peter Grace, a multimillionaire industrialist, asking him to recommend the best criminal lawyer in New York. Grace recommended Arkin, and Stanley said he was happy to represent Fiers, whom he considered a loyal public servant who believed he had acted in the best interest of his country. Fiers pleaded guilty in the summer of 1991 to two misdemeanor charges of withholding information from Congress. In the plea, he admitted that North had told him in mid-1986 about using profits from the Iranian arm sales to fund the Contras. Fiers said that he ultimately told Clair George about this and in October 1986 George instructed him to conceal the information. Fiers's decision to cooperate with prosecutors after his plea led directly to Walsh's prosecution of George.

Testifying in open court was an ordeal for everyone. Walsh ended up indicting Fiers, George, Clarridge, and others. While the four of us had not always agreed on policy, these clearly were strong leaders and operators of substance. I was highly annoyed to have been put in the position of testifying against them and had trouble understanding what I might possibly know that would help the prosecution's case. The prosecution lawyers never talked to me about their interest and left me in the dark about why I was relevant. Other officers who were subpoenaed had an even stronger reaction: some of them reportedly got physically ill at the thought of exposing Agency activities to the public.

When I was called to the witness stand on August 7, 1992, ground rules had been established to protect my identity, since I was still undercover at the time. I wrote my name down on a small piece of paper, which was circulated among all the members of the jury and returned to the judge. The prosecuting attorney then projected for the jury two indecipherable pages of notes I had kept during an inconsequential May 1986 meeting in Clair George's office in which we discussed an upcoming trip Richard Secord would make to Iran. There was nothing relevant in my notes.[6] He started asking questions about these notes, but his line of questioning was going nowhere. Then he changed subjects without warning and asked about my depositions. I responded, "Which one are you referring to, the one that's accurate or the one that was badly flawed and had to be corrected?" He and the defense attorneys rushed to the bench and began whispering to the judge, within my earshot, that I should be impeached as a hostile witness. Judge Royce C. Lamberth turned and gently dismissed me from the stand, which was a great relief. The account in *The Washington Post* the next day described me as "the broad-shouldered" undercover officer. I could certainly have been described in less flattering terms.

Alan Fiers testified as part of the agreement that Stanley Arkin had worked out for him when he pleaded guilty to withholding information. There are those who have never forgiven Alan for his testimony. Clair George, who died in 2011, was chief among them, and gently chided me when I became partners with Arkin in a private intelligence business in New York City in 2000. Stanley defends the Fiers deal to this day. He says Fiers was reluctant, and did a lot of soul-searching before ultimately agreeing to the deal because he thought it was the only thing to do. In the end, Fiers was pardoned by President George H. W. Bush on Christmas Eve in 1992, as one of the president's last acts in office, along with former defense secretary Caspar W. Weinberger and four others involved in the Iran-Contra scandal, including George and Clarridge. Their careers were ruined, though, and the Agency suffered. As we now know, Clarridge allegedly would surface again two decades later, running agents for the Pentagon in Afghanistan from his home outside San Diego.

Were there at least lessons learned from this debacle? There were for me. It helped solidify the principles I believe must be adhered to in any covert action. First, covert action policy must be consistent with the officially stated goals of the United States and supported by the American people and Congress. This concept is a basic tenet of the democratic process. Any initiative that is at variance with publicly stated goals is bound to have lasting negative legal and political fallout when revealed, as occurred in the Iran-Contra affair.

The second consideration is to make sure that all covert action proposals go through the carefully constructed interagency coordination process. In the name of expediency, many covert action proponents prefer to bypass this process, but it almost always ends up a disaster when allowed to proceed in the back rooms of the NSC or anywhere else. The coordination process can be tedious, but through it you gain the invaluable benefit of the State, Defense, Justice, and other agencies' information and insights, which often add greatly to the texture of the proposal. Leaks are an issue, but they can be contained by appropriate security management.

Likewise, consistent with the regulations, Congress needs to be notified of an operation in a timely fashion—seventy-two hours. If you cannot get through the interagency process and develop consensus within the congressional intelligence committees, serious thought needs to be given to the likelihood of a plan's long-term success. Also, within CIA and other participating government entities, the chain of command must be followed or you will end up with a collapse in professional discipline and with destructive operational confusion. One of the most troubling and unique experiences for me was to see fellow Agency officers during the Iran-Contra affair decide, for ideological reasons, to take it upon themselves to work outside the bureaucratic structure. This was an extraordinary breach in the rules of the game. If we are to run secret intelligence agencies in a democratic system, the letter of the law must be followed. Finally, as I noted earlier, working with exile groups is often a necessary precondition for running a covert action operation in certain parts of the world, but the intelligence and stated capabilities of these groups must always be taken with a large grain of salt. As Walsh's prosecution ground on in what I thought was an increasingly desperate attempt to nail anyone in the CIA he could get for anything he could find, no matter how picayune, I always felt it worth underscoring that Iran-Contra was a White House–made scandal. I have no problem holding the CIA accountable for its misdeeds—I believe that it is essential to our democracy—but I have a problem with those who blame the CIA for the misdeeds of others.

It was with much relief in 1986 that I watched the agonizing Iran-Contra endgame play itself out in my rearview mirror.

FIVE

"Jack, This Changes It All, Doesn't It?"

Washington/Afghanistan, 1986–87

In a conference room just off my office in New York City hangs a print of an official Central Intelligence Agency oil painting. The CIA is fastidious about its history and recording past glories. Not long ago its historical office began commissioning paintings of key moments in Agency history. The moment mujahideen fighters stood up, shouted, "Allahu Akbar!" and fired the Stinger for the first time at a Soviet helicopter gunship was second in the series—it was that big a deal.

By the spring of 1986, before the American people and most of us inside the CIA knew anything about the illegal diversion of funds from the Iran arms sales to the Contras, I had taken over the Afghan Task Force and become the official responsible for moving vast quantities of arms and matériel across the Pakistan border and into Afghanistan. By summer, the first Stingers were in theater, waiting to debut.

Given my belief in well-planned, muscular covert operations, I had favored introduction of the Stinger from the outset. If it performed in theater the way it had on practice ranges in the United States, the Soviets would quickly figure out where the weapon was coming from. They could choose to up the ante and retaliate against us, but I thought the odds were better that they'd begin questioning the wisdom of their occupation of Afghanistan. None of this mattered, though, if the mujahideen couldn't be trained to use the weapon.

That had been one of the arguments against the Stinger, and training the mujahideen proved arduous. We began by sending two soldiers who had just completed their army training on the system. They began to instruct mujahideen teams in the field. Later, the two soldiers trained Special Operations officers detailed to the CIA, who expanded the curriculum. The mujahideen, unlike the Taliban today, preferred fighting at a distance, especially against the Russians, recalled Dempsey, the former Marine captain who was my weapons specialist. They therefore required extensive experience not just with the new weapon system but in weaning themselves away from this "fire-and-run" approach.

In late August 1986, the mujahideen got off a lucky rocket shot and blew up forty tons of ammunition at the Soviets' Kharga ammunition dump outside Kabul. As one bunker ignited another and then another, like dominos, the night sky filled with a giant fireball. I showed videotapes of the explosions to all the key players at Langley, the White House, and key agencies, but especially up on Capitol Hill, to make the point that all was not lost in Afghanistan. Casey even showed the video to the president. Within a few days, we had satellite imagery of the destruction flown out to Pakistan and shown to the mujahideen leaders.

The positive vibes from this attack paled in comparison to those of late September, in response to the attack we had all been waiting for: on September 25, mujahideen gunners a mile from the Soviet air base at Jalalabad popped out of their hiding places in the rocks and brush and aimed their new heat-seeking Stinger missiles at an approaching squadron of Mi-24D Hind helicopter gunships. Luckily, Bearden was ahead of his time and had armed some mujahideen fighters with video cameras. Later I saw what they had managed to capture on videotape. The mujahideen fighter stood defiantly, shouted, "Allahu Akbar!" and fired. The first shot bounced off the ground, but the next three scored direct hits and blew three Hinds out of the sky. At first there was no immediate proof of what had happened beyond a field report from Bearden that didn't include the videotape. Confirming shootdowns with spy satellite imagery was often impossible—Afghanistan is a big country, with lots of mountains and hills. But because we had the general coordinates of the Soviets' Jalalabad air base, the CIA's imagery analysts were able to quickly produce eighteen-by-eighteen-inch pictures of the destroyed Hinds. "A picture tells a thousand words," said Tom Sheridan, who was in charge of securing whatever imagery we needed on the task force. "The imagery was proof of the report." As soon as I got the photos, the day after the attack, I called Near East chief Twetten and told him what I had.

"You better tell the director," he said.

I called Casey's office and went up to the seventh floor by myself with the imagery. I must have looked agitated, because his secretary showed me right in to see him.

"Mr. Director," I said, "we had a tremendous breakthrough yesterday. We deployed the Stinger and we shot down three helicopters."

I laid the photographs out on his desk.

"Jack, this changes it all, doesn't it?" Casey said. It would be his last taste of victory. With the Iran-Contra scandal engulfing him and the Reagan White House, he would suffer a stroke at the end of the year and never regain consciousness. He died the following spring.

Viewing the secret spy satellites in his office, though, he could immediately sense the implications. For the past two years, the issue had been how to get arms across the border. Everything was bottlenecked and wasn't moving through the mountain passes because of the Hinds. Within two weeks of the successful shootdown, though, the Soviet military started flying the Hinds above the fifteen-thousand-foot range of the Stinger. Once they did that, their gunships could not hit anything on the ground. It's rare that a single weapon changes the course of a war. I would like to say I knew when we sent the weapon out that summer that the Stinger would force the Soviets to change their rules of engagement, but I didn't. Even after the first three Hinds were shot down, I still thought we were looking at a long, protracted campaign. Within weeks, however, Bearden and I realized that the Soviets had indeed changed tactics and were no longer willing to fly low and risk losing their gunships. The Khyber Pass became a superhighway, with guns, ammunition, and matériel pouring through, and the Soviets were suddenly powerless to stop them.

While I was showing the video of the helicopter shootdown to various congressmen, the analysts back at Langley were squaring off in a predictable debate. The Soviet experts from SOVA demanded additional photographic proof before they would accept reports from the mujahideen that they were shooting down Hinds at the rate of about one per day, even with the Soviets' change in tactics. With such convincing evidence of the Stingers' ongoing success, I thought the SOVA analysts were wasting their time and missing the forest for the trees. The Stingers had forced the Hinds to fly higher, which meant they couldn't hit anything moving through the mountain passes. Twetten, who notes he had been slow to accept the idea of using the Stingers, came around in the end. "I thought covert operations should remain covert and that we could find another weapon somewhere else," he said. "But the Russians knew we were involved. By then, the size of the program was already very large. They weren't stupid."

Bob Williams, the task force military analyst, remembers that the Pakistanis had reservations of their own, even though they clearly saw pushing the Russians out of Afghanistan to be in their national security interest. "The Pakistanis didn't want the American hand seen, and they were reluctant at first to let the Stingers into the fray because of that," he said. "But they agreed because the Russians were inflicting very serious casualties." Like Twetten, Williams agreed in the end that using the Stingers was the right course. "It made a tremendous difference," he said. "When the mujahideen started knocking down the helos, the Soviet pilots had to fly beyond the reach of the Stinger and therefore were not able to provide low air-to-ground support to the Soviet troops. In essence, the gunships were taken out of the combat equation. Without the support of the people, the Soviet troops were very limited in their ability to move about the countryside." Frank Anderson, a veteran Middle East operations officer who replaced me months later as head of the task force, considered the Stingers a game changer. On top of a tenfold increase in assistance, Anderson said, the Stingers produced "a hundredfold increase in our efforts—which made the difference."

Indeed, by late 1986 and early 1987, the situation on the ground in Afghanistan was clear. From the field, Milt Bearden and a case officer were reporting the Soviet retreat. "The reality was that we never looked back after August 1986, and by 1987, I figured, I knew the Russians weren't going to prevail and would withdraw," Bearden said.[1]

With the Russians on the ropes and our success ever more likely, a steady flow of government officials from Washington wanted to go out and have a look for themselves. "You have to remember this was the hottest thing the U.S. government was doing—we were the only ones actually fighting the Soviets and were authorized by the president to do so," the case officer said.[2] "Everyone wanted to get a piece of the action." One of the first to travel from Washington was Bob Gates, when he was Casey's deputy. Gates, a Russia expert and experienced analyst who would later serve as director of central intelligence and secretary of defense, was among those who were beginning to realize the Soviets were in deep trouble. Bearden and I took him to a mujahideen camp along the Afghanistan-Pakistan border, which was a fascinating experience for him. This place was so remote that they had to haul water up a steep hill to the camp by hand from the stream below the outpost.

The night before we left Peshawar, Gates told Bearden he was concerned about food contamination in the bush, and asked that box lunches be brought along instead. When we arrived, one of the mujahideen leaders stepped out of his tent overhang and motioned us under it for a local feast.

"Where are the box lunches?" Gates asked Bearden.

"Where the hell are the box lunches?" Bearden barked at one of the drivers. "I told you to put them on the truck. Where are they?"

He turned back to Gates. "The Pakistani drivers forgot to bring them," he told him.

Of course, there never were any box lunches. Bearden was simply acting to keep everyone happy. I'm afraid Gates went without lunch that day as he moved his mujahideen food artfully around his plate so it looked as though he had partaken in their feast.

When we headed back to the airport after the Gates visit, Bearden glibly noted that the deputy director of central intelligence and his security team would have been horrified if they'd known that the safe house where we had spent the evening was located on top of a weapons warehouse. I'm sure he was right, and I wasn't exactly delighted to learn about it, either, since one misfire would have brought down the entire building. From there on in, I was extra careful in getting the lay of the land of any place I went with Bearden. He was not an inordinate risk taker, but when you reside in a war zone, your sensitivities wear down and you become used to a higher risk standard.

Among the many trips to Afghanistan with eager observers, one that remains memorable was with the then third-ranking official at the Department of Defense, Fred Iklé, who oversaw special operations, foreign arms sales, and military assistance during the Reagan administration and had pushed hard to deploy the Stinger in Afghanistan. When we arrived at the airport in Islamabad, the Pakistanis handed out dozens of little green books to senior officials from both governments that listed members of the arriving party, including "Fred Iklé of DOD and Jack Devine of the CIA." I was still undercover, which I took very seriously. "Milt, what the hell is this?" I asked Bearden, fuming. Somebody should have made sure that we didn't have the names of undercover people printed in a widely circulated little green book. Bearden and I had a curt back-and-forth over this, but it lasted only a few minutes.

Sometime later I made a trip to the Afghan border with Charlie Wilson. Before we left, Tom Twetten called and told me the congressman wanted to go to the region and was taking with him a journalist, George Crile of *60 Minutes*. Both of us felt this was nonsense, very unprofessional, and very un-CIA-like. It was virtually unheard-of to have covert CIA operations officials travel abroad with a journalist. But Casey himself had agreed to it. And if Wilson was going, he needed someone from CIA to go along. Despite Crile's presence, I was glad to be going, because it would give me another opportunity to develop an even closer relationship with Wilson. I also needed to be there so that Pakistani officials didn't come to the mistaken conclusion that Wilson was negotiating on behalf of the U.S. government and that they could orchestrate an end run around the CIA through him. "Charlie was a complicated handling problem," Twetten said. We stopped over in Egypt on the way to Karachi and unexpectedly met with President Hosni Mubarak. Wilson and I talked with him in between tennis matches; I wouldn't exactly call it a meeting. But Wilson had arranged this on his own and didn't notify Ambassador Frank Wisner, a friend of the Agency whose father was the first head of the CIA's Clandestine Service, then known as the Directorate of Plans. Wisner, needless to say, was annoyed.

Once we landed in Pakistan, we experienced a clash of titans. The momentary rift I had had with Bearden during the Iklé trip was nothing compared to Bearden's first meeting with Wilson. The two got off to a bad start. Maybe it was because they were both Texans; I'm not sure. Wilson didn't like the feel of Bearden, and Bearden had read too much about Wilson's celebrity status. He had a perception of Wilson as a policy dilettante, lacking in substance. I tried to play the role of peacemaker, and it took them a little while to reset their relationship. Things got better as the trip proceeded. Eventually, they became very friendly and mutually respectful.

We headed up to Peshawar, where we went into the Afghan refugee camps. There were more than three million people living in these camps along the border. It was a daunting challenge for the Pakistanis to take care of their needs, especially the hundreds of children who had been maimed by land mines. When we approached one of the medical tents, Swedish doctors asked us to donate blood. Wilson sat down and without hesitation rolled up his sleeve. I advised the doctors that I had been taking malaria tablets because of my international travel. With that, the doctor gestured me into the tent and pointed to the many maimed children. Do you think that matters? he said. That was the end of the discussion, and the reused needle was shoved into my arm to draw the blood. While I hoped the needle had at least been sterilized, it was a privilege to help these children.

Later, we met under a huge tent, fifty yards by fifty, with all the Afghan tribal leaders, who had gathered for a conference moderated by Abdul Rahman Akhtar, the head of Pakistan's intelligence agency, the Directorate for Inter-Services Intelligence, or ISI. At one point I whispered to Wilson that you could cut the tension in the room with a knife. He replied, "If you think this is bad, last year we had to bring the tribal leaders in a half hour apart and disarm them." He was right. We were in fact making slow progress with the likes of Gulbuddin Hekmatyar, Burhanuddin Rabbani, and Abdul Rasul Sayyaf. Hekmatyar was the most powerful mujahideen leader and the ISI's favorite. We considered him adept at fighting Soviets despite his anti-Western, radical Islamist views. Rabbani, an Islamic scholar trained in Egypt, based in Pakistan, and supported by the ISI, had built his militia with Pashtun, Uzbek, and Shi'ite fighters. Sayyaf, like Rabbani a Cairo-educated Islamic scholar, enjoyed strong Saudi backing.

Meanwhile, my deputy, Joe Malpeli, was responsible for running unilateral operations in Afghanistan—operations that we did not handle through the Pakistanis. We obviously worked closely with the ISI, but we also wanted to make sure we had eyes and ears trained on the Afghan program independent of the Pakistanis, so we knew what they were doing and not doing. We also ran operations directly with Ahmad Shah Massoud, a Tajik guerrilla commander in the Panjshir Valley who had turned back four Soviet assaults between 1980 and 1982 before agreeing to a truce in 1983 that deeply angered Hekmatyar and the ISI. We considered him one of the best and most reliable fighters. He and Hekmatyar were rivals and squared off in a civil war after the Soviet withdrawal. Massoud would go on to form the Northern Alliance before he was killed by suicide bombers immediately before the 9/11 attack, for fear that he would be at our side in the inevitable fight afterward.

After Akhtar's meeting with mujahideen commanders in Peshawar, Wilson and I went down to Darra, in the unruly North-West Frontier Province of Pakistan, close to the Afghan border. It was a "Wild West" town and an open-air gun market about twenty-five miles south of Peshawar. The Pakistanis were not enthused about the idea of our side trip, but they did not want to say no to Wilson. At the gun market, people fired guns into the air, and it would have been easy enough to get off a round directed at Wilson's entourage. But we were under very heavy military guard the entire time, to discourage anyone from taking a shot.

The market was exactly what it advertised itself to be: every store was literally a gun store, and you could buy every make of weapon (and knives and swords), including some from when the Brits were in Pakistan in the nineteenth century. The visit gave me a firsthand opportunity to see for myself if any of our weapons were being sold on the black market. We didn't see any of them, and there was never significant reporting of anything turning up in Darra or the other gun-toting towns.

At one point, Milt wandered off and came back with a ratty-looking, bloodstained Soviet army vest. I asked him what that was about, and he proceeded to tell me that one of the CODEL (Congressional Delegation) members we had left behind in Islamabad had requested a bloodstained relic from the fighting with the Russians. We rolled our eyes contemptuously. What a crass request; how demeaning of the loss of life associated with warfare. Before I had a chance to express my misgivings, Milt said he had picked up the vest in the market and had had one of the locals smear it with chicken blood. I hope the congressman didn't mount his souvenir on his office wall for display.

The Pakistanis saw Wilson as larger-than-life and key to U.S. support for them. They had seen the covert weapons program expand, and

they rightfully believed that Wilson's role in this was critically important. President Mohammad Zia-ul-Haq clearly respected and valued his
relationship with Wilson. Wilson and I once met with Zia and General
Akhtar during a trip to Islamabad. Wilson was smooth and used the
right measure of Texas charm and wit, blended with a clear understanding of what was relevant on the ground from Zia's perspective. (As
for Zia, I've met a number of national leaders through the years, and by
any measure, he was one of the most impressive. His presence projected power and stability, and his deep-set black eyes added more than
a hint of mystery. He spoke in quiet, measured tones, which added to
the overall effect of strength and left visitors hanging on his every word.
It was a great tragedy for all of us when he perished in a C-130 airplane
crash in 1988, along with General Akhtar and American ambassador
Arnie Raphel. At the time of the crash, I felt sure it was a terrorist act,
but the Defense Department's official investigation declared it a mechanical failure.)

Despite Wilson's stature in the eyes of the Pakistanis, it was always
quite clear to me and everyone else at the CIA that aid to the mujahideen was a U.S. government program, which by law the Agency, not
Wilson, was responsible for running. We greatly valued his support, but
we kept him professionally at arm's length while maintaining a productive and cordial personal relationship with him. "We all loved Charlie,"
Bearden said, but it was "Charlie Wilson's War" only in Charlie Wilson's
mind. "We had moved way beyond his involvement at that point, and it
was then a major U.S. government program," Bearden said. Indeed, this
is one of my biggest problems with the movie about Wilson, which creates the impression that he and a handful of other quasi-rogue Agency
operatives brought the Stinger to Afghanistan and ran the entire covert
operation independent of policy or chain of command. Wilson had
nothing to do with the Stinger decision. George Crile stated as much in
his book, though this fact got lost in Hollywood. Nonetheless, Wilson
was critically important to the effort because of his commitment and
the amount of money he was able to appropriate. Wilson had developed a reputation as a hard-drinking partier, especially during his
earlier years in Congress. But he was a complicated, serious person,
too—very helpful to us and truly dedicated to the cause. He was a
keen fan of the *Flashman* adventure series and fashioned himself in

Flashman's image: a swashbuckling adventurer. He tried to impart his enthusiasm for *Flashman* to all of us, and at one point, he presented key players on the Afghan team with leather jackets with *Flashman* and other warrior emblems sewn onto each. I have kept mine fondly, as a reminder of our time together. Charlie had found the jackets on a CODEL trip to South Korea on other business, but Afghanistan was obviously always on his mind. "When he was working on something he cared about, he was serious—and he was serious about the war," said Tim Burton, our logistics chief. Anderson, my successor, remembered that Wilson was "constantly looking for things he could do to keep our feet to the fire." There was a "prove it to Charlie Wilson" refrain at the Agency because of the amount of money Wilson brought in and his relationships with the Pakistanis, who from time to time would be convinced the Agency was not doing enough and would call Wilson directly to complain, Anderson said.[3] But Anderson knew that Wilson was not calling the shots. I can't remember him ever trying to ride roughshod over the task force. We just had to be responsive and keep him informed about what was going on. If it made sense, he stood aside.

At home, the task force team continued working on new weapons systems, even with the success of the Stingers. Wilson had about $30 million set aside in the defense budget for research and development. One of the things that really interested me were efforts to develop a device for clearing land mines, because they were such a terrible problem in Afghanistan, causing serious injuries to so many fighters and civilians, including children. We were also looking at bullets that would penetrate a tank and a device that would temporarily blind a helicopter pilot with a flash and cause him to come crashing down. The lawyers decided the flash device was not consistent with the Geneva Accords. I agreed. War is war, but if you have ground rules, you've got to follow them. Usually, the rules are predicated on sound reasoning. Do you want those same techniques applied to American troops? Shooting down a helicopter with a rocket is an acceptable action, because both sides authorize combatants, and the Hinds could fire back with everything they had. Blinding pilots, it seemed to me, was another matter. The lawyers also objected to a plan we were working on for developing a small drone that we could fly into the window of the

Soviet officers' quarters at Bagram Airfield outside Kabul and blow the place up. This struck them as a prohibited form of assassination. Interestingly enough, the mini-drone became the forerunner to the unmanned aerial vehicles (UAVs) that have become such a prominent part of the CIA arsenal and, like the Stinger, a game changer in the war on terrorism.

Still, when it came to attacking Soviet facilities with high technology, we were undeterred. Shortly after he was detailed to the task force, Clifton Dempsey began developing a long-range precision weapon. The 107-millimeter and 122-millimeter rockets were highly inaccurate, and we couldn't rely on luck to win the war, no matter how spectacular the mujahideen attack on the Kharga ammunition dump had been. Dempsey had to not only develop the weapon but make sure it could be carried on the back of a mule. In his research, he came across a Finnish Tampella 120-millimeter mortar that could travel almost four miles. This weapon was licensed and manufactured in Spain with monies from a special R&D fund Charlie Wilson had set up at DOD. We purchased 20 mortars and 125 rounds. With the army's help, we increased the mortar's precision by replacing the sight with a north-seeking precision module and changing out the tripod design with a bipod. The army also helped us adapt a computer that provided the azimuth (arc), propellant, and elevation needed to improve the mortar's accuracy. The Tampella eventually became standard in all U.S. Army mortar systems.

But the most exciting addition Dempsey introduced was the now-ubiquitous global positioning system, a constellation of Pentagon satellites that none of us had ever heard of. Smaller, shorter-range mortars left the mujahideen vulnerable to Soviet counterbattery fire, which enabled the Soviets to quickly determine a mortar's location and return fire before those manning the weapon had a chance to move. But from about four miles away, mujahideen fighters firing the giant Spanish-made mortars would be out of the Russians' counterpunch range, and the GPS satellites would tell them how to guide their mortars to the target. Once the coordinates of the mujahideen location were fed into a computer, along with the coordinates of their target, the computer could tell them the exact compass direction and elevation at which to aim the mortar tube. There was some skepticism about this at the

Agency, but Dempsey convinced me to go with him to Fort A.P. Hill, about an hour and a half south of Washington, for a demonstration.

It was pouring rain when we arrived. I had on a business suit, so I reached for a sensible umbrella as I started to get out of our car.

"Jack, I'll do anything you want, but please put that umbrella away," Clifton said.

In the army, when it rained on the battlefield, you got wet. So I put the umbrella away, got drenched, and watched the GPS-guided simulated mortar hit its target with stunning accuracy.

I also went to the Nevada desert to see the GPS 120 system tested, originally intending to use all the rounds in the testing. But I was so impressed with the system that I stopped the test after several volleys and decided to deploy the system to Afghanistan immediately, as we were in a rush to ramp up the pressure in sync with the deployment of the Stinger. The only disagreeable part of the test involved the CIA project manager coordinating the effort. It was his job to provide all of the necessary logistical support. He seemingly did not have his heart in it and was dragging his feet. His attitude was getting in the way. When that happens, there is no choice but to remove the manager from the project, which I told his superior needed to happen as soon as possible. The man was quickly replaced with a quality officer, who helped make the GPS-guided mortar work, and fast.

But making sure it worked was only half the battle. We had to figure out how we were going to deliver this large, heavy weapon to Afghanistan. Burton, my logistics genius, began working with his staff to develop a special saddle, so that mules could carry the mortars on their backs into the country. We had to procure the mortars from the Spanish without telling them what we planned to do with them. In the end, we sent about twenty of them to the field, and about seven of these were used in a devastating attack on the Spetsnaz battalion in the Kunar Valley, in eastern Afghanistan, in November 1987. This was the first time the GPS system was used in combat. A mujahideen team launched the mortar barrage right through the Soviet installation there, almost destroying it entirely. The Russians had no idea what hit them and had nothing in place with which to counterattack. Before and after photographs from spy satellites showed how completely the GPS-guided mortars devastated the Spetsnaz base.

The White House also started pushing for the introduction of the French-made Milan antitank missile once Soviet armored tanks replaced Hind helicopter gunships as the most lethal threat on the battlefield. My feeling was if the Milan worked to knock out the tanks, put in the Milan. After the Stinger went in, concern about sophisticated weapons, which the Milan was, dissipated. The Milan, guided by a thin copper wire, had ten times the range (about two miles) of an RPG-7, which was then the preferred shoulder-held antitank rocket-propelled grenade launcher. After we decided to deploy the missile and created the procurement pipeline, the Milan made it out to the field. By this time it was 1987 and Anderson had taken over the task force. The Milan soon did to tank formations what the Stinger had done to helicopter squadrons. By the fall of that year, Anderson said, the field report on troop illnesses and other tactical information made it clear to those running the task force that the Soviets were fighting with a "dead army" and we were winning the fight against them.

By the time I left the program in 1987 to become chief of station in Rome, the war was winding down. The Soviets under Gorbachev announced their plans to withdraw, but the covert war raged on as the CIA continued arming rebels fighting to topple the Communist government of Mohammad Najibullah. When the last Soviet unit rumbled out of Afghanistan across the Friendship Bridge into Uzbekistan in February 1989, Bearden sent out a simple cable from Islamabad: "WE WON." It had been a huge team effort. With the Soviets gone, the Bush administration quickly lost interest in Afghanistan. The Berlin Wall fell in November, consuming the administration's foreign policy focus. The CIA kept pushing arms through the mountain passes as the rebel factions tried to close in on the Najibullah regime, but with the Soviets gone from the equation, Congress cut its secret appropriation for Afghanistan by 60 percent in 1990. The 1991 Gulf War made Afghanistan a distant memory. The CIA's authority to arm the warring rebel factions formally lapsed on January 1, 1992. The Najibullah government finally fell later that year, but there was no outside power with enough interest left to broker a peace. Kabul descended into civil war among rebel factions, and paved the way for the rise of the Taliban in 1994.

With a quarter century's hindsight, it's hard now not to conclude that there was a better way to exit Afghanistan. America's abandonment of the country is an often-cited mistake for which many believe we are still paying. For years after leaving the Afghan Task Force, I believed, along with Charlie Wilson, that we should have extended our covert presence, as well as provided substantial overt U.S. aid to help rebuild the country, despite all the advice to the contrary from the area experts inside and outside the Agency. With the passage of time and considerable reflection, however, I'm honestly not sure today that in the end it would have made a difference. One way or another, Afghanistan would have fallen into a chaos of tribal rivalry, and terrorists would have found their way there under one of the tribes' protection. Because of this, I have little hope in the substantial U.S. efforts going on today to build a democratic Afghanistan.

Our close alliance with Pakistan's ISI throughout the covert war is also worth noting, in terms both of our ongoing relationship with Pakistani intelligence and of the ISI's role in shaping Afghanistan's future once we lost interest. As we draw down in Afghanistan, if we have any hope of having a stable outcome there, we will need Pakistan and the ISI's support. Pakistan not only shares the most important border with Afghanistan, but a large segment of its population belongs to the same Pashtun tribes that reside in Afghanistan. While the relationship has rough edges today, we have a long history of cooperation, and I hope we will return to a strong partnership.

Critics of our covert war also look at the CIA's alliance with Saudi intelligence and its arms pipeline to rebel factions across the ethnic and ideological spectrum, which helped provide the underpinnings for the network of armed Arab jihadists that would spring up across the region. However, it is important to emphasize that there is no evidence that Osama bin Laden ever received weapons or other matériel support from the CIA. He was a minor blip on our screen and his support came directly from the Arab states. To connect the dots and conclude that the CIA's covert war in Afghanistan created al-Qaeda and led directly to the terrorist attacks on September 11, 2001—as some of the CIA's most virulent critics have done—is wrong. The CIA's network of tribal relationships established in the 1980s made it possible for the CIA and U.S. Special Forces, along with devastating American air power, to topple the Taliban within months of the terrorist attacks on New York and Washington.

As I wrote in *The Wall Street Journal* in July 2010, after 9/11 we should have concentrated on getting Bin Laden and destroying al-Qaeda, not on nation building and counterinsurgency, as a block against the Taliban. The Taliban was an indigenous Islamic fundamentalist force that was not involved in the 9/11 attacks against the United States and did not have international ambitions. The real culprits were foreign Arab terrorists who trained in al-Qaeda camps in Afghanistan and have now dispersed to Pakistan, Yemen, Iraq, North Africa, and other parts of the Middle East. Invading Iraq in 2003 on a false premise that Saddam Hussein possessed weapons of mass destruction only made us lose sight of Afghanistan's true significance yet again. And when President Obama finally shifted the nation's focus back to Afghanistan in early 2009, after six years of war in Iraq, it was essentially too late. The Taliban had regrouped, and we were replicating the Russian and British mistakes of trying to maintain a long-term military presence in the "graveyard of empires." Many of my colleagues on the Afghan Task Force would agree. Milt Bearden has said it is "crazy to bring a big army into Afghanistan. There is no such thing as a well-conducted long war there . . . the Afghans don't get defeated." Bob Williams, our military analyst, who had fought in Vietnam, said that the best part of the Agency's support to the mujahideen was that there was no loss of American lives. The reason for our success of the Afghan operation in the 1980s—as compared to the situation today—was that we empowered the Afghan people to fight the war themselves. Tom Twetten agreed that the key ingredient was the Afghan fighters. He said it did not matter how much suffering they went through: they were absolutely united in their goal of expelling the foreign invader, which strikes an ominous chord today. Frank Anderson has also expressed skepticism about the manner in which we have conducted the current war in Afghanistan: "Military force is only useful when killing people and destroying property advances your interests. That certainly happens. One needs to be alert for the point at which it is no longer true, however." As the Obama administration pulls our troops out of Afghanistan, we should maintain a CIA covert action component aimed at al-Qaeda and other terrorists as part of a robust U.S. mission that includes diplomatic, economic, and antinarcotics components. If we've learned nothing else from the way we ended our involvement in Afghanistan in the early 1990s, it must be this: we need to leave in place a covert action structure. We simply cannot withdraw our troops in a way that leaves a vacuum to be filled by our adversaries.

SIX

Do I Lie to the Pope, or Break Cover?

Italy, 1988

As a reward for running the Afghan Task Force, the deputy director of operations, Clair George, offered me the plum job of Rome station chief. But in the hunting preserve of the Agency barons—highly experienced senior officers who had run multiple overseas stations and operational divisions—Rome for me possessed a special allure. It also came with a hazard that I came to sense only vaguely: my colleague from my precareer training days, Aldrich Ames. When I arrived in Rome in the fall of 1988, Rick had been posted there for more than two years, working against the Soviets. He supposedly considered me a friend and was pleased when he found out I was coming in as station chief.[1] My predecessor in Rome, Alan Wolfe, a hard-edged operator, had been critical of Ames's performance. He'd reportedly been frustrated with Ames's failure to file reports on his meetings with the one and only Soviet with whom he seemed to have contact at that time, Aleksey Khrenkov. Apparently, Wolfe had been pressing Ames on this, but Ames insisted there was little hope in recruiting Khrenkov. None of us knew at the time, of course, that Ames was working for the Soviets and that Khrenkov was his official go-between.

Shortly after we arrived in Rome, Ames and his second wife, Rosario, invited Pat and me over to dinner. The couple lived near the Forum, in a modest-size two-bedroom apartment, with one of the rooms converted into a study for Rosario. The walls were crowded mostly with bookcases. Whenever one of them filled up with books, Ames said, he would go out and buy another bookcase. The apartment had

Danish-style furnishings, and on one wall hung a high-quality oil painting of which Ames was proud. Rosario, a Colombian, was friendly and
sociable. A good deal younger than Rick, she had been taking courses
for a master's degree, and she was seven months pregnant. They were
anxious about the arrival of the baby. Rosario had had a miscarriage
the previous year, and Ames had asked to extend his tour of duty for a
few months so that the baby could be born safely in Rome. The Agency
was always sympathetic to such requests, and Ames was granted a
six-month extension. Otherwise, he would have left shortly after I
arrived.

I couldn't help noticing, as they greeted us that evening, that Ames
had spruced up his appearance since we last saw each other. I attributed this to Rosario—she wore a stylish maternity dress—remembering
his unfashionable look back in Washington. He was dressed in good-
quality slacks and an oxford cloth shirt. I noticed that his teeth were
in the process of being fixed. Before we sat down for dinner, Rick
went to one of the bookshelves and pulled down the volume I had lent
him twenty years earlier, when we first joined the Agency: Harold
Lasswell's pre–World War II work *Psychopathology and Politics*. The
ideas in the book were influenced by the Freudian theory that early
upbringing results in predetermined adult behavior. In essence, by
extrapolation, if you are weaned on the left, you will be liberal, and if
weaned on the right, a conservative. I would come to appreciate the
irony, since, to my mind, Ames's upbringing and his father's rather
uninspiring CIA career were major factors in his decision to become a
Soviet mole. I mentioned that I had enjoyed the book he had lent me,
A Coffin for Dimitrios, the spy novel by Eric Ambler, whose writer-
narrator descends into a netherworld of treachery and counterespionage and becomes indistinguishable from the characters in his books.
More irony.

Rosario had prepared a meat and vegetable dish. It was well presented but nothing fancy or memorable—and not Latin or Italian,
which I would have found more interesting. They served a decent red
wine to go with it. Because the spouses weren't cleared, and we were
taught that we should never discuss business at home, we didn't that
night. The discussion centered on life in Rome, Rosario's background,
and her pregnancy. Ames at the time was driving a used Jaguar, which

he had smartly purchased on credit, but there wasn't anything else conspicuously excessive about their lifestyle. Because we were still in temporary quarters without a washing machine, Pat, as a matter of course, would ask to bring our laundry along when we were invited out. And she did so this evening as well.

The atmosphere was convivial, but our relationship had changed, and I'm sure Ames understood this, despite his nonchalance. As I had learned from my three previous station chief postings, it's lonely at the top. It is difficult to be friends with staff and at the same time exercise leadership and command authority. I was Ames's boss, and a professional relationship had to be maintained. There would be no hanging out and socializing. Pat and I would socialize mostly with senior officers in the embassy in Rome and with foreign liaisons. These relationships were professionally and personally rewarding, but those outside the Agency culture don't completely understand the challenges, stresses, and issues you face because of the secrecy embedded in our business. The truth is I felt closer to station chiefs whom I would see at conferences and back in Washington, even though I had much less contact with them.

Still, that evening at dinner with Ames, it was hard to get past the fact that I had risen to station chief and that Ames was still a mid-level officer. This hung over the room like a ghost, though he showed no outward signs of envy or discontent with the situation. It is conceivable that he saw it purely as a social evening and that he blocked out his other life for the night, but what he felt inside is impossible to say.

•

Compared to the other stations I had run, Rome was considerably larger, with more complexity and greater responsibility. Despite the job's stature and prestige, there had been no formal selection process. Clair George had been looking to replace Wolfe, and someone I knew quite well in human resources suggested my name. George reportedly trusted me, given our history with Iran-Contra and Afghanistan, and liked the idea. He called me into his office one day and told me, "You're going to Rome." Wolfe supposedly wasn't as enthusiastic, since he had served as a station chief and chief of the Europe Division before Rome and thought the Italians would find my relatively less senior status at the time off-putting, which did not turn out to be the case. Nonetheless, Wolfe was gracious to Pat and me during the transition.

The main mission there focused on "hard targets," including the Russians and all their Eastern Bloc allies, who had a huge presence in Rome. Thousands of Jewish refugees were coming out of Russia then, arriving in Rome before going to their ultimate destination of Israel or the United States. Many of these refugees were engineers, scientists, and others with highly technical backgrounds who possessed valuable intelligence, and they had to be debriefed as they arrived. Rome and the other European stations were still very large, given the importance of Europe and our shared history since World War II. More power has shifted back to Washington in recent years, given rapid advances in communications technology and more than a decade of war in Iraq and Afghanistan. But back when I arrived in Rome, the European chiefs truly were barons—a term you don't hear much in the CIA anymore— and the stations they ran made them the equivalent of three- or four-star generals in the military.

By this point in my career, I had learned to avoid the debilitating syndrome known in the Agency as "clientitis"—falling in love with the host country and overestimating its importance and the challenges it faces. Rome was incredibly dynamic, and the Italians certainly had their charms, so it was good that I had developed the experience to accurately determine Italy's priority in the context of the overall U.S. national interest.

The CIA and Italy go back a long way in the covert action field. The Agency's earliest and most important "influence operation" took place during the 1948 parliamentary elections. At that time, the Americans and Russians were just starting to face off in the Cold War international power struggle for the "hearts and minds" of free men. President Truman had already put down a marker that we would not let Russia spread its Communist system to Western Europe. There was already great concern about the Soviet Union gobbling up Eastern Europe. Truman knew that, on the heels of World War II, a military confrontation with the Russians would be disastrous for everyone. So he moved his fight below the radar and to the back alleys. He put the CIA at the forefront of this fight, and Italy was the first of the political battlegrounds. To counter the very strong Communist Party influence in Italy, Truman authorized the CIA to pour money into the elections there, through newspapers and magazines, radio broadcasts, posters, leaflets, and political organizations. According to Ambassador Hugh Montgomery, who spent three decades working in Western European postings for the Agency from 1952 to 1981, including a stint as station chief in Rome, the CIA was critical to preventing a Communist takeover in the Italian elections of 1948. "Without the CIA, the Communist Party, in which the Soviets had huge interests, would definitely have won," he said.[2] In the end, the conservative Christian Democracy Party defeated the leftist pro-Soviet Popular Alliance by a margin of 48 percent to 31 percent. This election set the standard for future fights, and the pro-West coalition prevailed in Italian parliamentary elections for the next fifty years. As time passed, the democratic parties were strong enough to stand on their own two feet and no longer needed to rely on clandestine Agency funding and support. Our effort in Italy was so successful that it endured for years as a model for effective political covert operations. In fact, much of the doctrine was still in vogue when I arrived in Allende's Chile in 1971. We all took a few pages from the Italy playbook.

•

When I arrived in Rome, I was amazed at how thoroughly the CIA's political influence remained ingrained in the Italian psyche, for good and bad. There was an inflated sense of the power of the CIA. I was able to take advantage of this mind-set with many of my contacts, one of whom, the chief of police, would go out of his way to be seen seemingly conspiring with me at the U.S. embassy's annual National Day party. As a matter of routine, he would take me by the arm and walk me very slowly around the perimeter of the embassy's garden, in plain view of hundreds of top dignitaries. Using the most secretive body language, while everybody looked on, he would whisper, "Aren't these gardens attractive?" and go on at length about the foliage. In this way, he accomplished his objective of being seen with the CIA station chief and ensuring that everybody knew he and the Agency were very close. He wasn't quite convinced, despite his position in the government, that we weren't still involved in calling the shots. It was to our advantage that I be complicit in this deception, and I gladly participated in the farce on the Fourth of July.

The chief's assiduous attention continued until I left Rome. As a farewell gesture of respect for the CIA representative, he invited Pat and me to dinner at an upscale restaurant. When we walked in, he and his wife were already seated at a table, the piano player was tapping away, and the waitstaff was lined up at the door. Everyone was exceptionally attentive. After fifteen minutes, I realized that no one else had entered the premises. When I asked him why, he said, "I closed the restaurant down for the night so we could have a special farewell." The unmistakable message was that he had great power, which I frankly had never doubted.

Our interactions with locals were enhanced by our ability to speak their language. While many Italians in the business and technical world speak English, a surprisingly small percentage of Italians in politics, law enforcement, and intelligence do. The Agency prepares people very well for postings abroad by providing rigorous predeployment language training for both agents and spouses. The language classes were arduous—and very small, so there was no place to hide. Our class consisted of Pat, me, and my soon-to-be-deputy, Doug Hokenson. Neither Pat nor I thought much about it ahead of time, but we quickly realized that married couples studying together present unique challenges that would test just about any relationship. We eventually felt sorry for Doug, who was the better linguist yet tried not to outshine his future boss while at the same time studiously ignoring the occasional tension between Pat and me. Like most things, Doug handled this with ease.

One of my most vivid memories of discord during training occurred when Pat and I were practicing our Italian lessons in the car while driving to the Jersey Shore. I made the terrible mistake of correcting Pat about a subjunctive verb ending. I don't know who was correct, but Pat found it so irritating that she rolled down the window and threw our textbook out of the car and onto the congested Route 95. Neither of us shone in class the following Monday, and we never practiced Italian again in a speeding vehicle. When we finished the training, we could converse in Italian across a broad spectrum of subjects. Our teacher even went so far as to spend a day on Italian hand gestures, some of which I still use.

We prided ourselves on our language skills, which made navigating the cultural divides, not to mention recruiting foreign agents, far more manageable. In Rome, speaking Italian also enabled us to enjoy and understand the country's incredible cuisine. I grew up believing that tomato sauce needed to cook all day and that there was only one recipe—a couple of cans of Hunt's tomatoes, a can of tomato paste, a teaspoon of sugar along with a dash of salt, pepper, and garlic. It remained my favorite sauce until I tasted authentic Italian cooking. Later on, I learned that the key to Italian cooking is using fresh, natural ingredients. When I think about my favorite sauce, I probably come back to the basic pomodoro and basil recipe, which goes well with just about anything. A very close second, particularly as a specialty, is spaghetti in the black ink of squid. It is hard to find on the menu, even in very good New York Italian restaurants, because the squid ink sac must be fresh and spoils easily. I was delighted to find a similar risotto dish at my favorite local Italian restaurant in New York, Cellini, in Midtown, run by Dino Arpaia.

Besides the great cuisine, there was wonderful opera. Pat and I had become opera lovers in Argentina, which is renowned for the Teatro Colón, one of the world's best acoustical opera houses. One of the lovely ways to enjoy the opera in Rome during the summer is at the Caracalla Baths, an outdoor site that in ancient Roman times accommodated as many as five thousand bathers. The ruins of the baths remain, with the addition of a huge stage constructed under the stars. It is a marvelous experience to witness Verdi's *Aïda* performed with live animals, including, on special occasions, elephants and horses. Our contacts in Italy were flattered by our interest in Italian opera and invited us one season to opening night at the famous La Scala opera house in Milan. It was an extraordinary event, not only listening to great opera, but also observing the cognoscenti decked out in capes and tiaras. The Italians take their opera seriously and are vocal in their appreciation of and displeasure with the performers. One has to be brave to sing at La Scala.

Far to the south, in Naples, I was involved in another bit of theater that required some fortitude—landing on the deck of the USS *Forrestal*. Ambassador Peter Secchia convinced the U.S. Navy that it would be a good idea to arrange for a group of us to land on the deck of the aircraft carrier when its port call was Italy. I took my seat on the airplane next to a Roman Catholic priest, who turned out to be Cardinal John Foley from Philadelphia. A close mutual friend from our hometown,

Dick Doran, had been urging both of us to meet each other in Rome. At the time, Cardinal Foley was serving as the Vatican's director of communications, and over the months ahead, we became good friends. The plane touched down on the carrier deck with a jolt that I braced myself for. The whole experience—landing an airplane on a ship bobbing in the ocean—was fascinating and memorable.

It had been my hope during my assignment in Rome to get a private audience with Pope John Paul II, who had had a great deal to do with encouraging democracy in Eastern Europe. I was reluctant to infringe on my friendship with Cardinal Foley, but once, when I mentioned that Pat's and my wedding anniversary was approaching, he suggested that we celebrate with a private Mass with the Pope.

Shortly thereafter, we received instructions about where Pat, our son, Conor, and I should go in the Vatican, very early in the morning, to be escorted to the Pope's private chapel. About twelve people had the same privilege that day. The dress code for men was business coat and tie, but the women were required to have their heads covered. When we walked into the small chapel, the Pope was kneeling in prayer in front of the altar. It was a solemn and special occasion for all of us. After the Mass, we were placed in a semicircle, and the Pope proceeded to walk around and address each person individually in his or her own language. When he reached me, he asked me in perfect English an unexpected question: Where do you work? My mind raced—do I lie to the Pope, or break cover and identify myself as the CIA station chief? "Your Holiness, I work for the U.S. government," I said, with slight hesitation, having found an inspired answer that allowed me to avoid lying to the Pope or failing my next polygraph. I thought I detected a knowing smile on the Pope's face.

Italian cuisine, the opera, a private Mass at the Vatican—all this contrasted with what I will always remember as the dark side of my time in Rome: Rick Ames. He constantly reminded me that the spy game could be a hall of mirrors (and as far as Ames went, of course, I did not yet know the half of it). I had been told at headquarters before I left that he had a drinking problem and had been brought back from Rome to Washington to dry out. A later inspector general's report on how Ames had been able to function inside the Agency as a KGB mole for nearly a decade would conclude that he had been known to drink during lunch and sleep at his desk. But now he was back in Rome and reportedly sober. One of the first things I did when I arrived was call him in to address the issue head-on. I told him, "Rick, you're a potentially talented officer and I know you've had a drinking problem, but I'm not going to tolerate it if you start drinking again. If there's any backsliding, you're out of here." He apparently was staying sober because his wife was pregnant, and he was on relatively good behavior. Nevertheless, I asked my deputy, Doug Hokenson, a first-class officer and experienced operator, to keep an eye on him as well. This was hard to do, since Ames was located in a separate area. I knew that it was important to check up on him, so I would from time to time seek him out in the afternoon and stand very close to him, as I would with my teenage children, to see if I could detect any liquor on his breath. I never did. But a question I've asked myself many times was whether it might have been a mistake to alert him to the fact that we would be watching his drinking. He was smart enough to stay out of our presence. At the end of the day, I would do it again, because the alternative of ignoring the issue would have been worse. Of course, years later the irony wasn't lost on me. While I was saying, "Shape up, try harder, you'll be successful," he was probably thinking, "You have no idea how successful a Soviet spy I am," as he went about stealing U.S. government secrets.

Not long thereafter, we took a ride together because he wanted to show me some of the Soviet installations in Rome. It seemed like a positive gesture, but I had an eerie sensation that something was wrong, although I couldn't put my finger on it. I couldn't imagine at that time that he would betray his country, the Agency, and his family and friends. By that point, at least ten of our best Russian agents had been arrested because of Ames's betrayals, and the KGB was systematically executing them. Ames was the only one inside the CIA who knew how the Russians had identified the agents. He never seemed troubled that he had, in effect, issued death warrants for these heroic men. The only thing that occasionally worried him was getting caught—and during his days in Rome, he was concerned that the KGB's aggressive moves against those whom he had betrayed might get him caught.[3] By then, he had deposited more than $1 million in blood money from the KGB into a secret Swiss account. However, as time went on, Ames's concerns apparently seemed to fade.

Upon my arrival, Doug Hokenson, who started in Rome before me, informed me that Ames, during Alan Wolfe's tenure, had a pattern of failing to file routine reports on what he was doing and whom he was seeing. "Rick," I told him, "you're going to produce, and if you don't produce, I'm going to be on your case." Hokenson and I stayed on him and nagged him—where's your report, whom did you see, where is your accounting this month? He complied, but slowly and resentfully. Hokenson and I were determined to keep Ames on the right path; inattention to small tasks can result in serious breaches. After he was caught, and the Agency started reviewing everyone who had managed him, the investigation team noted that we had been on his case on these issues.

My final encounter with Ames involved an Eastern European government official who walked into the station and offered his services as a spy. Most of the time, you have to work hard and be visible if you want to find assets. If you are out there moving around, they will find you; you cannot just sit around and wait for them to knock on your door. But in truth, many of our best assets were "walk-ins," people who simply walked into our embassies and volunteered to work for us. We sent Ames to do an initial interview with the Eastern European official, code-named Motorboat. In his book *Confessions of a Spy*, Pete Earley provides a bizarre account of the case from Ames himself. Among several authors to write about the Ames case, Earley was the only one able to interview the spy extensively.

Ames told me that after he met with Motorboat, Jack Devine asked him to arrange for Motorboat to be taken to a safe house so that he could be debriefed. "I was dead set against it," Ames said, "because I thought it would put Motorboat at risk . . . I said, Well, Jack, you are just going to have to order me to meet with him, because I don't think it is safe. And Devine told me, Well, I think it is worth the risk, and he sat down and wrote a memo to the file, saying that I didn't want to do it but he was ordering me to do it."

Ames told me that he was required to meet Motorboat at a safe house. "I must admit it was a very strange situation for me to be in," Ames said. "Here I was, I mean, I was working for the KGB, right, and here I am interviewing —— who is telling me about a penetration of our government by a U.S. citizen, someone who the KGB had under its control. It was a rather weird situation."

Ames told me that he later passed everything that he had learned about Motorboat to the KGB. "Only a few days earlier, I was arguing strenuously with Jack Devine about putting Motorboat in danger. Now, I was telling the KGB all about Motorboat. All I can say is that I had been genuinely worried about protecting Motorboat at the moment when I was arguing with Devine. It is just another sign of how compartmentalized I was."[4]

Ames's comment about being compartmentalized is oddly self-serving and nonsensical. And he tells only half the story. His concern for Motorboat's safety is ludicrous, as he himself notes, since Ames gave him up to the KGB several days later. His operational concerns about putting Motorboat at risk by taking him to a safe house were equally so. We regularly met assets far more sensitive than this Eastern European, and in places considerably more hostile than Rome. It is my strong view that with proper tradecraft, the CIA should be able to conduct a secure meeting just about anywhere in the world. But Ames didn't tell Earley the entire story. I also told Ames to polygraph Motorboat, which is standard operating procedure for assessing the veracity of agents and controlling their behavior. Polygraphs are usually administered in safe houses, far from the public eye. It's now clear why Ames wanted to avoid polygraphing Motorboat and came up with a flimsy excuse not to do so.

Under duress, Ames ultimately did conduct a polygraph examination of Motorboat over the weekend, and the polygraph operator reported that there were indications of possible deception in Motorboat's initial answers. My policy when deception was indicated was clear: come back to the station, report the results, and ask for guidance. Simply readministering the test only further distorts the results, but this is what Ames did, in violation of my guidance. I learned this Monday morning from the polygrapher who had conducted the tests. I was livid and angrily marched down the hall, got in Rick's face, and yelled, "What the hell do you think you were doing?" He had a lame excuse, but I detected for the first time what I thought was a high level of resentment and superiority. While he didn't say it—because he was at heart passive-aggressive—I felt he was thinking, "How dare he challenge me. I understand the Soviets and their Eastern Bloc allies far better than he ever will." And then I saw the flash of resentment in his eyes. It was an *Ojo* moment, as the Latins say—watch out. I didn't understand exactly what the look meant at the time, but it sent out a negative brain wave. When the mole hunters at headquarters came to see me much later, it all started to make sense. Not long after this encounter, Ames departed Rome for an assignment in Washington.

•

Shortly after arriving in Rome, I combed through the station's files on everyone we'd had relationships with, going back a number of administrations. This is something I did routinely with every new posting. While doing this, I identified an old contact, not an agent, who was a very experienced politician, having served in the government in different positions over decades. He was a reservoir of wisdom and understanding about Italian politics. Meeting with him also gave me a good opportunity to work on my Italian over a relaxed lunch. He always ordered the same thing—spaghetti basilica, which is basically spaghetti with tomato sauce and basil. He would proceed to sprinkle it with freshly crushed dried red pepper. He was convinced that it was the best and purest traditional Italian pasta. Over time, I came to the same view. We met every three to four months during my stay in Rome. While he was extremely well-informed, he gave no indication that he was still personally heavily involved in day-to-day politics.

The other unforgettable figure from my years in Rome was my Italian counterpart. Although he was highly regarded and powerful, he lived humbly. He came to our house several times and on occasion insisted on bringing the pasta sauce himself. This annoyed Pat to no end, as though he were suggesting she didn't know how to prepare sauce, but we let him do it because it was part of the rapport building that cements a special relationship.

Needless to say, the locals had exceptional on-the-ground surveillance and technical capabilities in Italy that enhanced our local presence—most of the time. Surveillance and countersurveillance are art forms. They can involve anything from small two- and four-man teams to complex operations involving large numbers of personnel. The FBI and Britain's secret service have often run them on this scale, with overhead flights, tracking devices, and concealed cameras. Certainly the Russians know how to mount massive surveillance operations in Moscow.

On any given day, anywhere in the world, an intelligence officer can become the subject of surveillance—to his everlasting embarrassment if he doesn't pick up on it. In this environment, officers are trained to develop a pattern of behavior over time that allows them to identify hostile surveillance. This must be done in a natural way, so whoever is watching the CIA officer can't figure out what he is up to and is not tipped off that the officer is carrying out a clandestine operation. Looking in the windows for reflections and bending over to tie your shoe is only for the movies and is a dead giveaway to surveillance teams.

Officers are trained to look for a natural route—known as an SDR, for surveillance detection route—that allows them to maintain routine travel patterns, all the while trying to draw out the surveillance team. This is best done using a combination of walking, mass transit, and taxis that will greatly complicate a relatively light surveillance team. Even a good team loses its target with more frequency than is generally realized. It also is useful to build in patterns that bring an officer face-to-face with a surveillance team—for example, entering a store and then heading back the way he came in. Sometimes spies spend hours on an SDR to break away from surveillance for a few minutes or hours in order to carry out a clandestine operational task.

The most important thing is to let your inner ear speak to you. If an intelligence officer is under regular surveillance, he can actually become accustomed to feeling its presence. There's never any foolproof means of detecting it, so officers must remain vigilant at all times. The lazy operator who cuts corners runs huge risks of detection. Before I went overseas on my first foreign tour, I sat in on the debriefing of the military attaché to the U.S. embassy in Santo Domingo, in the Dominican Republic. Lieutenant Colonel Donald J. Crowley had been kidnapped one Easter Sunday, off the capital's polo grounds, by members of the Dominican Popular Movement (MPD) and held for two days before being released in exchange for the release of twenty MPD members being held in Dominican jails. In his debriefing, Crowley described the ordeal in detail: how he was blindfolded and thrown to the floor of a speeding vehicle while his abductors held a gun to his head and, as in a game of Russian roulette, repeatedly pulled the trigger with empty chambers in the pistol. What grabbed my attention most, though, was the way he described the days before his kidnapping. As he left his house for his daily run each morning, he sensed something unspecific wrong in the environment. He couldn't pinpoint it, but his inner antenna told him something was amiss. This reinforced a belief I already had—that, when abroad, it's important to trust your instincts. If something doesn't feel right in the environment, stop and recalibrate. With each successive foreign posting, this lesson was affirmed, over and over again.

During my tenure in Rome, we would take pains to clean ourselves of surveillance when we were meeting somebody we didn't want the Italians to know about. It wasn't that we were trying to penetrate their government, but if we were going to meet a sensitive source from out of the country or local hard targets, we wanted to do it "in the dark." Even as chief, I had to be careful in any clandestine meeting I had in-country. I devised SDRs and followed procedures by the book. I did not want the Italians knowing whom I was meeting with, particularly since you always had to take seriously the possibility that the local intelligence service might have been penetrated by hostile forces. Once, I was surprised to learn from sensitive sources that the Italians had actually put heavy surveillance on me. Fortunately, it was a day that did not include a sensitive meeting. I was curious about why they might be zeroing in on me. Sometime later we learned that they were concerned that on that particular day I might come across their first sensitive meeting with Russian intelligence. Up until then, the Italians had had no formal relationship with the Russians. They were worried that I might accidentally spot the meeting. I hadn't spotted the surveillance that day, because I wasn't looking for it. I wasn't carrying out any unilateral acts, so I did not use an SDR. It was an important reminder that you can come under friendly surveillance for defensive reasons, and that you can never let down your guard.

Near the end of my stay in Italy, I made an official trip back to Washington with an Italian for a meeting at the CIA and the National

Security Agency. We flew Alitalia to Dulles, and Dewey Clarridge, then chief of the Europe Division, sent a stretch limousine to pick us up. I would never have ordered a stretch limousine; it was too visible. I would have preferred a more modest Lincoln Town Car. But this was Clarridge's style, so we got into our stretch limo and headed off to Fort Meade, about an hour away. It felt terribly conspicuous and unclandestine, especially pulling up in front of the NSA. The NSA officials who greeted us were not used to this level of display and probably passed it off as the CIA flexing its muscles. Frankly, I was embarrassed.

We had our meeting in the dining room with Vice Admiral William O. Studeman, the NSA director. It turned out that of the four top NSA officials around the table, two were named Devine—they were brothers, both deputy directors—John Devine and Jim Devine. As we were having lunch, the Italian asked, "Jack, is everybody named Devine in the intelligence business?" Everyone laughed. Before that day, I'd known of only one other Devine in the entire U.S. government. I never imagined a clan of Devine spies.

After the meeting, we headed for New York in the limo to share a meal before he had to fly home. He said he knew "a special restaurant," and I guessed that he had someplace exquisite in mind. After the long ride up I-95, our driver dropped us at a greasy spoon hamburger joint in Manhattan. We ordered hamburgers, and this official proceeded to take the roll off; remove the onions, lettuce, and tomato; and then cut the hamburger with a knife and fork. After a few minutes of this, I could no longer contain myself. "You tell me we're going to go to New York and you have a special place, and here we are having a hamburger, and you're not even eating the hamburger the way it should be enjoyed," I said quizzically. "What's up?" He replied without missing a beat: "This is where they filmed Popeye in *The French Connection*, right in this restaurant!" He loved that movie.

Back in Rome, shortly before the end of my tour, I got blindsided by press reports that the CIA had devised and implemented a plan in the mid-1950s to organize a clandestine network of operatives in Italy and across Western Europe whose job it would be to form a resistance movement should the Soviets invade or should the Communists prevail in Italian elections. Supported with secret caches of money and weapons, the network had subsequently been placed under NATO auspices until Giulio Andreotti, Italy's prime minister from the Christian Democracy Party, revealed its existence to the Italian parliament. The whole thing seems far-fetched today, but in the climate of the time it was a real concern that the Communists would seize power throughout Western Europe or that the Soviet Union might take control by military force. This was particularly true in Italy, where the second-largest European Communist Party that existed outside Moscow had a real shot at coming to power in the 1950s. It was from this fear that Operation Gladio (from the Latin word for sword) was born and would continue to operate after the fall of Europe.

Gladio provided not only real material support to the resistance, but also a guarantee of U.S. loyalty to Italy. "They knew that the U.S. was serious about supporting Italy and giving them a means to defend themselves," said Hugh Montgomery, a former Rome station chief. "It was a major factor for stability in Italy and across the region."[5] Gladio did outlive its usefulness, however, and should have been quietly dismantled, as many similar activities throughout Western Europe were. I first learned about Gladio from the local press when Prime Minister Andreotti revealed to parliament the existence of a clandestine network of between six hundred and a thousand operatives and more than one hundred weapons caches in secret locations throughout the country, a network that had been dormant for decades. It created huge local headlines but was hardly a blip in the U.S. media. According to Andreotti, Gladio was put under the command of Italian military intelligence in the 1980s, and though technically still in existence, most of the weapons caches had been dismantled. Apparently all postwar prime ministers had been briefed on Gladio. Andreotti's hand was forced by a Venice magistrate who stumbled on documents describing Gladio while investigating a decades-old car bombing. The media and political figures quickly fell to speculating about Gladio's possible involvement in the political violence that had plagued Italy over the past three decades, culminating in the Bologna railway station massacre. These stories included outrageous allegations and preposterous speculation. But they certainly had their believers, and the blowback from them continues today in some Italian quarters. There wasn't much for us to do except weather the firestorm.

The controversy kept me busy until the very end of my tour. Wrapping up a family's affairs in a foreign country after a two- or three-year posting was always fraught with entanglements. When it came time to leave Italy, for example, we engaged in the ritual garage sale. There was a strict agency weight allowance for shipping, so we needed to strip down our belongings. Pat enjoyed running the sales and was an expert at it. She could sell anything to anybody. I wisely ended up in the background, organizing the items and setting up tables. Near the end of one sale, a dapperly dressed young man came into the house and started looking through Pat's dresses. He said he wanted to purchase them for his sister, but it soon became apparent that he was a transvestite, which was not as socially acceptable then as it is today. The children and I sat on the staircase watching in fascination as Pat put him at ease, bantering about how well her blue dresses matched his eyes and how a tuck here or there would make a perfect fit. She sold most of the dresses to him, and he left extremely pleased. Once again, I couldn't help thinking that my wife should have been working full-time doing recruitment pitches.

When we left Rome, Daniel Serwer, the State Department's deputy chief of mission, gave me a plastic sword as a going-away gift. Despite his good humor and our good working relationship, I had the feeling he thought I had been holding out on him by not telling him about the long-inactive program. His suspicions notwithstanding, the Agency had lost interest in Gladio many years earlier and had no hand in what emerged years later as some of these same stay-behind individuals became involved in rather unseemly local political action.

It was around the time of our departure that Howard Hart came through the station on a farewell tour of sorts. Hart was the first director of the CIA's Counter Narcotics Center (CNC), a standing interagency task force set up at Langley to fight global drug trafficking and all the related crime, from murder to money laundering (the name was later changed to the Crime and Narcotics Center). Hart's position at CNC spoke to his closeness to the man who had replaced Casey as CIA director, William H. Webster, the only man to serve as head of both the FBI (from 1978 to 1987) and the CIA (from 1987 to 1991). Given his law enforcement background, Webster, a former federal judge, was intensely focused on the war on drugs, as was the White House.

As for Hart, he had served as a spymaster in the Middle East, and now, at fifty, he was determined to retire. We spent a fair amount of time together while he was in Rome. We had known each other for some years, and we had a good, though not close, relationship. Near the end of the visit, he announced that he planned to tell Judge Webster when he returned to headquarters that I should replace him at CNC. Was I interested? I said I was, and that it sounded like a very intriguing task, running one of the new interagency "centers," which reminded me of the multidisciplinary nature of the Afghan Task Force.

In this age of war and terrorism, it's hard to properly convey how important the war on drugs was for the White House and Congress— and in turn for the CIA, the FBI, the Pentagon, and other agencies. Many agencies, including the CIA and the FBI, had resisted this particular struggle for years. But as the White House focused attention on the problem and appropriated large amounts of money to stop the drug trade, it was not surprising that everyone in the intelligence community was looking to play on this field.

Hart was as good as his word. He recommended me to Judge Webster, and I flew to the States to interview with him. Soon after, Pat and I started preparing to leave the wonders of Rome behind.

SEVEN

Selling the Linear Strategy, One Lunch at a Time

Washington, 1990–92

I took over the Counter Narcotics Center in December 1990, more than a year after Pablo Escobar's *sicarios* assassinated Senator Luis Carlos Galán, the Liberal Party candidate for president in Colombia. Galán was about to address a rally of ten thousand in Soacha, south of Bogotá, when a gunman, spraying bullets that wounded ten others onstage, shot him twice in the stomach. Earlier that day in August 1989, hit men from Escobar's Medellín Cartel had murdered Colonel Waldemar Franklin Quintero, a provincial police chief who had been leading the fight against the organization responsible for about 80 percent of the world's cocaine. By day's end, Virgilio Barco Vargas, Colombia's president, promised in a nationwide address to renew Colombia's treaty with the United States for extraditing suspected drug dealers.

Because the war on drugs was then regarded as a top national security priority, President Reagan had signed a classified National Security Decision Directive in 1986 authorizing the Pentagon to become involved in stopping the trafficking of narcotics across the U.S. border, which the document called "a national security threat." Shortly after Galán's murder, President Bush then signed NSDD 18, which authorized $250 million for the Pentagon, the FBI, the CIA, and other agencies to fight the drug cartels. He also authorized U.S. Special Operations Forces to train the Colombian military and police.[1] By the time I arrived at the CNC, the administration had unveiled an $8.8 billion Andean strategy for funding the Drug Enforcement Agency, the State Department, and the CIA in a major thrust to take down the drug cartels.

Judge Webster, in his second year as director of central intelligence, created the Counter Narcotics Center in April 1989, making counternarcotics his top priority. He was a highly regarded public servant, having served as a federal judge and director of the FBI, where he was praised for his integrity and political soundness. I, too, respected the judge and found him to be a gentleman in the true sense of the word.

The "center" construct called for bringing together into a coherent unit the CIA's three primary disciplines—operations, analysis, and technology—and including representatives from the FBI, the DEA, the National Security Agency, the Defense Department, Customs, Immigration, the Coast Guard, and other agencies. The CIA's Counterterrorism Center was the first interagency center, and it was formed in 1986. It resided in the Directorate of Operations and was the first major experiment in creating an interdisciplinary team that could combine CIA operations officers, analysts, technologists with SIGINT (signals intelligence), specialists from the NSA, FBI agents, and military weapons experts, among others. A counterintelligence center was created two years later, also in the Directorate of Operations.

Webster placed the Counter Narcotics Center within the Directorate of Intelligence because the DI leaders had complained when the first two centers went to the DO and had made a hard pitch for a center of their own. The DO was only too happy to let the DI have it. Historically, the Agency had run away from narcotics. There was a conviction that if we became involved in the drug war, it would contaminate our officers and corrupt the Agency. Within the DO, going after the hard Soviet, Chinese, and Cuban targets had been considered noble and necessary during the Cold War, while "drugs and thugs" seemed less part of the geopolitical game and more of a law enforcement concern. So it is not surprising that no one was sorry to see DEA take the lead in the war on drugs. However, when counternarcotics became Webster's number one target and the CIA started receiving greatly enhanced budgets, more personnel, and White House attention, everyone became more interested in this target. The can-do spirit and perseverance of the Agency, said Jerry Svat, a former deputy chief of the Latin America Division and later deputy chief of Africa division, won over those in the CIA who were reluctant to get involved in something seemingly intractable, with difficult targets, turf battles among U.S. agencies, and high risks for those operating in the field. By the time the Berlin Wall fell and the Soviet Union collapsed, the CNC was growing rapidly in significance.[2]

Two major narcotics cartels operating out of Colombia, Medellín and Cali, virtually controlled the world supply of cocaine, a multibillion-dollar business when I took over the reins of the CNC. While the Cali Cartel maintained a low profile, the head of the Medellín Cartel, Pablo Escobar, the "world's greatest outlaw," was an international celebrity, drawing worldwide publicity, which he seemingly relished. As late as 1989, *Forbes* magazine named him the seventh-wealthiest person in the world, with an estimated personal fortune of $25 billion. While he had been born into poverty, he managed to climb the criminal ladder quickly, from petty thief and bodyguard to major drug smuggler. He reportedly was a millionaire by the age of twenty-two. By the mid-1970s he was well positioned to take advantage of the steep demand for cocaine in the United States, and at the peak of this epidemic, he was allegedly shipping twenty to thirty tons of cocaine monthly to the United States.

Escobar was able to control his share of the market by mastering the art of intimidation and corruption. His approach was straightforward and became widely known as *plata o plomo*—"silver or lead." In other words, you either accepted his bribe money or you were shot. It was not a hard choice for many. Escobar was brash in using violence, even under circumstances that guaranteed international publicity—the Galán assassination, the bombing of Avianca Flight 203, and the attack on the Colombian government's security headquarters not long thereafter. (Avianca 203 blew up shortly after takeoff from Bogotá on November 27, 1989, killing all 107 people on board. The headquarters bombing, an attempt to assassinate the Colombian security chief Miguel Maza Márquez, killed fifty-two and injured hundreds.) It would be wrong to assume that all officials and policemen would succumb to this corruption. Quite to the contrary: despite the risk to life and limb, thousands of honest policemen, judges, and government officials paid with their lives for resisting Escobar's threats. Sadly, in the process of fighting the traffickers, Colombia became the murder capital of the world. In the fall of 1998, the country was averaging thousands of murders a year.

Webster put me in charge when the center was approaching its second year. I think he liked my background in Latin America, a track record in covert action, and highly valuable experience from my days running the Afghan Task Force, which required bringing different disciplines under one roof, much as the CNC was now doing. The Afghan experience had made me a believer in the value of locating analysts and operators and military and technical experts in one office. The center took this model to another level.

As head of a relatively new center with a lot of high-level attention, I needed to set the tone and establish two strategic priorities to help guide our work against the drug cartels and meet the objectives as articulated by the policy makers. The first priority was to overcome historic inter- and intra-agency rivalries, so that the various departments and agencies could work together against this difficult target. The second was to build up the resources, capabilities, and esprit de corps of the center that were necessary to carry out counternarcotics programs successfully.

Webster had created the CNC after the new headquarters building was completed. The only space that Howard Hart, its first director, could find was on the bottom floor, an underground area without windows. Most of those on the CNC's large staff of around two hundred found it depressing to work all day without sunlight, especially when many reported to work before the sun rose and did not leave until after it had set. But the work was challenging and exciting, and no one complained. The workforce was divided fairly evenly among analysts, operations officers, and technologists working together as one team—the big idea behind the center—and it worked. There were also between twenty-five and thirty representatives from the DEA, the FBI, the NSA, the DOD, Customs, the Treasury, and the State Department. A torrent of intelligence flowed into the center around the clock, from agent reports to imagery from spy satellites capable of seeing through thick jungle foliage to detect clandestine airstrips in coca-growing regions.

Leading the CNC required stamina and a lot of heavy lifting. Marty Roeber, my deputy, and I routinely worked on Saturdays. We had both come up through the ranks with a focus on Latin America. Roeber came from the Agency's analytic side and had served as the CIA's national intelligence officer for Latin America for three years. He demanded rigor and made it clear that there would be no slanting the intelligence one way or the other. He had grown up in Texas, an air force brat. He graduated from the University of Illinois in 1966 and then went on to graduate school at SUNY Albany. He applied for a job at the CIA and then forgot all about it as the process dragged on. But when a job offer came from Langley out of the blue, it took him about ten minutes to pack up his car and head south.

Any leadership expert will tell you that individuals lose and teams win, and Roeber and I made a good team. He was a detail person, focused on consistency and continuity; I developed the strategy and worked to build support for the center's work from its partners across the federal government.

As we were gathering momentum early on in my tenure at the CNC, we adopted what became known in the intelligence and law enforcement communities as the "linear strategy." Working closely with Doug Doolittle, one of our top analysts, we developed the concept for focusing the combined efforts of all U.S. agencies as well as our foreign intelligence partners in a top-to-bottom effort that spanned the Southern Hemisphere and the globe, enabling us to target entire drug-trafficking networks, not just individuals. Roeber said, "Executed properly, the linear strategy provided an opportunity for intelligence and law enforcement to cooperatively target trafficking organizations. It was a blueprint for simultaneously conducting strikes against crops, labs, and trafficking and distribution networks from South America to the United States." It was a logical outgrowth of the center construct, locating representatives from more than a dozen agencies under one roof at Langley so as to concentrate U.S. efforts. We worked hard to go beyond the center and break down the silos and "need-to-know" classifications that agencies had built around their most valuable information to zealously guard it from others in the federal government who should have been their partners—something the intelligence community continues to struggle with today, in the post-9/11 landscape.

For instance, I convinced Robert C. Bonner, administrator of the DEA, to let us send over a few CIA analysts from CNC to rummage through his files looking for data relating to the Cali Cartel. Bonner was friendly and open, but clearly had long-standing concerns about the Agency being up front with him and sharing everything that was appropriate. Over the years, a number of U.S. agencies and officials have been suspicious of the CIA, its motives, and the possibility that it is withholding information. Sometimes this suspicion has been grounded in truth, but much of the time it is just a natural reaction to the fact that the CIA's collection and analytical capabilities expand beyond those of others in the U.S. government. At the same time, there is a significant cultural difference between how intelligence and law enforcement officers approach information and the purposes for it. In its simplest terms, intelligence officers spend their time collecting information to put together a strategic mosaic, while law enforcement officers try to collect evidence for a judicial prosecution and assiduously work to avoid contaminating that evidence. Two months after our analysts had dug through the DEA files, they produced a very thorough and rich report. We sent it to DEA, and a few days later I received a call from a very upset Bonner. "I thought we had an agreement," he said. "How could you produce all this information without sharing it with me? This is all new information to me. I feel sandbagged." To his relief and slight embarrassment, I pointed out that it was his own information. We had merely given it some analytical horsepower, in the spirit of broadened collaboration. After that, he became more trustful of the CNC, and a number of his senior leaders became major supporters of the center.

Beyond this new trust and cooperation among federal agencies, the other new and innovative component of the linear strategy was the way we started dealing with our liaison partners in foreign intelligence agencies. Brian Bramson, a veteran CIA operations officer and Latin America hand, led the way here—and has never been fully recognized for this achievement. Traditionally, we tried to give liaison partners as little support and intelligence as we could get away with to stay in the game. We did not want to develop their skills to the point where they could jeopardize our other unilateral operations if they turned against us. I understood this reluctance, having seen trusted liaison partners become criminal liabilities.

Nevertheless, when it came to attacking drug cartels at the CNC in the early 1990s, we made a decision to truly build up liaison capabilities and share with the locals even high-end resources—everything that could be used to damage the narcotic-trafficking networks. Our strategy was to use our liaison partners as a genuine force multiplier. Combining their on-the-ground knowledge, language abilities, and existing networks with our skills, training, and equipment, we went from minimal bilateral liaison to enhanced multilateral liaison. "The kind of information we were looking for had to be gathered in-country by our good liaison contacts that we trusted . . . liaison relationships were key," Brian Bramson said.[5]

Soon we were building powerful and effective intelligence collection units. An Andean region drug-trafficking organization was dismantled from "stem to stern" in the early 1990s due in large part to a carefully cultivated liaison relationship. This was a classic example of how good liaison relationships could result in significant advances against these cartels, Bramson said. We had not, in my view, structured an intelligence-collection program quite so coherently up to that point in time.

In order to sell the linear strategy, I felt I had to become a regular user of the CIA's Executive Dining Room, which—thanks to Bill Casey—had the best kitchen in federal Washington. Apparently, he had found the cuisine at Langley wanting and called upon the other CIA, the Culinary Institute of America, to infiltrate the kitchen. Since it was against regulations for the federal government to pay for meals for government employees, I used my own scant money as I sold the linear strategy over lunch to most of the heads of the sixteen agencies, whom I invited one by one. This strategy remained for many years a cornerstone of what is now the Crime and Narcotics Center. The CNC's focus expanded in 1994, a couple of years after I had departed. One of those who came over for lunch was Rich Haver, then secretary of defense Dick Cheney's chief of staff at the Pentagon. He was instrumental in talking to all the Defense Department intelligence people and getting them to support the CNC. He invoked Cheney's name and told them the defense secretary was fully behind this strategy. In the end, all the agencies signed on to it and moved forward in implementing it. The power of cooperation, instead of competition, was so obvious that the linear strategy remained a "blue plate special"—highlighted annually to Congress for more than a decade as an example of the intelligence community's effectiveness at a joint endeavor—and was used as justification for continued funding.

It wasn't hard to sell the CNC's ability to target an entire network or cartel. Indeed, the linear strategy helped make "targeting" a recognized discipline at the CIA and "link analysis" a necessary tool for mapping connections, one that has since become critical in mapping and attacking al-Qaeda and other terrorist networks. Targeting is a means of identifying the most important people in a network by using link analysis to understand their roles, their connections to one another, their communication patterns, their locations, and the way they move money.

Just as targeting became a recognized discipline thanks to the linear strategy, counternarcotics started to become a recognized focus at the Agency. The linear strategy had become so well embraced and well funded that it moved the CNC toward a career service, as opposed to a rotating assignment, which served to boost morale and attract top talent from within the Agency.

The counternarcotics mission required an unusual bureaucratic arrangement to keep all our efforts aligned. The CIA's Latin America Division, headed at the time by Terry Ward, controlled those who worked out of the stations across the region. We controlled the money they received for counternarcotics operations and provided, with Bramson leading the way, technology, direction, and powerful analytic support. Because the cartels extended beyond country borders, Agency case officers across Latin America benefited greatly from feeding the raw intelligence they were gathering from human and technical sources to the CNC in Washington, where analysts were able to connect the dots with what their counterparts were collecting. And the fruits of that analysis went back out, not only to the CIA stations, but also to DEA, the State Department, and military units working in the field on counternarcotics. While my immediate supervisor was John Helgerson, head of the Directorate of Intelligence, Roeber noted that he is still amazed how much time we spent up on the seventh floor meeting with the Directorate of Operations, which spoke to how operationally oriented the CNC had become.

The power of the linear strategy, and enhanced liaison with the Colombian military and intelligence service, was evident throughout the collaborative campaign to take down Escobar and the Medellín Cartel. Shortly after President George H. W. Bush signed NSDD 18, he dispatched U.S. Army Special Forces trainers to work with the Colombian police and military on quick-strike tactics. Roeber and I heard from a fair number of people that we were never going to get Escobar. But the linear strategy put pressure on him from every angle, and we remained confident. "When you start putting the full weight of the U.S. against a target, you will get him," Roeber said. "Getting Pablo Escobar was a cumulative effort, and intercepts played a huge part in counternarcotics." The Colombians were then able to zero in on Escobar's movements by intercepting his communications.

Back at the CNC, Bramson was rightfully convinced that the only way to get the upper hand on traffickers was to arm the local police and our intelligence counterparts with first-class equipment, including analytic and operations hardware. I visited one of the units in Colombia and was very impressed with the caliber and skill of the officers. The chief of the unit bluntly noted that part of their success came from the fact that they had handpicked the police recruits and put them undercover so that they never worked the streets. Otherwise, he noted, these officers would be approached by a trafficker their first day on the job and be offered a bribe "they couldn't refuse."

Escobar understood politics and used substantial sums of money in developing a Robin Hood image, spreading some of his wealth among the poor. It won him goodwill among the masses. Nevertheless, his violence against the political system became unsustainable. As pressure mounted against him, he was able to negotiate his surrender to the Colombian authorities in June 1991 in exchange for a reduced sentence and special imprisonment conditions. Colombia's Constitutional Assembly voted to prohibit his extradition to the United States, ensuring he would not be tried here and receive a long, hard sentence, or worse. His confinement in La Catedral prison became an international joke, given the royal treatment he received there, as well as the ease with which he could exit the prison under seemingly loose controls. Still, the linear strategy had worked. When I took over the CNC, Escobar and the Cali Cartel were virtually seen as untouchable. Now Escobar was in prison and the cartel was collapsing.

EIGHT

Jousting with the Soviets: When I Knew It Was Over

Washington 1990–92

Escobar may have been our number one target, and Latin America was clearly our focal point at the CNC, but the war on drugs was global. In the spring of 1991, Milt Bearden phoned, hoping I could help him cultivate a new relationship with our old enemy, the Russians. My presence, he realized, would underscore for them our mutual interest in combating the drug trade. It wasn't hard for Bearden to talk me into this escapade.

"I've got a sweetener," he said. "I think I can cut a deal with the Russians if you come, and we can make them take us to the poppy fields of Uzbekistan, along the border of the river that flows under the Friendship Bridge. I can get us out there."

"That would be great," I said. "You and I cavorting with the KGB on the bridge where the Russians retreated from Afghanistan."

Bearden had become head of the former Soviet Division, now called the Russia Division, of the Directorate of Operations after he left Pakistan. The Cold War was coming to an end, a new world order was at hand. I saw it as a sign of the changing times and something we needed to do. I thought we should have more heartily embraced the Russians when the Berlin Wall fell in November 1989, but the policy then was "They're still the Russians." This reticence eventually contributed to Vladimir Putin's rise to power. If we had moved aggressively to work with more reform-minded forces in Russia, things might have been different.

Philosophically, Bearden and I were on a similar track on this point.

Despite our role in fighting against the Soviets in Afghanistan, we shared a conviction about the need for a new approach. But a lot of the old-timers at the Agency thought Bearden's cultivation of KGB contacts was virtually treason. I may have disagreed with them, but it wasn't hard to understand why they felt that way, given the years, the decades, all of us had invested in the Cold War maniacally focused on the Soviet threat.

Even though I spent my first five overseas tours in Latin America, I constantly found myself dueling with Soviet officers. I was trying to recruit them; they were trying to recruit us. Central America was a rich hunting ground in the late 1970s and '80s. The Soviets maintained one of their largest missions there, both to gather intelligence and to project propaganda in the region. Similarly, our operation was a flagship there for the Latin America Division, which had a legacy of robust counterintelligence operations. This was the era of the KGB's "Golden Boys"—smart, well-educated officers with excellent language skills who would stay in a post for years perfecting their knowledge of the local geography and culture and building a network of contacts. They would taunt us with the ease they had moving about, dropping into a conversation a reference to a recent trip to Dallas, for example, then taking it back when we called them on it, as if they had let it slip by accident.

I was particularity interested in a Russian Foreign Ministry officer who reportedly had shown signs of disaffection on an earlier assignment. I tried a number of ploys to get to him. I knew he was a fan of the band Chicago, which was coming to the city for a performance. I obtained tickets and invited the official and his wife. His KGB controllers allowed them to go, but he clearly was instructed to beg off any follow-on socializing after the performance. We all enjoyed the show immensely, but the entire auditorium was a mist of marijuana smoke. No doubt, we all ended up with a bit of a contact high.

We learned shortly thereafter that the officer was returning to Moscow, and we decided to make an unusually forward advance. I arranged to drop by his apartment unannounced when we knew he would be alone. The intent was not to pitch him but rather to allow him an opportunity to step forward if, in fact, he was disaffected. He handled my arrival smoothly. We shared his bottle of Courvoisier, and as Russians tend to do, he waxed philosophical about the meaning of life and human nature. While the conversation was deliberately oblique, I'm sure he understood why I was there and was telling me between the lines that he was contented enough with his lot in life and that I should not expect him to show up on my doorstep anytime soon.

We were not above using artifice to curry favor. My colleague Brad Handley had a famous cousin, Peter Benchley, author of the book *Jaws*, on which the blockbuster movie is based. Back in 1975, we arranged a special showing of the film for our Soviet counterparts and told them we were able to get a copy of the movie, still in its first run, only because of Brad's relationship with Benchley. Brad had another great in, this one with the international community: he played rugby. His team was well-known and played regularly, which put Brad in contact with a whole different group of people. He often told me what a rich source of potential targets this was and urged me to join him. Finally, one day in the elevator, he implied, not so subtly, that if I didn't join him in the scrum, it was because I was just another "empty suit" case officer. This hit the right button, and I soon found myself on the rugby pitch, at the bottom of a scrum where the Australian beside me had a French opponent by the neck of his jersey and was yelling, "If you bite me one more time, I'm going to smash in your teeth." I knew I was in the right operating environment!

These occasions were often diverting, but they were never just for fun. We would all have our targets, and we would plan in advance our method of approach. If one of us was rebuffed, another would move in, and there was always a plan C and plan D. We planned meticulously and left nothing to chance. When it came to seducing and recruiting potential assets, we considered and reconsidered every detail and always had contingencies. All this would have been invisible to the uninitiated, but Brad saw it from the inside. On those occasions when Pat and the children were able to join me, we were, for all appearances, just energetic hosts—throwing parties, arranging special entertainment, organizing outings. Each occasion, though, was carefully devised to build a strategic social network and to cement relationships in the international diplomatic community in the hope that eventually we would persuade our new friends to become agents.

I don't think I was fooling the KGB. The Russians were working us the same way we were working them. We made it a habit of crashing each other's National Day celebrations, usually going along with an embassy official who had been officially invited. Once they spotted me, the KGB officers would take turns making a beeline for me to offer a toast, hoping that the repetitive vodka shots would get me intoxicated. You play that game only once. On one occasion, I spotted the Russian embassy code clerk, the most protected target in the mission, and quickly headed toward him. Almost like a Western wagon train, a group of KGB officers suddenly appeared and literally formed a human circle to block my talking to him. Too bad—that would have made for an interesting report for both of us the next day.

The KGB's Golden Boys were also very active. One of their tactics was for one of them to ride the same bus that a number of female U.S. embassy staff used. One male KGB agent boarded the same bus each day but didn't sit down beside his target right away; he sat in various spots for several days, until there was a natural opportunity to sit next to the U.S. embassy employee. Little by little, he followed up on the light banter until it seemed natural to suggest a rendezvous, with the objective being a sexual tryst that would lay the groundwork for the ultimate goal: a pitch for classified information. All his careful planning was for naught, however. He had hit up the wrong employee. She reported the incident immediately, and we were able to gracefully break off the relationship and alert other members of the staff to this clever technique. It's not hard to imagine that this ploy didn't always fail.

We also ran some interesting technical operations, including one that nearly ended in disaster. A senior Communist leader from Central America came to town and we were able to install an audio device in his hotel room. Not a great idea in retrospect, since he was sexually ambitious and spent most of his time frolicking in bed with his mistress. Our bug produced no intelligence whatsoever. At one point, the interaction with the mistress became rather vigorous, and the bed actually broke. We heard the mistress screech, "A bug!" and we thought the audio device had been exposed. After a few moments of panic, it became clear that she had seen, in fact, an insect! In another case, our "tech op" went smoothly from a technical standpoint but failed for the worst of reasons. Our technical staff had manufactured a sophisticated voice-activated audio device to be installed in the ambassador's office in an unfriendly embassy. It was a masterpiece of craftsmanship, and we were able to observe from a discreet distance its flawless installation. But it never worked. We wrongly assumed that it had somehow been picked up by their "sweep team," the team that searches a room for such devices. We later learned from a defector that the unfriendly government had a penetration agent in the government service who had alerted them to the device.

Setbacks, of course, are as much a part of the game as successes, and they serve a purpose. There was the time we imported a "locks-and-pick man" to gain entrance to the apartment of a high-value target who was on temporary duty. I don't know how one becomes a specialist in picking locks, but this man was very good at it. In my office, he demonstrated his dexterity with a range of complicated door locks. There didn't seem to be any kind of lock that could keep him out. But when we got to the actual door we needed unlocked, he was stymied. During his unsuccessful attempt, our surveillance had to keep in view the corridors and the target himself for over twenty minutes, which seemed like a lifetime, with the man exposed in the hallway, working to no avail. He was dejected by the experience, as was the entire team. Nevertheless, we gave it a go a few days later, and it worked like a charm. That operation proved very successful.

Recruiting Soviet agents was a primary focus for us in Buenos Aires, where there was a substantial Soviet Bloc delegation because of the agricultural trade between the two countries. One of the station's senior case officers had met the East German chargé d'affaires at several parties, and I encouraged him to work on the relationship. The case officer was skeptical. The East Germans were among the best. Succeeding with an East German—well, it was tougher than succeeding with a Soviet. And this official was a typical hard-core operative.

Defection is a mysterious calculation, with a cost and a benefit to all involved. My best information on what it must be like for the defector comes from Yuri Nosenko, a KGB officer who defected to the CIA in 1964. Nosenko changed sides just as the CIA was trying to determine whether there was a Soviet connection to the assassination of President John F. Kennedy, a scenario that would have had grave political consequences. Kennedy's killer, Lee Harvey Oswald, had lived in Russia, and there were suspicions that Oswald had been recruited by the KGB. Nosenko, though, told his debriefers that he had handled Oswald in Russia and that Oswald had been surveilled by the KGB but never recruited because he wasn't considered bright enough and was deemed mentally unstable.

I had the opportunity to have dinner with Nosenko when he visited Argentina during my tour there. During the dinner I asked him how he had been able to make the decision to leave behind his country and his family so suddenly. He said that he had been thinking about defecting to the West for years and that his own situation had become so desperate that he couldn't stand it anymore. Once he made up his mind, he said, he realized that he would have to forget about his family for their sake and just walk away and never look back.

"I simply had to cut out my heart and go on living," he said.

Nosenko's case also shows what can happen when you become the poster child for the excesses of counterintelligence paranoia. Nosenko was locked in solitary confinement by the CIA for three years and interrogated by officers who were convinced he was lying and that he was actually a KGB plant meant to sow disinformation.[1]

Nosenko's imprisonment is often blamed on the famously distrustful chief of counterintelligence, James Jesus Angleton. Nosenko actually was held by the Agency's Soviet Division, but the suspicions about his motives no doubt grew from Angleton's convoluted and controversial theories about Soviet espionage strategy. Angleton had been heavily influenced by an earlier Russian defector, Anatoliy Golitsyn, who had claimed that the KGB had infiltrated the CIA and that its agents were manipulating the Agency to get it to advance the KGB's agenda unknowingly. He said in essence that all other defectors were part of this plot.

Angleton began to see these "moles" everywhere, in what he described—borrowing a phrase from T. S. Eliot—as "a wilderness of mirrors." He hunted relentlessly for these double agents and destroyed careers along the way, the impact of which I saw in a small way early in my career. I had an instructor at the Farm who impressed me tremendously. I praised his skills to a number of seasoned officers and each time received in response a wince and an indication that something unspecified about the instructor wasn't quite right. I assumed it might have been a drinking problem or other indiscretion, until I learned years later that Golitsyn had told Angleton that one of the Soviet plants in the CIA was a Slav whose name began with a *K* and ended in *-sky*. My instructor fit that description, as did a few other officers. At the suggestion of the CIA, these officers later sued the U.S. government because their careers had been derailed by Angleton's suspicion that they were Soviet plants.

Angleton's paranoia became extreme; he was forced to resign in 1975. But a certain amount of distrust is the fate of any spy. When you are acting covertly, it's reasonable to assume that the people you are dealing with have motives as murky as your own. It is necessary to triple-think interactions and to keep your antenna up for signs of subterfuge. Why is this person cooperating? Is his information verifiable? Who stands to gain from it?

So it was with this Eastern European. Our case officer cultivated him slowly, aware that he might be working his own angle. Perhaps he thought he could get something out of our officer, even convert him. The officer received no indication he would ever drop his guard, but he kept working him, because you never know. Shortly after I left Buenos Aires for Washington, our persistence paid off. He came to us, asking for help to defect to West Germany.

By then we had repaired relations with the civilian Argentine government following the junta's fall after the Falkland Islands war. We would have had great difficulty getting him out of the country quickly if the relationship had still been in the state it was in when I arrived.

This and a dozen other operations aimed over the years at Soviet Bloc officers came to mind with a surreal quality as Milt Bearden and I flew to Moscow in June 1991. Even more surreal was the fact that we visited KGB headquarters, toured the KGB museum, and met the head of the KGB. In the museum, black curtains were pulled down over a few exhibits. We were told these were photographs of Americans caught in flagrante delicto.

The other thing that Bearden wanted to do was visit the Silk Road. So we flew to Samarkand, to the land of Genghis Khan. With the Russians, we stayed in the dacha once inhabited by Stalin's infamous security chief, Lavrentiy Beria. I'm sure it was adequately wired to pick up any indiscreet conversations among our team.

We were traveling with our chief from Moscow and the KGB's head of counterintelligence—the general who had been responsible for overseeing Aldrich Ames, we would later learn. On their side, there was a Ukrainian colonel plus a couple of midlevel Russian colonels. A senior staff member from the CNC rounded out our delegation. Everywhere we went, there was ritual toasting. The Russians would toast President Bush, so there were Milt and I, toasting Gorbachev. I'm sure if anyone on our counterintelligence staff had gotten word of this they would have concluded we were nothing but spies all along for the Russians.

As part of the trip, our Russian guests arranged a private boat ride on what appeared to be a desolate lake. At midday, the boat anchored close to the beach for an impromptu picnic. Communications among us were less than ideal, because we were speaking in many tongues, including French, German, Spanish, and Russian, depending on where we had served abroad previously. At one point, for an inexplicable reason, our German-speaking CIA officer asked our Russian hosts if one could swim in the "nude" (*nackt*). The German-speaking KGB officer thought he'd asked if one could swim at "night" (*nacht*), to which he casually responded, "Of course." With that, our officer dropped his swimsuit and ran to the water's edge stark naked. With a look of horror, and shouting "women and children!" the KGB officer leapt up and ran after the CIA officer. It turned out to be a public beach, and a family was strolling toward us about a hundred yards away. We had a good laugh, and the Russians must have been shaking their heads in disbelief later that night, but we were all reminded how easily miscommunications can happen when working in a foreign language, even by experienced officers. After the lake excursion, we boarded a helicopter to fly over the poppy fields and the Friendship Bridge. The Russian pilot flying along the river explained that we were going to have to fly a little farther west, because the people on the other side, in Afghanistan, had these very dangerous missiles. At that, the KGB general got on the radio and calmly said, "Captain, you don't need to explain that to these men."

There was no miscommunication there. Everyone laughed nervously, but the context was clear: the Russians understood that by introducing the Stinger missile to Afghanistan, we had been doing our job and trying to win the war. And they were doing their job, and afterward, life had gone on in a civilized manner. That certainly isn't the case now, with al-Qaeda, with whom there can be no dialogue or operational understanding. The task is simply to destroy them.

There was another incident that occurred before we went to the Friendship Bridge, this time in Moscow, that was incredibly illuminating. The Russians took us to a historic museum just after five o'clock in the afternoon. There was a corporal guarding the museum gate. The KGB colonel told him we wanted to go inside.

"It's after five; you can't come in," the guard said.

"I'm here with the KGB general!" the colonel said, whipping out his KGB credentials. In the past, this would have terrorized anybody.

"Well, it's after five, and I don't care who you are. You can't come in," the guard said.

We all walked away sheepishly, which was an extremely humiliating experience for the head of KGB counterintelligence and the colonel. The next day, the colonel called our local chief and told him that the museum guard had been replaced. But I wasn't sure they even had the power to get rid of him. When I went back to my office at the CNC in Washington, I wrote a trip report and told many people that story. At that point, I knew the Soviet game was over, because they had lost the intestinal fortitude to clamp down and instill the fear in their people that is necessary to hold a dictatorship in place. That was in June 1991, and the government fell in August.

NINE

A New Boss, a Bad Penny, and a Principled Heroin Dissent

Washington, 1990–92

Shortly after my return from Russia, at the end of August 1991, Webster stepped down as DCI and was replaced by Richard J. Kerr, who held the position as interim director while Congress considered President Bush's nomination of Robert M. Gates, who had been forced to withdraw his nomination four years earlier because of concerns that he knew more about Iran-Contra than he'd acknowledged. As we now know, with the perspective of more than twenty years, Gates served with great distinction as secretary of defense under George W. Bush, who brought him in to smooth out the situation left behind by Donald Rumsfeld, as well as under Barack Obama, who kept him on at the Pentagon as a gesture of bipartisanship. At Defense, Gates engendered support from the troops, who genuinely liked and respected him. In fact, he mastered serving the needs of soldiers and of the White House. At the time he was nominated to run the CIA, I thought he was a very smart analyst, particularly with respect to the Soviet Union. Above all, I thought he knew how to work the bureaucracy better than anyone else I had ever met in government. He was finally confirmed by the Senate in early November, in what was a personal vindication, with both Republicans and Democrats saying they did not believe Gates had ever tried to cover up the Iran-Contra scandal.

Shortly after Gates moved into the director's spacious office on the seventh floor, Roeber and I met with him at around seven o'clock one evening. Unlike the more modest approach I had taken with Casey in setting up the Afghan Task Force, I told Gates that we were expanding operations and needed more resources; Roeber had developed a solid visual presentation to support the requested increase. Gates had just returned from downtown looking frazzled but had squeezed us in to hear our pitch. When we entered, he motioned for us to sit down on his sofa. The office was dark except for a small light on his desk. He sat directly across from us and looked us in the eye. He listened to us motionless for about twenty minutes, without any questions or body language. At the end of our presentation, he returned to his desk without a word, and we exited the room. When Roeber and I were outside his office, we looked at each other and agreed that we clearly had bombed. We returned to our office dejected, thinking of how we would adjust our plan to press ahead. However, Gates's assistant called the next day and, to our amazement, reported that the DCI had authorized the increase. As good as his word, he had the money and staff reprogrammed shortly thereafter.

As director of the CNC and then director for Latin America, I made a couple of trips to Colombia to better understand the operations against Escobar, the Medellín Cartel, and the Cali Cartel. It was by far the most dangerous place we were working at the time. On one of the trips there and to Bolivia, I accompanied Senators Dennis DeConcini (Arizona) and Bob Graham (Florida) and Representative Henry Hyde (Illinois) on their chartered aircraft. CIA officials in the region opened the door wide for us, granting broad access to the highest levels of government and our joint intelligence programs. We visited the liaison facilities and made helicopter trips into the interior to check out cocaine labs that had been set up in the jungle.

All of us benefited from the firsthand experience. Everyone on the ground extended themselves and provided us with an excellent opportunity to "kick the tires," whether it was the helicopter trip into the jungles of Bolivia where we looked at a recently raided drug production site, or our sit-down with the special police team in Bogotá that later had a direct role in the takedown of Escobar.

Travel as a CNC director came with many lessons—and not all of them were related to the drug war. On a trip to Asia, I stopped in Japan en route to Thailand to meet with the Japanese minister of justice to talk counternarcotics. Feeling a bit groggy from the long flight but seeking to break the ice with the taciturn minister, I commented on his elegant fish tank, asking if it was difficult to feed so many diverse fish in one tank. He replied that it was no problem at all, and we went on to have a productive discussion about our efforts to fight the opium trade in the region. I was pleased with myself for being able to open him up with the question about his fish—until the next day, when a carefully wrapped miniature fish tank from the minister arrived at my hotel. It was full of mechanical fish—exactly like those in the minister's office—which naturally did not require any feeding whatsoever. I smiled, thinking about the laugh the Japanese must have had at my expense, and made a note to be more aware of my surroundings even when jet-lagged.

On a visit to Colombia, I stayed at a colleague's residence in Bogotá. He was an old friend, and we had served together in Chile. He may have regretted my stay. When I got up around six o'clock one morning, I used his guest bathroom to freshen up, but somehow I grabbed the sink faucet so hard that I ripped it off the wall and water began spurting all over the apartment. I snapped him out of his deep sleep with a shout that startled him so much that, as I recall, he reached for his weapon and ran in to join me. He thought that we had been raided by the traffickers. We couldn't find the turn-off valve, and the water kept flooding the room. Finally he was able to rouse the building's superintendent, who managed to turn off the water. What a way to start the morning. We packed up quickly and joined the ambassador in a heavily armored convoy to visit Colombian president César Gaviria. He probably thought he was safer there than in the flooded apartment with me.

As I was approaching the end of my time in the center, Rick Ames ended up on my doorstep again, like a bad penny. This time a friend delivered him—Milt Bearden, my colleague from the Afghan Task Force days. Bearden was chief of the Russia Division, which had a billet in the CNC, and he implored me to take Ames off his hands. He seemed to be concerned about Rick's reliability in handling sensitive Russian data, given his history with alcohol. At the same time, Bearden touted Ames's Russian-language skills, though these were not in high demand at the CNC at that time.

There was something in Milt's voice that suggested this was more than just a favor. My first question was "Is he drinking?" The CNC was a large operation, and it would be hard to track Rick and keep an eye on his intake. Milt assured me he wasn't.

In the end, I agreed to it. We put Ames on a Turkey project, which he seemed to take genuine pride in, even though by then he was a long-term agent of the KGB. I had little interaction with Rick and no social encounters with him.

Unbeknownst to me, Ames by now had become a suspect in a great mole hunt being conducted by our colleagues in another part of the CIA. His name had first surfaced on a list of almost two hundred CIA employees who had had access to the identities of all the agents we'd lost in the Soviet Union. Several days before Bearden called me, Ames had been interviewed by the mole hunters. By the time he reported for duty at the CNC, one of them was convinced he was a spy.

Equally problematic—and more directly related to the drug war—was my responsibility as CNC chief for producing national intelligence estimates on drug production. Every year there were battles royal over our findings. These estimates impact policy makers' decisions about how to spend counternarcotics funds and how to allocate personnel. Every agency had a vested interest in the outcome, and it was the CNC's job to serve as an honest broker and to produce the most objective product possible.

In 1992, Roeber led one of the most controversial estimates on heroin production. Many of the law enforcement agencies and the military wanted to downplay the spike in poppy production worldwide, since a high number would mean they might be forced to commit more of their stretched resources. Again, it is worth remembering that at this time counternarcotics remained a top national security priority. The world was at peace, and terrorism was not the overarching problem it would become in the late 1990s.

Roeber was a strong leader in any meeting and knew how to press hard on people who came to the table with shoddy data and analysis. This made him an extremely valuable ally for me but did not endear him to those who felt the sting of his penetrating questions. The 1992 CNC data clearly showed a substantial increase in heroin production, but the rest of the intelligence community wanted no part of this conclusion. Some of the participating agencies became so vexed by the numbers that the level of dissent had reached DCI Gates. He was, in turn, pressing John Helgerson, the CIA's top analyst, to see what all the fuss was about. Helgerson rarely became involved in counternarcotics matters, but on this occasion he set up a special meeting to tell me that many in the intelligence community were accusing Roeber of the mortal sin of the "politicization of intelligence." The charge made no sense. I explained the situation to Helgerson and assured him that Roeber and the CNC were just doing their jobs.

In the end, the estimate produced by the intelligence community went against our views, which were voted down by representatives from other agencies. The assigned non-CIA writer drafted a vanilla product. To his credit, Gates signed off on a CNC dissent of the key judgments in the heroin estimate. We were proud in the CNC that we had dissented. It epitomized what I believe to be key to good analysis: independence of thought. As it turned out, heroin continued to grow as a worldwide problem and remains a major problem today in Afghanistan, where it has greatly complicated our efforts to combat the Taliban there.

It was around this time that Pablo Escobar "escaped" from prison. Government authorities tried to move him to a more rigid prison, but he was tipped off and escaped under highly suspicious circumstances. Thus, the hunt for Escobar began. He was hounded from two sides. On one side, we intercepted his communications. And four days after his escape, U.S. military forces arrived in Colombia to train the Colombian police and military in his capture. On the other front, Escobar's rivals in the Cali Cartel financed the creation of "Los Pepes" (Los Perseguidos por Pablo Escobar), led by the infamous right-wing paramilitary officer Carlos Castaño. He led the group of vigilantes who helped hunt down Escobar and were thought to have ties to the Colombian National Police. The CIA didn't run Los Pepes and didn't give it any support. The Cali Cartel obviously benefited the most from the activities of Los Pepes, but the Colombian military and police did, too. One colleague said, "Thank goodness for Los Pepes. We didn't support them, but they provided a service that we couldn't do. These people had the Medellín Cartel scared to death." The U.S. ambassador to Colombia at the time, Morris Busby, said that "Los Pepes ended up being an excuse for any and all killings," and we made it clear to President Gaviria that we would pull our support if we learned the Colombian government was behind them. Jay Brant, an experienced Latin America case officer, said, "As far as I know, no U.S. government organization had any contact with Los Pepes. They were a bunch of terrorists."

There was, in fact, a standing rule that if it was discovered that any of our assets were involved in a breach of human rights or a violation of U.S. law, the Agency would have to cut off contact and/or turn them over to Justice. Brant remembered a highly legalized environment in the CIA at the time and stressed that there was great sensitivity about human rights. The Agency's lawyers were all over it. There was some concern at the State Department, the Pentagon, and even in the Agency's Directorate of Intelligence that some of the intercepts and other technical information we were passing to our liaison partners in Colombia were ending up in the hands of Los Pepes. When information is passed to legitimate liaison counterparts, there are never guarantees that some of it will not be siphoned off. All you can do is put down markers with liaisons and try to keep an independent check on things. To the best of my knowledge, we were never aware of information ending up in the wrong hands in Colombia, but I can't really prove it. Los Pepes was quite effective in countering the violence of the traffickers at first. But as time went by, it, too, became corrupt and indiscriminately violent. It certainly was not our creation or our tool.

As I approached my second anniversary at the CNC with Escobar still on the loose, Tom Twetten, my old friend and mentor, who had risen to deputy director for operations, asked me if I would like to accompany him on a trip to India, He thought it would be worth asking the Indians to cooperate with us on counternarcotics. George Crile, in *Charlie Wilson's War*, notes that Gust Avrakotos did not hold Twetten in high regard. Avrakotos not only missed Twetten's essence but greatly underestimated his intellect, operational acumen, and tough-mindedness. While Twetten may have appeared mild-mannered, he had that exceptional blend of political acumen and sharp operational skills. I never sat in on a meeting with him and foreign dignitaries or U.S. government officials when he wasn't constantly assessing the situation or analyzing the next move on the board. He also was not afraid to ask the tough question: "Will you work for me as a spy?" We had worked closely together going all the way back to Iran-Contra and Afghanistan.

On the trip to India, Twetten, an old India hand, took me to "Old Delhi" to see how the other half lived in the poorer sections of the city.

He convinced two rickshaw drivers to ride us through the rougher part of town. At six five, I felt rather silly being pulled along by a bony, one-hundred-pound young man, but it was the only way to do it. On foot would have been impossible. Twetten particularly wanted to show me a "factory" that bound books with homemade paper liners and gold gilt. He was an avid collector of antique books, and after retiring he would study bookbinding and set up an antiquarian book company in Vermont. When we got to the site, I was amazed to see what passed for a "factory": it consisted of a dozen Indians sitting on the floor, hammering out the artwork. I felt I was somehow intruding, even though they seemed immensely proud of their work. It reminded me in no uncertain terms what a privileged life most of us in America live. I later sent half a dozen personal books to them for rebinding, which I cherish to this day.

When we settled back in New Delhi, we relaxed over a few beers and very spicy food. Inevitably, we returned to talking about the business, and Twetten said that he wanted to run by me a couple of positions that would be coming open soon, to see if I was interested in either of them. The two jobs he was looking to fill were chief of the Latin America Division and chief of the Counterintelligence Center staff. Which one would appeal more to me? He said he couldn't tell me the whole story but made it clear that there was something really significant happening inside the Counterintelligence Center, something he described as "critically important." He knew what I didn't—that the mole hunters were closing in on their prey. It was like the moment, fourteen years earlier, when I was offered the choice by Ray Warren between being a base chief or a station chief in Latin America. This time, it took me about as long to decide.

TEN

The Rooster and the Train

Washington/Haiti, 1992–94

Latin America was home to me, the part of the world where I'd served five overseas tours—three as chief of station—and overseen the drug war as head of the Counter Narcotics Center. When Tom Twetten gave me the choice of running either the Counterintelligence Center or the Latin America Division, I chose Latin America in an instant, with a sense of pride. Ever since I was a young operations officer in Chile, I had wanted to be division chief. And Latin America was the obvious choice; after all, I'd spent the first half of my career there. After Chile, I had traveled frequently on assignment to Mexico and other countries and then served as station chief in Argentina before returning to head-quarters' Near East Division.

The job that Twetten was offering me was the rough equivalent of a three-star general in the military. It was a position that required a new set of skills and offered challenges that tested my mettle and political agility. There are only two jobs above division chief in the Directorate of Operations: the deputy director for operations and the associate deputy director for operations. The chief of the Latin America Division could influence Agency policy and operations in the region and have a say at the DO board level. And two of the men whose leadership I most admired in the Agency, Ray Warren and Nestor Sanchez, had both held the position with distinction. Warren was station chief during my first tour in Chile and remained a mentor throughout my career, counseling me, encouraging me, promoting me. Some of us referred to him as the "Gray Fox," for his wavy gray hair. He was six four and could have easily passed for an ambassador or Fortune 500 executive. He was measured in his demeanor and thoughtful and balanced in his deliberations. When, as chief of the Latin America Division, he sent me off on my first assignment as station chief, he gave me only a few words of caution: "Remember, most people in your position break their pick on the ambassador. Watch that." In other words, don't tangle with the ambassador on trivial issues and, even more important, develop a close collaborative relationship with him or her. Ultimately, you are expected to work out problems locally and not bring them back to headquarters for adjudication, which rarely works to a chief of station's long-term advantage. It was invaluable wisdom that applied well beyond the embassy, to relations with liaison partners in foreign intelligence services, Congress, and other U.S. agencies. Warren was a man of impeccable judgment.

Nestor Sanchez succeeded him as chief of the division. He was yet another Agency legend. Born in New Mexico and fluent in Spanish, Sanchez, as a young case officer, ran a Cuban agent named Rolando Cubela, point man in the CIA's plan to assassinate Fidel Castro. Sanchez and Desmond FitzGerald, one of the founders of the Agency's Clandestine Service, met with Cubela in Paris in early November 1963 to talk about the latest Castro assassination plan. At the meeting, Sanchez gave Cubela a ballpoint pen made by the Technical Services Division that was actually a hypodermic needle filled with Black Leaf 40, a poison. As the meeting broke up, Sanchez and FitzGerald were informed that President Kennedy had been assassinated in Dallas. As a consequence, the operation was aborted.

Nestor, a consummate operator but also good at Agency politics, rose steadily through the Agency. He became the top-ranking Hispanic officer in the DO at the time and had a great feel for Latin American political and operational life, which he combined with passion and humor. He was an especially effective recruiter, exuded leadership skills, and was broadly liked in the division. With almost no introduction in 1980, he asked me to go abroad. The assignment was a plum, and there were many people in line in front of me. Not only that, I was only a GS-14 in the civil service system, and the work I would be doing was at a GS-16 level, roughly the equivalent of a one-star general in the military. At the time, there was a rule that you couldn't jump two grades for a new assignment, so Nestor said he was going to downgrade the post temporarily so I could do the work—not a common occurrence and no doubt the cause of some hard feelings among those waiting in line for a senior posting.

I assiduously observed Warren's counsel on maintaining harmonious relations with the ambassador, and this cordiality was broken only once, when Sanchez visited. I brought him down to pay a courtesy call on the ambassador, and in a flash, both of them were agitated and practically yelling at each other. I wasn't sure what exactly had set it off, but I quickly hustled Nestor out and back to my office. But for the next hour, I received calls from the ambassador telling me in no uncertain terms what he thought Nestor needed to know, and Nestor in turn instructed me on what to tell the ambassador. I was amazed that two exceptionally bright and talented professionals could push each other's buttons so easily and dramatically. The ambassador, to his credit, did not hold this against me. It did, though, earn me some points with Nestor, for dealing with what he perceived to be a very difficult ambassador. The truth, of course, is that it took no especially adroit effort.

I saw Nestor again when I was back at Langley for a visit. I had lunch with him and a colleague who was running another station in Latin America, and he told us both that we should be putting in for the station chief's job in Tegucigalpa, Honduras. We both laughed. Tegucigalpa was a three- or four-man station; to say you were going to Tegucigalpa was like saying you were being sent to Siberia. Sanchez was visibly agitated by our reaction. "You know how many times I've been upstairs to talk about your stations in the past week? None," he said. "You know how many times I've been up there to talk about Tegucigalpa? Ten times. It's going to become the biggest station in Latin America."

That was my first introduction to the brewing operation to arm and train the Contras. Nestor's skepticism about certain aspects of that operation seemingly cost him his job at the CIA. Casey is said to have told others that Nestor wasn't "bold" enough for him. The operator who, as a young officer, ran the Cuban agents the CIA was counting on to assassinate Castro wasn't a big enough risk taker? No, the real problem was that Nestor apparently did not fully share Casey's enthusiasm for the Contra program. Here, again, we see the line between good covert action and bad covert action. Nestor reportedly thought using exiled members of the deposed Nicaraguan dictator's National Guard was not the way to go. He questioned having other Latins training the Contras in Honduras. It likely was because of his resistance to parts of the operation that Nestor was eased out of the CIA, to become assistant secretary of defense for Latin America, a position he filled admirably.

Like Warren and Sanchez, I was not intimidated by the challenge of running the Latin America Division, perhaps because I didn't fully appreciate what lay ahead. The country was banking on a peace dividend, having won the Cold War, and looking to a new leader after the U.S. presidential election in November 1992. Most officers at the Agency do not wear their politics on their sleeves; for a civil servant, it is unprofessional. I suspect most were silently rooting for President George H. W. Bush to beat Democrat Bill Clinton that fall, not so much for Bush's politics, but because he had been a popular DCI, from 1976 to 1977, and was respected as a serious public servant himself, with extensive international experience. But the CIA workforce took Clinton's election in stride. There was no gnashing of teeth about what it would portend. We were more concerned about the general depreciation of CIA stock because of the end of the Cold War, and what the peace dividend would mean, with both parties in Congress deemphasizing intelligence.

Clair George, the former operations director who had sent me to Rome, was convicted in the Iran-Contra scandal in December for reportedly misleading Congress six years earlier about what he knew about a cargo plane shot down in Nicaragua. Notwithstanding a Christmas Eve gift of a pardon of George from the lame-duck president, this was not, by any stretch of the imagination, a good time to be taking over the division, or any division. With the Cold War over, the focus had turned to transnational threats, such as counternarcotics and, to an extent, counterterrorism—with good reason. On January 25, 1993, a Pakistani national named Mir Aimal Kansi opened fire with an AK-47 on CIA employees stopped at a traffic light on Route 123 in Langley, just outside headquarters. While not initially considered in the context of the al-Qaeda–inspired terrorists attacks of today, the Kansi attack was particularly stunning to those of us working at Langley. Agency officers Lansing Bennett and Frank Darling were killed in their cars, and three others were wounded in the attack. That year the general assumption at headquarters was that Kansi was a lone deranged Pakistani. No one linked his singleton action in late January to the bigger plot behind the truck bomb detonated below the North Tower of the World Trade Center a month later, or to any fundamentalist Islamic terrorist organization. But like Ramzi Yousef, the mastermind of that 1993 bombing in lower Manhattan, Kansi said in 1997, when captured by the FBI in Pakistan, that the Langley shootings were in retaliation for U.S. policies in the Middle East and for how Muslims were treated by the CIA in that region. Though Kansi could not be connected to any group in Pakistan or elsewhere, in hindsight, it's clear that he, too, was a forerunner to Islamist terrorism à la al-Qaeda. After his capture, Kansi was rendered back to the United States, where he stood trial for the murders. He was found guilty and executed by lethal injection in 2002.

•

The Latin America Division was on the third floor of headquarters. I had the largest office of all the division chiefs, because it once had been the deputy director of operations' office, before the DDO was moved up to the seventh floor. It even had its own bathroom, a novelty for an office in that building. There were numerous stations in the division reporting to me. I had a division staff of about twenty, including reports officers, counterintelligence officers, a lawyer, and a human resources officer, but all field operations were run out of the individual stations. I brought with me my deputy from the Counter Narcotics Center, Marty Roeber, and made him deputy of the division, because I needed someone I could rely on and trust to pay very close attention to the day-to-day operational and intelligence details. It had been natural for me to choose Roeber, a career Latin America analyst from the Directorate of Intelligence, as counternarcotics deputy, since the CNC resided in the DI. But my decision to bring him over was fraught with peril and risk— for both of us. It is hard for an outsider to appreciate how rare a move this was, given the closed nature of the DO. To many in the directorate who had waited years for this job to open up, it appeared that I was bringing in an outsider unfamiliar with operations. But Roeber was a great partner, the most knowledgeable person I knew on Latin America in the Agency. He knew Latin America in a way that was different and more substantial than I did, even though I had lived there, and since counternarcotics remained a huge account in the division, it was a natural transition for us. Indeed, the overlap between the CNC and the Latin America Division was great, given that much of the money being channeled to the region in the early 1990s was for the purpose of counternarcotics. Marty helped immeasurably with the continuity and with coordination. He was also a bulldog in the Latin America office, and we worked extremely well together. I normally came in at 7:00 a.m. and would leave at 7:00 p.m. Roeber was there when I arrived and when I left at the end of the day. It must have been the Dr Pepper, which he drank incessantly, that kept him awake.

DO officers did not like the way Roeber dispensed with diplomatic polish when critiquing performance. He was a stickler for accuracy and detail. He wasn't reluctant to tell people, "You got it wrong." The DO, for all its wonders, did not like being challenged on its facts. But the DO performs best when it is challenged. Roeber would hold the line on facts—and most DO officers, schooled in cultivating relationships, did not like this. Roeber demonstrated to me just how valuable the analytic role could be in managing the intelligence gathered by the DO. As a consequence, I began to bring more analysts into the directorate in the reporting area. Coming off my experience running the CNC—and being in the midst of the hunt for Pablo Escobar in Colombia—I was acutely aware of the value of having analysts and operators work together. Having said that, these analysts were influenced by being so close to operations and so were not involved in producing the finished intelligence read by the top-level consumers in Washington. For our purposes, the analysts needed insight into what was going on in the operations and the quality of the sourcing, but their objectivity was inevitably influenced when they were on the team and were expected to be "true believers" in the cause at hand. That's why we tried to maintain a "cellophane wall" between the analysts and the people running operations, especially covert action programs, because it's so important that the analysts stay independent and objective. Analysts cannot be "part of the program." Even though Roeber took off his DI badge for this assignment, he still brought intellectual and analytical rigor to the DO, and unfairly took a number of hits for it. DO officers blamed him for being hard on their reporting and operations, but they did not have the perspective to understand that he was doing exactly what I wanted him to do. They simply had a hard time accepting that "one of them" might actually think this was a good thing.

Latin America is one of the areas of the world where the CIA has a larger-than-life reputation. The Agency's involvement in the region, both real and imagined, goes back many years and is centered on hard targeting of Soviets, Cubans, and Chinese, as well as covert operations designed to stave off Soviet penetration there. Robert Gelbard, who served as ambassador to Bolivia in the late 1980s and early 1990s, believes that an exaggerated fear of the Soviets by U.S. policy makers led to "dramatic mistakes" by the U.S. government in the region—the coup in Guatemala, the Bay of Pigs, the shadow cast over the Agency by supporting the opposition to Allende, and aiding the Contras. "The whole game back in those days was part of the Cold War—everything has to be presented and understood in the context of this overarching conflict with the Russians," Ambassador Jeffrey Davidow explained.[1] Davidow and I served together in Chile in 1973 and remained friends throughout our careers. He would become assistant secretary of state for Latin America. From the policy side and the intelligence side, we both experienced this environment of hostility toward the Cubans and the Russians, and saw how it played out in Latin America—sometimes for the good and sometimes not.

Brian Latell, who served as national intelligence officer for Latin America at the Agency and focused much of his career on Cuba, believes the Cuban intelligence service helped to perpetuate the David-and-Goliath imagery and portray the United States as the evil, imperialist hegemon to the north. "The role of Cuban intelligence in propagating these myths cannot be underestimated," according to Latell, author of *Castro's Secrets: The CIA and Cuba's Intelligence Machine*.[2] Propaganda against the CIA came straight from the Cuban playbook. Cuba was looking for a scapegoat to blame for the failings of its own economic system. The Cubans were not alone. Many other Latin American governments were more than happy to point the finger at the CIA if it meant giving themselves some cover and a bit of political space to maneuver. The Cubans played the spy game hard. Once, they actually tried to gain access to my house through our Chilean housekeeper, Bernarda, who had come to us in Santiago when she was only seventeen. She'd been trained in Old World–style service, with a uniform and gloves and very formal interactions. But because of her youth and our informal American manners, she loosened up considerably while keeping her impressive command of setting and serving meals at formal dinners and cocktail parties. Most important, she was a loving nanny to our young children. She became a member of the family, and when it came time for us to leave Chile, it was too hard for all of us to part with her. We brought her with us, and she spent half her time working for us and the balance completing her education.

The Cubans clearly did not know how close and loyal she was to the family. A Cuban official who attended a holiday party at our residence tried to follow up with a call to Bernarda to see if she would meet with him privately. She turned him down without hesitation and alerted us to the approach. I suspect the Cuban was hoping to use her to gather classified documents in the house or to install an audio device in a strategically located room. These types of operations are commonplace abroad. Most intelligence professionals assume their phones are tapped, their residences bugged, and their staff on someone else's payroll. Thus, no documents are ever brought home and no Agency meetings ever take place there. So even if Bernarda had been persuadable, very little could have been gained. I regarded the Cuban's overture as ill-advised and ham-handed, but I knew I couldn't be too smug.

The CIA's larger-than-life image in Latin America also worked to our advantage. The Agency came to be known as "the Company," in Latin America, which is what CIA means in Spanish, and it was both revered and feared throughout the region. This image enabled us to develop strong liaison relationships with host governments and to recruit sources to our cause, which became essential to our counternarcotics efforts in the late 1980s and early 1990s, when we needed to train and coordinate with host country security services in the fight against organized crime elements and the drug trade. In some cases, a chief of station in Latin America had better access to information and government officials than the ambassador. For Latin Americans in the region during this time, Davidow said, "The image of the CIA was that they were so overwhelmingly powerful that everyone in the embassy must be spies." This naturally caused friction between the CIA and the State Department, especially when an ambassador felt upstaged by a chief of station, but this was based on the belief in the region at the time that the CIA had eyes and ears everywhere.

Even more dramatic than these CIA–State Department tensions was the sea change brought about by the Carter administration's emphasis on human rights. The Agency was placed in the difficult position of trying to balance Carter's ambitious human rights imperatives against the pragmatic need to recruit assets and collect intelligence. "They were difficult times, when sources or liaisons had to be cut off if they were even suspected of human rights violations," said Ed Boring, a retired CIA officer with long experience in Latin America.[3] Boring believes human rights concerns were even greater under Clinton than they had been during Carter's presidency. Someone on the ground would propose using a colonel as an asset, Roeber similarly noted, and "the decision would come down to figuring out how dirty he was." Many assets would take polygraphs, but others would not. It was a real issue at the time: "There's no way to get it exactly right. You make the best judgments you can," Roeber said.

Roeber was very helpful in managing our response to the Commission on the Truth for El Salvador, which started investigating human rights abuses. Its three international commissioners were appointed by the secretary-general of the United Nations. Having grown up in the Directorate of Operations, my initial reaction was that we could not talk to these commission outsiders. But Roeber was convinced that if we showed a little ankle and goodwill to the commission members, they would likely throttle back. Roeber felt the commission members were not as hostile as depicted. Together, we worked with them, and the potential problem went away. I learned an important lesson from this experience: you don't always have to say no to the outside world. To everyone's benefit, it pays to talk to potential critics, provided you have your act together and have prepared well for the exchange. Roeber had it right. Engagement can be a successful strategy under certain circumstances.

Another big challenge within the Latin America Division involved streamlining our mission and cutting budgets. Money continued to flow for counternarcotics, which remained Washington's top priority in the region. But it was the exception that proved the rule: personnel accounts and budgets were coming down, and in an organization where our tradecraft depended upon the steady recruitment of assets and training, this was not going to be an easy adjustment. Every time this has occurred in the life cycle of the Agency, as it has too often in the CIA's history, there has been a monumental disruption. A similar cut during the Carter administration led to personnel disruptions many years later. The hiring freezes in those years led to a bubble in staffing and a missing generation of A-plus officers. We need to be very careful today that we do not repeat this mistake as we wind down the Iraq and Afghanistan wars.

"It's never a happy camp when you're downsizing," Roeber noted. "We spent a lot of time closing down counternarcotics programs, based on the philosophy that if it's not contributing to the linear strategy, let's not do it."

Not all the cuts were ill-advised. Some of the stations we were downsizing had grown out of all proportion during the Cold War and had far larger staffs than their new missions required. Inevitably, the most troubled stations, with the biggest personnel, fiduciary, and morale problems—and the biggest problems getting along with their embassy counterparts—were the ones being downsized. It is in that transition that things fall apart. For this reason, the most problematic station in 1994 was a country in Central America that, because of our efforts during the 1980s, was one of the largest stations in the world. We could not bring it down fast enough to match the new reality.

I sent Roeber down there to size up the situation. The station chief was a Latin America veteran who had a good record up until then and was generally well liked. He was close friends with Terry Ward, my predecessor, and a number of other Latin America hands, and though I had not known him before, I found him to be operationally savvy and personable. But while he was aggressive in his operations, he was not effective at managing personnel tensions in this downsizing environment, which would have been challenging for anyone. In the mode we were in, his style was becoming a problem, and we were getting a steady stream of complaints, official and unofficial. After Roeber did an initial review, and several delicate issues came to the fore, I decided I had better pay a visit to see if the situation was salvageable. Unfortunately, and not surprisingly, cliques had already formed at the station, pro and con, with regard to the management, which almost always results from a major personnel shift. It was clear that in order for things to start healing, the station chief would have to move on. Likewise, for morale purposes, we also tried to switch out most of the staff as quickly as possible.

To deal with problems as they arose at this and other stations in similar straits, I set up accountability boards to help chiefs talk through their management issues and figure out how to fix problems with reporting, personnel, and operations without the sometimes heavy hand of the inspector general's office. Accountability reviews were also designed to help stations examine their force structures, cover arrangements, and platforms for collecting intelligence, and their relationships with their embassies and the rest of the intelligence community. The accountability boards helped us to assume responsibility for our own stations and personnel within the Latin America Division. Roeber believes these reviews actually helped to boost the "can-do" attitude of our officers. Creating them ended up being a deft bureaucratic move that often succeeded in sparing us most of the pain of review by the inspector general.

The equilibrium of an overseas station could be upset in all sorts of strange ways, often completely unexpected. In a South American country, a popular math teacher at my children's elementary school was very active in the community, including serving as the assistant Boy Scout leader, and was reputed to be so patriotic that one of our officers suggested we use his apartment as a safe house. But Pat thought the man was "suspiciously strange," and I felt very uncomfortable about such an arrangement. Months later, my daughter Jennifer walked one of her timid sixth-grade male classmates to the principal's office, where he reported inappropriate behavior by the teacher. Sometime later, the teacher was arrested in one of the barrios surrounding the capital. He turned out to be a pedophile living in alias and on the country's Most Wanted list, using his apartment to seduce children from the school. His arrest was not only a local cause célèbre, but his face and story were flashed around the world, and all I kept thinking was what an operational disaster it would have been if we had used the man's apartment. I could picture the headline: CIA SAFE HOUSE USED AS SEX DEN BY PEDOPHILE. A slipup like that would almost certainly have been career ending for me. You just couldn't explain something like that away. Luckily, Roeber's reviews turned up nothing so salacious when I was running the division.

•

From our time together in the Counter Narcotics Center, Roeber and I had begun to appreciate the value of analyzing management data. This was largely alien to the Directorate of Operations culture. If you talked to most DO officers, they would stress at some point that espionage is "an art, not a science." That attitude tended to excuse everything—"We're artists." It sounds good, and I subscribed to this view for years, and a number of times used the same expression myself. But the more I thought about it, the more it seemed nonsensical. It is true that espionage had a human dimension to it that wasn't easy to quantify. For example, how and when to pitch a target. But that didn't mean that analyzing management data wasn't helpful, even essential, or that we should have been immune to accountability for the sake of this "artistry." The DO, in many ways, was almost mythic in the way it viewed itself and hated to be evaluated, resisting basic questions such as "How many people do we have here?" and "What are they doing in comparison to other offices?"

At one point, after Ted Price had replaced Twetten as the deputy director of operations, I arrived at a meeting of division chiefs with an analysis that Roeber had done of staffing levels across the directorate. We also looked at how many agents each division had and how much reporting they were doing. We were meeting off-site to discuss the budget and personnel downsizing problems, and I was there to insist that Latin America needed more people and that these new slots should be reallocated from other regions. I was clearly the skunk at the party, since we all were expected to say how much of a hit we were prepared to take, not to ask for more manpower. But I wanted to see the hits taken from the bloated, overstaffed locations. When it came time for me to speak, I handed out color analytical packages to everybody and said I would like to open this part of the session with a discussion about rationalizing how the directorate was organized.

My colleagues took their packages, turned them facedown, and decided it was time "to take a break." When everyone returned, we moved on to the next point on the agenda. My colleagues simply refused to discuss a rational analysis of manpower and resources. This was a distinguishing and annoying characteristic of the DO with which I never made peace. There we were, resisting rigorous analysis and replacing it with "gut instincts," believing that we were artists even in the management arena. It had been risky to challenge this perception, but I genuinely believed it was the right thing to do and did not mind raising the issue. My colleagues did not enjoy it as much and would probably still disagree with me today.

There had also been a long-standing tendency in the directorate to resist technology, although things have improved substantially in this area in recent years. When the Agency's IT people first offered e-mail to the DO, nobody in the directorate would take it, but having relied on it more heavily in the CNC, I volunteered Latin America to be the guinea pig, and we were the first division to have e-mail. I don't need to explain that, since today it is so much a part of U.S. government and private-sector communication. The debate over e-mail mirrored a fight that took place earlier in my career, over satellite phones, specifically STU-IIIs. John McMahon, when he was deputy director of operations from 1978 to 1981, not only threw most of the lawyers out of the DO but would not accept the STU-IIIs despite our obvious need for fast international communications. If station chiefs were talking on the phone, he reasoned, they would not be making a record of what they were doing. They would not be writing cables, which would inevitably lead to a breakdown in the chain of command. So the DO was nearly the last place in the CIA to have the satellite phones. His motive for this way of thinking was good, inasmuch as there has to be good command and control, but you can't hold off technology in the intelligence business. New policies on the technology were soon drafted, however, and STU-IIIs became ubiquitous at the DO. Even the most technology-averse officers eventually had to yield to modernity.

•

Working as chief of Latin America necessarily meant dealing with Cuba and Haiti, two troublesome countries I had managed to avoid up until that point. By virtue of their proximity to the United States and their history, Cuba and, to a lesser extent, Haiti have long been a preoccupation for the White House and the seventh floor of the Agency. For those of us who have spent our lives studying and working international relations focused on U.S. national security objectives and intelligence collection abroad, we found that working Cuba and Haiti was about not just foreign policy but also domestic policy. Both countries have significant diaspora communities in the United States—with both adversaries and advocates in the U.S. Congress. Their proximity to Florida, the growing significance of their exile communities in American politics, and the specter of mass migration made Cuba and Haiti priorities within the Latin

America Division in the early 1990s. No one in the Bush or the Clinton administrations wanted to see poor immigrants taking to the seas as Cubans had in the Mariel Boatlift of the 1980s and as Haitians had in 1991 following the coup d'état that overthrew President Jean-Bertrand Aristide. Whether economic migrants or political exiles in fear of persecution, they were seen as an unwelcome problem in Washington by both political parties.

From the perspective of operations, Cuba has always presented a challenge for the Agency. This is partly because it is an island without easy access or, since January 1961, an official U.S. embassy presence from which to operate. After the Cuban Revolution that brought Fidel Castro to power in 1959, leftists throughout Latin America flocked to Cuba for training and ideological inspiration, making Cuba a hotbed of anti-American sentiment and, needless to say, a particularly hostile environment in which to operate and recruit sources. Roeber said, "Cuba is a miserable hard target. The Agency's record [there] over the years was less than stellar."[4] From the outset, Castro invested heavily in intelligence and placed the responsibility for espionage in the hands of guerrilla fighter Manuel Piñeiro Lozada, the infamous "Barba Roja." As early as 1961, Piñeiro set up the first professional intelligence organization in Cuba, known as the Directorate General of Intelligence (DGI), whose mission was to collect intelligence on political parties, international organizations, private businesses, exile groups, and foreign governments, especially the United States. Hundreds of Piñeiro's officers received extensive and excellent operational training by the Soviets and East Germans, who provided them with deep insights into the CIA and our methods of operating. Piñeiro and I crossed paths in Chile, where he spent months in the early 1970s before Allende was ousted. Piñeiro provided support to the Chilean government's security apparatus and pro-Cuba organizations there at the time—of course, to no avail. Throughout the 1970s and '80s, he went on to support revolutionary activities in Argentina, Bolivia, Nicaragua, Uruguay, and Venezuela.

The DGI quickly became one of the most effective smaller services, and over the years, one of the biggest threats Cuba posed to us was one of counterintelligence. In 1983, former DGI agent Jesus Mendez defected and reported that many of our agents in Cuba had been doubled against us. In 1987, Juan Antonio Rodriguez Menier, one of the founding and most senior members of the DGI, passed on a treasure trove of information that revealed the DGI's very aggressive operations against the United States over the previous twenty years. It was also the DGI that played a major role in the 1970s in the defection of former CIA officer Philip Agee, who from exile in Cuba published the true identities of hundreds of undercover CIA officers. More recently, in 2002, the hand of the DGI was revealed with the conviction of Ana Belen Montes, a senior Cuban analyst with the U.S. Defense Intelligence Agency (DIA), as a Cuban spy who had spent sixteen years working for the DGI.

Despite the robust efforts of the Cuban intelligence service against us and the difficulties that the operating environment presented, Cuba was no longer considered a real threat to U.S. interests by the time I became Latin America Division chief. Nonetheless, we were always looking for ways to approach Cubans. As division chief, I would have off-site strategic sessions to discuss this topic. Jerry Komisar was the head of Cuban operations in the division at the time. I was glad to have him working this issue, since it was difficult to find top-notch people to work the discouraging Cuban account. As part of our efforts, we brought together people from across the intelligence community to look at the issues and think more strategically about Cuba and how to approach it. Komisar and I also traveled to Florida to talk with leaders of the Cuban-American community and strategize about ways to maintain the pressure on the Castro brothers. Meanwhile, Latell, who focused much of his career on assessing Castro and the situation in Cuba, was closely tracking this so-called special period in Cuba after Soviet subsidies had dried up in the early 1990s. Indeed, the economic situation on the island was bleak, with Cuba sorely lacking energy supplies and basic foodstuffs. The military did not have the resources to train troops, acquire new equipment, or even maintain what they had, including their planes, which were in dilapidated condition. In September 1993 two Cuban MiG fighter pilots attempted to defect, one landing in Key West, Florida, and another at our naval base in Guantánamo. One of the pilots said he was fleeing the country due to the economic situation there. We also learned from the two defectors that Cuban pilots hardly ever fly because of fuel shortages and their aircraft being in such poor condition. Aside from this information, there was little to gain from the pilots from an intelligence standpoint. Looking back, I see that there might have been an opening to do more on the island at that time, when the Cuban economy was so fragile, but ultimately, the policy-making community in Washington did not have the appetite to do much more than keep a close watch.

Haiti was another story. Beginning in 1993, Congress put a lot of pressure on the Clinton administration to do something there. In September 1991, Haiti's first freely elected president, Jean-Bertrand Aristide, was forced out of power by a military coup engineered by three Haitian generals less than a year after being elected with approximately two-thirds of the popular vote. First President Bush and then President Clinton pursued economic sanctions along with the OAS to force the military junta to the negotiating table. The Governors Island Accord was signed in July 1993, but from the outset the generals failed to adhere to the agreed-upon measures and time lines. In October 1993, the USS *Harlan County*, carrying a small implementation force of U.S. military engineers, turned around and came home when confronted by a gang of armed paramilitary thugs at the Port-au-Prince pier. President Clinton was assailed from the right for what they perceived as an erosion of the nation's ability to project power, and he was criticized from the left for pursuing the Bush-era policy of picking up fleeing Haitians at sea and forcibly returning them to face a repressive regime. In April 1994, the head of the House Appropriations Committee, David R. Obey, called for an American-led invasion to oust the junta, and Randall Robinson, head of the TransAfrica Forum, was undertaking a highly publicized fast until the administration reversed its policy of indiscriminately returning refugees. Finally, the White House decided that it had to take action, and it turned to the CIA.

During a previous posting in the Caribbean, our household help, as in most of the community, had come from Haiti, which shares the island of Hispaniola with the Dominican Republic but is far less prosperous. Once, after Pat let a recently hired housekeeper go for stealing our children's clothes and throwing them over the wall to her friend in an adjoining apartment complex, she discovered what looked like a tiny altar in the maid's bedroom. Upon closer inspection, the "altar" turned out to contain a letter from Pat's mother, its edges burned, and a lock of hair surrounded by little rocks and chicken feathers. One of the things the housekeeper had told Pat prior to being fired was that her mother was a voodoo witch doctor, and it was hard to mistake the altar for anything other than an arrangement for a voodoo ceremony, probably overseen by her mother and directed against the evil spirits of our family. Of course, we didn't believe in voodoo, but it was uncanny, the series of mishaps that immediately followed. My fourteen-year-old son, Joe, decided he would take the family station wagon for a spin. While he didn't make it out of the driveway, he did manage to rip the front door off the car. That same day, Antonio, our industrious gardener, received a bad electrical shock from our metal gate, which apparently was wired somehow to hot circuitry. He survived, but the incident gave us all a fright. Finally, when I opened my bank statement, I was notified that I had overdrawn the account by several hundred dollars. Later, it turned out that "the bank record system had skipped a line" and hence, according to the bank, it was only a technical mistake. I still don't put any credence in voodoo— most of my days are filled with commotion of one sort or another—but it was hard not to feel like I was experiencing the wrath of the witch doctor that day.

This would not be my last brush with voodoo. In 1993, I played a part in the Clinton administration's effort to restore Jean-Bertrand Aristide as president of Haiti. I believed that if the White House wanted to pursue a policy to remove a military dictatorship in Haiti and reinstall a democratically elected president, it was worth considering seriously how this might be done effectively. So I threw myself into a seemingly endless round of meetings to accomplish this policy. In the end, we had an approach that everyone got behind.

Out of the starting gate, the Clinton White House wanted efforts coordinated with robust public diplomacy and possible military intervention. "There was a lot of interaction with the military in the lead-up to the intervention," a colleague, John Kambourian, said. "We had a very good relationship with many military personnel working directly, and it worked very well."[5] Indeed, liaising with the military and sharing intelligence were both important parts of the mission. In Norfolk, Vice Admiral Thomas Wilson played a key role in charge of military contingency planning in Haiti (and in Cuba), and we met often in strategy sessions and planning meetings before the U.S. military intervention the following year. "That was just when the military was starting to get their arms around 'jointness,' so for the CIA and the military to have a cooperative relationship was a bit of a rarity coming into that time frame," Wilson said.[6] There was definitely a sense that Haiti needed to be a joint effort, and those of us involved were determined to make it work.

I counted Senator John Warner, the distinguished Virginia Republican who served on the Senate Committees on Intelligence and Armed Services, as a strong supporter of the Agency. One afternoon he called me over to his office on the Hill to get an update on the situation in Haiti. At one point, he asked if there were any problems he could help with, and I made the mistake of telling him that Kambourian might be suffering from dengue fever. "I will call the navy and have a medical ship pick him up," Warner said, moving toward the telephone. I back-pedaled quickly, insisting that I was confident that Kambourian was on the mend. Warner looked at me quizzically, but returned to his seat. There was no doubt that he meant what he said and would have made the call, to our everlasting embarrassment. It was a good reminder to be careful what you wish for in the office of a powerful senator.

Around this time, I was surprised to get a call from Sandy Grimes, a colleague with whom I had gone through a midcareer training program, and Jeanne Vertefeuille, a gray-haired woman straight out of a John le Carré novel. Jeanne was a counterintelligence officer and Sandy spent her career supporting our Soviet assets. Could we meet outside my office, so as not to attract attention? When we sat down together, the two women told me they were on the trail of a mole working for the KGB. It was the first I had heard of it. In the mid-1980s, we had lost at least ten of our best agents inside the Soviet government. The mole hunters, toiling for the past eight years, had started with nearly two hundred suspects, CIA officers who had had access to all the assets, and had narrowed the file down to one. According to Sandy, they'd done this by asking everyone on the special counterintelligence team, plus six experienced officers familiar with Soviet operations, to write down a short list of suspects. Rick Ames was on everyone's short list, and the first person on Sandy's.

So it was that Grimes and Vertefeuille asked me about Aldrich Ames: Did I think he could be a spy for the Soviets? I immediately flashed back to my strange confrontation with him years earlier in

Rome, over ignoring my instructions about readministering a polygraph test to the Eastern European walk-in code-named Motorboat once he had shown deception on the first test. The look of resentment and defiance I saw in Ames's eyes when I challenged him about this had left a lasting impression.

"Yes," I said, "and he is the only employee I know I would say that about."

While the White House had been fully briefed on the top secret mole hunt, the president remained publicly preoccupied with the situation in Haiti. A mini-controversy erupted in October 1993 when one of the Agency's top analysts described ousted Haitian president Jean-Bertrand Aristide in highly critical terms in a closed-door, classified briefing before the House Intelligence Committee. This briefing was followed by others, including one in the Senate that had been requested by Senator Jesse Helms, the conservative North Carolina Republican who opposed intervention in Haiti. To some in the Clinton White House, this appeared to be a case of the CIA siding with the president's conservative opponents and playing games with intelligence. But actually it was the opposite. The CIA was not against intervention in Haiti or reinstalling a democratically elected president, if that was what the White House desired. Rather, we wanted to make sure the president and members of Congress had the clearest picture possible. James Woolsey, the director at the time, agreed with the Agency assessment, which represented a consensus across the intelligence community. But his stance made it difficult in the beginning for us to gain the trust of the White House.

At the time, I could not allow myself to get too caught up in the controversy du jour because there was always so much else going on. The Clinton administration's human rights focus in Haiti remained a top political priority in Washington, but in Latin America our number one operational priority remained the hunt for Pablo Escobar, head of the Medellín drug cartel. I made this abundantly clear to Jay Brant, a CIA officer who was in Bogotá at the time. Escobar had become more than just a drug trafficker. By then he was a real political problem, one that symbolized the drug war. Brant remembers my marching orders: "We have to get Pablo. We need to show real progress here. Put everything you have into it," he said I told him.[7] Brant knew that the relationship with the Colombian authorities was essential in the hunt for Escobar. He knew that a decision by them to put Escobar's wife and children in protective custody would help as a lure. "We were constantly looking for ways to flush him out, and this strategy was what ultimately worked, because we were able to find a way to cause Escobar to reach out more frequently to his family, especially his son, who he adored," Brant said.

The hunt finally ended on December 2, 1993, when a special technical surveillance unit of the Colombian police known as Search Bloc, commanded by then colonel Hugo Martínez, intercepted a cell phone call Escobar made to his son, Juan Pablo. Escobar was hiding out at a safe house in the Los Olivos neighborhood of Medellín. Police units immediately surrounded the house. Escobar and his bodyguard attempted to escape over the rooftops, but both were shot and killed.

However, that success was not long-lasting, since in the end the ever-present demand for cocaine resulted in a more decentralized network run by lower-level leaders who were able to keep the flow of drugs heading north. Jerry Komisar, as CNC director, noted that in many ways the Agency's successes against drug kingpins such as Escobar seemed to only make the job more difficult. Komisar has said, "We would take down a dragon but be left with a lot of little snakes," he said.[8] Despite our best efforts, innovative developments in using intelligence for tactical purposes, and such big successes as bringing down Pablo Escobar and breaking up the Cali Cartel, many of us knew right from the start that we were never going to fully accomplish the objectives of the program as set out by the policy makers. As long as there is a highly profitable demand for drugs, there will always be some enterprising group around the world that will find a way to meet that demand. The CIA deputy director Dick Kerr wisely commented that the drug business is the type of crime that will always be with us; the best we can do is "to keep beating it with a stick" to make it painful for the traffickers to engage in the business and, to the degree possible, make it harder and more costly for them to deliver the drugs. There has been some decrease in drug use in the United States in recent years, but it remains a multibillion-dollar business. The ambassador and former assistant secretary of state for international narcotics and law enforcement affairs Bob Gelbard said that on the supply side of the problem, one of our biggest mistakes is in thinking it is within the U.S. government's purview to interdict, convict, and eviscerate the scourge of drugs in the region, when really it is up to the foreign governments to take advantage of the tools and skills we share with them and develop the democratic institutions and system of justice necessary to deal with the illegal organizations profiting from the drug business.[9] Echoing Kerr, Komisar said it is frustrating to look back and see that, despite the successes, we did not eliminate the drug problem.[10] Indeed, many of us who worked against the narcotics threat over the years would agree. But good liaison cooperation with host governments and assets we can trust, a linear strategy that coordinates agencies and capabilities across the U.S. government, and, most important, increased demand-reduction efforts at home is perhaps the best formula for countering or at least containing a serious transnational threat such as narcotics.

Two months after Escobar was killed, the CIA's mole hunt came to an end that was even more dramatic. On February 21, 1994, Aldrich Hazen Ames, the man I had first met and come to know well in our training days, was pulled over near his home in Arlington, Virginia, by FBI agents as he drove his 1992 Jaguar to CIA headquarters. They had been trailing him and listening to his calls for months. There was some suspicion earlier that Ames and his wife were spending far more money than Ames made as a case officer, but it was assumed that was because Rosario came from a wealthy Colombian family. The real break in the case came after Grimes matched the dates Ames had reported meeting with a Soviet diplomat he was supposedly trying to recruit with the dates on which large deposits were made into one of his domestic bank accounts. According to Grimes, in an April 20, 2013, talk she gave at the National Archives, in 1993 an additional piece of information became available that pointed in Ames's direction, and lead the FBI to open a full-scale investigation on him. It is believed by many in intelligence circles that the information came from a source who said that the mole we were looking for had served in Rome. This narrowed down the list pretty quickly, and the FBI opened an investigation into Ames. I saw his arrest on television, and even though I'd had an inkling this was in the cards, it was a shocker. I found it particularly depressing because I knew him personally. His arrest led to one of the lowest morale moments in the history of the CIA.

What could possibly have led Ames to commit the ultimate betrayal of country, friends, and family? The question troubles me to this day. Paul Redmond, the head of the counterintelligence team that finally identified Ames, said that "it always boils down to money in the end." Ames, who was in some financial distress when he brazenly walked into the Soviet embassy in Washington back in 1985, admitted as much. In a number of interviews, he said his motivation was money. I suspect the picture was much more complicated than that. While Ames was intellectually smart, he had relatively poor people skills and was fundamentally lazy. As a result, he turned out to be a spotty performer as a case officer, but nevertheless had a highly inflated, if not grandiose, sense of his own capabilities, intellect, and importance. Dr. Kerry Sulkowicz is an insightful psychiatrist and founder of the business psychology firm the Boswell Group. We've discussed Ames, and he believes that Rick had very little insight into his own motivations. Sulkowicz surmises that the money Ames received from the Russians was a much-needed validation of his importance and self-worth. It was also a necessity for keeping Rosario happy. Joe Wippl, an experienced Europe operative, gained keen insight into Ames's motivation as the senior representative from the Directorate of Operations on the damage assessment team that studied Ames's betrayal. In transcripts of FBI wiretaps, Rosario repeatedly berates Ames about his competence and time and again grills him about the details of his encounters with the Soviets. Wippl pointed out that while Rosario's extended family was wealthy, her immediate family had limited financial means. Money was a symbol not only for Ames but also for Rosario. It is Sandy Grimes's belief that Ames would not have been a traitor if it hadn't been for Rosario.

Except for a brief moment after the Soviets had arrested the agents he betrayed, Ames continued to believe, right up to the end, that the Agency could never catch him—that he had outsmarted the system. At the same time, I do not doubt he believed he was gaming the Russians. According to Sulkowicz, this points to his narcissism—with low self-regard and the need for constant validation. Ames needed to boost his depleted sense of self-worth by turning himself into the opposite: a grandiose figure. "He built up this grand façade, but in fact he was nothing," Sulkowicz said. In thinking about Ames's motivation, it is also interesting to consider his apparently difficult childhood and his conflicted relationship with his father. Sulkowicz speculates that on some level the Agency was a stand-in for his father, and his desire to tear down this elite institution that he was admittedly proud to be a part of cannot be separated from his ambivalence toward his father, who was also an Agency underachiever. This analysis makes sense to me. But one thing is clear: Ames had a capacity for compartmentalizing, so he would not have to consider the consequences of his actions—what he called "file and forget." Only he knows whether signing the Soviet agents' death warrants haunts his nights at the high-security U.S. penitentiary near Allenwood, Pennsylvania, where he will spend the rest of his life. I doubt it.

•

By the time Director Woolsey embarked, midsummer, on a broad internal review of intelligence collection and analysis at the CIA in the aftermath of the Ames case, U.S. forces were practicing for their planned invasion of Haiti. The Clinton administration had been frustrated for months in its efforts to oust the Haitian military and restore Aristide as the country's democratically elected leader. But time, and international patience, were running out for Haiti's military rulers at the end of July. The UN Security Council unanimously authorized the use of force against the Haitian junta.

Prior to military intervention, I was asked by the White House to go to Port-au-Prince to meet with Lieutenant Colonel Michel François, the head of Haiti's secret police, and tell him to get out of town or the U.S. government would be visiting him in full force. Anthony Lake, Clinton's national security adviser, and Lake's deputy, Sandy Berger, liked to manage events carefully and wanted to prepare a script for the meeting. We spent a great deal of time going over a very detailed script, which was rather overdone. A meeting like this cannot be scripted line by line. Only the main message can be fully developed by committee. After that, normal human interactions play out. Flexibility and maneuverability are necessary in the real world. There was just too much give-and-take in this type of tough meeting. It was essential to develop a rapport before jumping to an ultimatum. In the end, I delivered the clear message the White House wanted, but took the time I needed to set the stage. I have always believed that Lake and Berger liked the fact that I was the one undertaking the task, because they thought, at six foot five, I could project a frightening presence, despite my friendly self-image, which I now recognize may not have been universally shared.

François was fearful of the meeting. We had clandestine reporting that he had gone to his witch doctor beforehand to fend off "the evil spirit from the north." Apparently, the witch doctor doused him in white powder as an antidote. It is rather amazing that he was frightened, since it was his country, and he controlled the secret police. In reality, I probably should have been concerned for my own well-being. During the meeting, François refused to eat or drink, perhaps thinking he might be drugged or poisoned. I told him a story that I was once told by a senior Latin American official in another country that addressed the issue of machismo, which I thought was apropos of this situation. Needless to say, this was not part of the script. I told François what the official told me: in a crisis, "we [Latin Americans] are like roosters on a railroad track, and the United States is the train. While we should get off the track, the roosters puff out their chests and stand pat." I suggested he did not want to play the role of the rooster. He did not accept my advice or financial offer to leave town right away, but he was gone by October. Sometime after that, François reported to the media from exile that an Agency official had threatened to kill him and his family if he did not leave Haiti, which of course was far from true. I did deliver a heavy message, for sure, but he allegedly interpreted it as a physical threat—or tried to score political points by publicly spinning it that way.

Kambourian and other CIA officers with long years in the Latin America Division agree that the Haiti operation was a successful one that met the president's objectives. It was a success because of the coordination between the Agency and the military. It was also a success in that no American lives were lost in the operation. After Clinton told the American people, in a nationally televised address on September 15, that the United States was prepared to use military force to oust Haiti's military rulers, I tracked developments from our headquarters command center on a daily basis. I was impressed by the way former president Jimmy Carter, at Clinton's behest, had traveled to Haiti and pushed relentlessly for a settlement. He would not give up, even after Washington started urging him to cut off the talks because the Haitian military seemed to be standing its ground. Carter supposedly received a White

House directive to leave the table because the invasion would be launched soon. He ignored this and went on jawboning the military. About that time, our attack aircraft started to take off from Miami. The Haitians likely had plane watchers in Florida, and they reported this quickly to the Haitian high command, which immediately yielded to our demands, and our aircraft were called back. It was a gutsy move by Carter and Clinton. Kambourian informed the U.S. military high command that the Haitians would not resist. U.S. forces started landing in Haiti the following day. Aristide returned a little over three weeks later, on October 15, 1994.

Back at headquarters, at the height of tensions prior to the troops' landing in Haiti, Woolsey announced that he had reprimanded eleven current and former Agency officials for failing to discipline Aldrich Ames during his lackluster, alcoholic career or not moving more aggressively once it was discerned that a mole was loose inside the Agency. He noted "a systemic failure of the C.I.A.—and most significantly, of the Directorate of Operations—a failure in management accountability, in judgment, in vigilance."[11] I went to the auditorium at headquarters to hear Woolsey announce the reprimands of my colleagues and explain his reasoning for them. The place was packed, and the atmosphere was thick with tension. I stood at the back. Most of those in the audience were expecting Woolsey to come down much harder and announce a spate of firings. But they'd clearly misjudged the man. He had approached the task like the lawyer he is. He reviewed the evidence carefully and realized that there indeed had been a series of small misdeeds by a number of people, rather than major mistakes by a few. I sensed that most of those on hand were not satisfied. They surprisingly seemed to want harsher penalties for their own colleagues, largely because of the pain and humiliation the Agency had suffered. This view was shared by Congress and the White House. Washington needed a scalp, someone to take the fall, even though there was not one villain whose failures had led directly to the fiasco. I'm not sure Woolsey understood this at the time, and he received no credit for his measured approach.

The CIA's inspector general identified twenty-three senior managers who in his view were accountable for Ames's betrayals. Not long after Woolsey announced the reprimands, Frank Anderson, my successor as head of the Afghan Task Force, with associate deputy director of operations John McGaffin's concurrence, headed off to Europe to give Milt Bearden, my close partner during the covert war in Afghanistan, a career achievement award. Bearden was among the eleven who had received reprimands. I did not know anything about this unauthorized award ceremony. But when Woolsey found out what Anderson and McGaffin had done, he immediately removed them from their positions, thinking it was an act of defiance on their part. They resigned instead of accepting their demotions.

McGaffin's departure created a vacancy in the second-most-powerful position in the Directorate of Operations, that of the associate deputy director of operations. Certainly I was interested in the position, but I would rather have ascended to the directorate's upper ranks under happier circumstances. The Ames case had shattered confidence in the Agency and crushed morale. The Clinton administration was downsizing and remained, at best, ambivalent about the value of the Agency, despite all the good counternarcotics work we had done in Latin America and our success in Haiti, where Aristide was back in power. Still, I had had my eye on the seventh floor since the day I joined the Agency, and I felt ready to take on a new challenge.

ELEVEN

Raising the Bar

Washington, 1994–95

A few days after Anderson and McGaffin resigned, I was surprised to receive in my office mail a formal letter from Woolsey saying I was a candidate for McGaffin's job and would be interviewed soon. In the past, the director of central intelligence would simply have conferred with his deputy director of operations and selected someone. This time, Woolsey and his deputy DCI, Admiral William O. Studeman, wanted a clear say in the decision. There reportedly were three of us in the running: one senior officer from the Far East and another from the Africa Division, where Somalia was a hot issue. I knew the competition would be intense. The interview took place around the conference table in Woolsey's office, with just me, Woolsey, and Studeman in the room, and lasted for half an hour, maybe forty-five minutes. It went by quickly. They began with a single, basic question: How would I propose handling the job? I took it and ran with it, setting forth an agenda for change inside the directorate that I had carefully thought through ahead of time. I told them I wanted to increase the emphasis on centers, bringing operators and analysts closer together, as we had done so effectively in the Counter Narcotics Center and the Afghan Task Force. We need to change our "tooth-to-tail" ratio, trimming staff in favor of more operators in the stations. We needed stricter accountability for our operational responsibilities. We needed more emphasis on counterterrorism, and we needed to push hard to upgrade the directorate's technological capabilities. I thought my enthusiasm came across and helped me win points. It was hard to judge how I had done, but I felt I had handled myself reasonably well, and when I left the room I remained confident that I was still in the running.

I received a call a few days later from Ted Price, the deputy director of operations, who told me the job was mine. He called a senior staff meeting that afternoon in his office to make the announcement. I called Pat to give her the good news and then advised my deputy in the Latin America Division, Marty Roeber. But I did not mention it to anyone else. I did not want it out on the street before the official announcement from Price's office. When Ted made the announcement to the division and station chiefs that he and Woolsey had selected me for the job, it came as a mild surprise to some, especially the other contenders. I enjoyed the moment, but like many moments in my life, I did not linger long on the good news and the shot of adrenaline that came with it. I moved on quickly, concentrating on how I would handle the job.

The news flew through the directorate instantly. Everyone in the Latin America Division was already aware of the development before I got back to my office. Price sent out a brief cable to all our field stations alerting them of my assignment as ADDO. Without fanfare, I took over my new office the next day and attended the directorate's weekly staff meeting. I sat down in the ADDO's chair at the table. I felt at home. The high-rolling clandestine chess match had begun.

As a psychological side benefit, I had a prestigious key to the director's exclusive elevator, an office on the vaunted seventh floor, and a parking space in an elite executive lot in the basement, small symbols of success. It was a long walk from West Parking Lot, where I parked the first day I arrived at Langley so many years earlier. The executive parking area had a limited number of spots: for the DCI and the DDCI, the DDO and the ADDO, the DDI and the ADDI, the inspector general, the general counsel, and the executive director. DDO Ted Price drove a Porsche; IG Fred Hitz, a Lexus; executive director Nora Slatkin, a Cadillac convertible. I drove a bright canary-yellow Ford Festiva with stick shift and no air-conditioning. Hardly James Bond! Fortunately, my spot was adjacent to that of ADDI Dave Cohen, who drove a world-class junker that leaked oil profusely.

The atmosphere on the seventh floor was unlike anything I have experienced, before or since. The pace was relentless. The days were filled with back-to-back meetings and an onslaught of operational and personnel decisions that needed to be made nearly instantly. It was simultaneously exhilarating and frustrating, an addictive challenge to see how far I could push myself. But there was never as much time to be as thorough as we wanted. It was tough to maintain control over the day. All too often I was scheduled to do a project or meet people, and a fire would ignite over a flap that was in the press, or something would come in from the field, or someone would need immediate consultation. We wanted to be sure we saw to all our priorities, but there were always loose ends, because we never had enough time. The results were never perfect, and we often had to hope that what we put together did not unravel due to one errant thread.[1]

But I believed in my ability to handle any contingency. By that point in my career, I had recruited agents, run stations, orchestrated a covert war, directed an interdisciplinary center, and led a division. I'd even run a black bag job in the Mediterranean Basin, a singular moment in command when I reinforced, under intense pressure, that I could indeed pull the trigger.

We were breaking into a government building to steal a set of highly sensitive documents, a foreign nation's crown jewels. We couldn't leave fingerprints, and things had to run like clockwork, because this was the only night of the year we could go. If we didn't do it that night, we would be out of business for a year. We had inside information telling us where the security cameras were and how the alarms worked, but the trickiest part of all was keeping tabs on more than a dozen foreign officials with access to the target area who could, theoretically, show up in the middle of the operation. We needed to know where all of them were when we went in at precisely 11:30 p.m. It was now 11:00, and we had them all under surveillance. So far, everything had gone according to plan. The insertion team from headquarters and all the extra surveillance teams, including some of our wives, had assembled with their fake documents and elaborate cover stories. They'd all been training together for weeks. It got down to every team member knowing exactly what he needed to do, including carrying a bag of coins so he could use a pay phone if his secure phone didn't work. This was one of the most sensitive things we did in the Agency. And the people who executed the break-ins in many ways engaged in the most professional part of tradecraft. If it went well, we would get a pat on the back, and no one would know about it other than a small group of people. But if it went badly, it would be a long road back for me. Inevitably, someone would come in and show how I hadn't taken proper precautions. The political and personal risks associated with this kind of operation were huge. If we were caught in the act, it could lead to the arrest of our entry team and create a political firestorm that could embarrass the highest levels of the U.S. government.

All this flashed through my mind when we lost one of the people we were supposed to have under surveillance, on the outskirts of town minutes before our insertion team went in. Up until then, the team had largely been directing the operation, because of its expertise and preparation, and seemed to want to call the shots. This now changed on a dime. No one wanted to sit in the middle of the room and take responsibility for what needed to be done next.

"Over to you, Chief. Now what do we do?"

They recognized that the risk had escalated substantially. They understood that I needed to make the call and take full responsibility for the operation. All the air was sucked out of the room, and all the risk was on me. Within seconds, I had to assess the options and outcome—where did we lose him? what was the likelihood of his returning to the building? could we pick him up in enough time to still vacate?—and then decide. And it all needed to be done in a matter of seconds. I couldn't say, "I want to go think about it, and we'll reconvene in an hour." Truth be told, I didn't need an hour. I had the facts. I knew that nothing new was going to develop over the next hour. I calculated that, given where we had last seen the target, we should be able to get in and out before he returned. I also doubted that on that particular day, at that hour, he would be headed back to the office. But it wasn't a certainty. I took a calculated risk.

"Okay, we're going," I said.

You could say it was foolhardy, or you could say it was a prudent risk-management decision. It all came down to whether we pulled it off. And this time it did indeed go off like clockwork. The team got around the alarms and the security cameras, broke the locks, found the documents we wanted, and got them out in minutes. We had to quickly copy them and put them back exactly where we'd found them. But then we hit a major snag no one had anticipated: the documents were sealed with an acrylic paint that, if they were opened, would show telltale indications of tampering. Since they had to be returned in pristine condition, we couldn't break the seal until we solved the paint problem. Fortunately, my wife, Pat, was out on one of the surveillance teams, method acting. She is an artist, and she was on the street posing as one, with all her paints. She came in, looked at the envelope, and worked up an identical paint. We broke the seal, and Pat restored it to normal without a trace. The team redeposited the documents. Mission accomplished.

•

If anything, the pressure, the risk, and the intensity only escalated all these years later as I was put through my paces on the seventh floor. Days often began before dawn and ended well after dark, with me lugging a large Samsonite suitcase loaded with an evening's reading, which was retained in an Office of Security safe within my residence. When I first got there, I wondered if I was the only one doing this, until one night I saw DDCI Studeman leaving with two suitcases! After dinner at home, I would spend hours plowing through documents, only to start again the next morning. Dottie Hanson, who was my wise and multitalented administrative assistant, recalls that I would arrive in the morning with a pile of little notes I had written overnight, which she would quickly review so we could plan our day from there.

Despite the intensity of the work environment, Hanson maintained her sense of humor. Most memorably, one day I accidentally shut a car door on her foot rushing to go downtown. Although she wasn't hurt, she decided to play a prank and immediately headed to the nurses' office and had them wrap her foot in a huge bandage. I was mortified when I returned to the office and saw her foot, but she could not keep a straight face and quickly broke out laughing, to my relief. The ability to laugh was an important quality for everyone working in such a fast-paced and high-stakes environment.

Another important trait in this type of environment is the ability to think strategically. I learned a lesson about effective leadership from an unlikely source when I was young. The lesson was to carve out time in my day, every day, just to think. I learned it when I was listening as a teenager to an unusually frank conversation between my father and his longtime friend Jim O'Neil, the head of Plumbers Union Local 690 in

Philadelphia and the leader of all the building trades in the city. In terms of power, he was second only to the mayor, who many thought had been elected by the powerful union bosses in the early 1960s. I was fascinated to see these very strong men talking about life and leadership. They exuded strength and decisiveness. O'Neil noticed me, turned, and apropos of nothing said, "Always have a firm handshake and never have your photo taken with a drink in your hand. But most important, take the first half hour of each day to reflect and game the day." These were simple thoughts, but they stuck with me. I have a reliable alarm in my head and almost never use an alarm clock. When I was on the seventh floor at the CIA, that internal alarm always woke me up—as it does today—half an hour early so that I could reflect on the day ahead.

To help in the decision-making process, the Directorate of Operations through the years had set up mechanisms to get necessary information in front of the DDO and ADDO and to reduce the amount of time needed for them to be awake at night. The front line for headquarters was our twenty-four-hour watch center, which monitored all the worldwide cable traffic and fast-breaking developments and crises. Most issues were handled at the branch or division level, but the duty officers would reach out via a secure phone to the DDO and DCI if people had been injured or if there had been an operational flap that would vibrate around Washington or a foreign government, which happened with some frequency.

What kept me awake at night when I was responsible for overseeing spy operations all over the world? Interestingly enough, it was rarely the operations alone. It was much more likely to be an operation complicated by a serious personnel problem for which there was not a Solomonic solution. While operations could be extraordinarily complex, both from a tradecraft and a political point of view, they tended to be relatively easy to deal with when all the data were in front of you. Adding personnel problems to the mix always created untold complexity.

My executive officer, Rollie Flynn, recalled the kinds of thorny issues we regularly faced: "By Friday afternoon, my in-box was a foot and a half high. It was filled with quarter-inch-thick packages of decision memos with relevant attached documents. They were just god-awful things that would require the ADDO or the DDO's decision. You could not make these things up. You might have a flap with an agent: perhaps the mother-in-law of a good case officer abroad is suspected of working with the Russians. Do you bring the valuable officer home from wherever he or she is in the world, pulling the kids out of school and disrupting the whole family on the suspicion that the mother-in-law might be out of line? The list of issues like this seemed endless. Every Friday night I'd have eight or ten of these binders that I would try to read over the weekend and highlight so I could put together recommendations for Jack by Monday. But there was never time to read it all."[2]

•

The unique mission of the Clandestine Service made running the DO a challenge unlike others. My job was to make decisions, and the consequences were always significant, so the pressure was high. As an officer working on the floor at the time described it, the days were made up of a constant series of risk/reward calculations, and there was no such thing as a risk-free option.

We also held a weekly DDO staff meeting, which was attended by all the directorate's senior officers. It took place in a plush, secure interior conference room, where the walls were adorned with the photos of all the previous DDOs and ADDOs. The ghosts of the past seemed to haunt the room to ensure that tradition prevailed.

I carried out a quirky operation for one of those legends, Ted Shackley. The "Blond Ghost," as he was known, for his aversion to being photographed, served as station chief in Saigon during the Vietnam War, having run America's secret war in Laos before that, and the CIA's Miami station in the immediate aftermath of the Bay of Pigs fiasco. Dressed in his black suits, white shirts, and black ties, he had always seemed to turn up where important activities were happening. I say this to keep my brief encounter with him in perspective. It barely rates as a footnote in his long and controversial career, but it left an impression on me.

It was 1976, and I was back at headquarters working for the Latin America Division after returning from a trip to Mexico, when I was summoned to his office on the seventh floor with a colleague. Shackley, the associate deputy director of operations at the time, was cut from the same cloth as Robert McNamara, the former defense secretary: enthralled by data, analytics, and the latest technology. Some found him intimidating and very demanding. But there was no denying he brought a certain energy to the table as he sat us down and told us that he wanted us to go to New York City and tell U.S. congressman Edward Koch, the New York Democrat who later became mayor of New York City, that a group of right-wing Uruguayan military officers had hatched a drunken plot to have him killed.

The CIA had learned more broadly of Operation Condor from its reporting on various Latin American intelligence services—Argentina, Bolivia, Brazil, Chile, Paraguay, and Uruguay—as part of a global effort to eliminate those whom they deemed to be dangerous leftists. In their eyes, this was often anyone left of center, including the Chilean politician Orlando Letelier, who was tragically assassinated on the streets of Washington that same year. It would take years to determine that he had been killed by Chilean intelligence operatives. The plot against Koch wasn't nearly as serious. A couple of Uruguayan officers had told their CIA counterparts that they were going to assassinate the congressman for sponsoring legislation that cut off military assistance to Uruguay because of human rights violations. When we obtained this kind of threat information, our policy was to brief anyone who might be targeted. Shackley wanted to make sure we gave Koch the facts without histrionics. After describing our assignment, Shackley wanted to know exactly what we were going to say. The meeting soon became a dress rehearsal of our session with Koch. As a case officer with two tours under my belt, I felt a little insulted by Shackley's micromanagement. But Koch was an important figure, our intelligence was explosive, and Shackley wanted to get everything just right. In hindsight, I would have done exactly the same thing.

We met Koch in his New York office. He was friendly, and I could tell that he was taking seriously what we were telling him. "Even though we have doubts about the source," I said to him, "we wanted to make sure you were informed about it." Nothing more came of it. After we briefed him, I learned that he formally asked for FBI and police protection, which means he took the threat very seriously.

The CIA was definitely not involved in this operation against Koch. At the time, we took it upon ourselves to voice to our counterparts in the Latin American intelligence services our objections to assassination plots and human rights abuses whenever we learned about them. We were prohibited from even uttering the word *assassination* after the Church Committee, a select U.S. Senate panel chaired by Senator Frank Church (D-Idaho), began to investigate intelligence abuses. The agency had released to the committee a series of fourteen reports in 1975 and 1976 on CIA assassination attempts, coup plotting, and domestic spying. This fundamentally put an end to the Agency's dabbling in assassination at the behest of the executive branch.

•

During my tenure as associate deputy director of operations, one of the issues that occupied a great deal of our time and attention in meetings was dealing with the aftermath of the Ames affair. Ames's arrest had dealt the Agency a devastating blow. There was instant and extensive disbelief, self-doubt, and demoralization, especially within the Directorate of Operations. The criticism we faced produced anger and frustration among the workforce. From the beginning, however, the blow was internalized, manifest only in a flurry of activity to prevent such a betrayal in the future. A palpable drumbeat was sounded that someone had to pay for the pain we were undergoing. At the same time, a steady stream of rockets was being fired at the Agency from the media, Congress, and other agencies in the intelligence community, including, at times, our allies at the FBI—who, it would soon become apparent, should probably have been spending more time scrutinizing their own counterintelligence apparatus than critiquing ours.

Part of my job was to see that we made the necessary changes without going too far and hampering operations. The Ames affair forced us to become more vigilant about making hard personnel decisions when red flags arose and when it became clear that people were not performing. At the same time, as one of my colleagues recalled, we did not want to create a frenzied atmosphere in which everyone was looking over his shoulder, feeling that people were questioning how he could afford his shoes or his tie, and we did not want to destroy the élan or the esprit de corps of the organization.[3]

Not surprisingly, countless initiatives were undertaken to tighten up our counterintelligence program, including additional training courses and extensive new rules and regulations. Some of these were important tools to allow us to highlight potential problems early on. One such highly worthwhile reform gave the security office access to selected employees' financial records, which had not been permissible before Ames's arrest. This would have been most useful for spotting Ames's treachery earlier—for example, when he carelessly paid cash for his new home in Virginia. This would have raised a red flag during his routine security evaluation, even allowing for his credible but untrue cover story to explain his excess funds: that his Colombian wife came from a wealthy family. Regrettably, when the mole hunters were closing in on Ames, the information coming back from Colombia wrongly validated this story.

Another outgrowth of the Ames scandal was a renewed focus on the compartmentation element of counterintelligence: making sure that, even in an atmosphere where everyone has security clearance, access to sensitive information remains restricted to those who truly need to know. In the Monday morning quarterbacking that followed the scandal, the Agency was lambasted for poor compartmentation. Many wondered why Ames had such broad access to information. Some within the organization believe that much of his access was actually informal "hallway intel" he was able to gather through friends, but the fact remains that our compartmentation systems and practices needed tightening up.

The challenge with compartmentation, of course, is striking the right balance between protecting your secrets on the one hand and, on the other, making sure the people analyzing information have access to what they need. In government, the pendulum tends to swing back and forth as a reaction to the events of the day, which sometimes leads to overcorrection. Many within the Agency felt that there was an over-reaction post-Ames, albeit in response to real mistakes that had been made. This overcorrection and hesitancy to share and disseminate information was a major criticism leveled at the Agency post-9/11. At the same time, much of the credit for successes such as the absence to date of CIA documents in WikiLeaks can be attributed to good compartmentation practices. The key bureaucratic and procedural question becomes: What is the right balance?[4]

At the end of the day, though, while most of the post-Ames internal control reforms were well-intentioned, the majority of the professional counterintelligence people knew these endeavors could be helpful only around the edges. When you scrape away all the bureaucratic security measures, you are left with the realization that the best and most effective defense by far is having a penetration agent in your enemy's camp who can tell you where *their* penetration agents are in *yours*. Good security and counterintelligence can help prevent penetrations, but you usually need a mole to catch a mole. The Russian recruitment of Ames illustrates this truism loud and clear.

Being in the business ourselves, we understood its nature and knew that our Soviet Bloc opponents had been working just as hard to penetrate our system as we had theirs. Nonetheless, it still hurt to have our dirty laundry aired in public. One of my colleagues from the time notes that, before Ames, we had been able to point at other agencies—the army, the NSA, etc.—and say that we were special and had not been infected by this problem. But even though we had helped build an image of invulnerability, it was always overstated. Ames forced us to admit that we were not invulnerable, which was humiliating. It was not so much that the Ames scandal set us back irreversibly on our mission or undid important things we had to do, but it did take some of the gloss off the organization for a few years.[5]

In my mind, we hit a low point in our response to the scandal when it became fashionable among some of the workforce to wear buttons pronouncing "Never Again." I refused to participate, because by that time I knew a terrible dark secret: the Ames damage assessment could not explain all our losses of top-notch Russian sources. The mole hunters had come to realize that the Soviets had executed agents whom Ames could not possibly have known about, leading them to an unmistakable conclusion: there had to be another mole in the woodwork somewhere. It was a professional nightmare.

The hunt was on, and we were piecing together tidbits of information that came to us in dribs and drabs from our penetrations of Russian intelligence. Much of the information was titillating, but it consistently led us down blind alleys. At this time, we had a contingent of more than twenty FBI agents at Langley headquarters rooting through our files, trying to develop counterintelligence leads. I asked to speak to the CIA analytical team that was putting together the mosaic of our penetration. It was bizarrely fascinating to observe their dealings with me. Since "no one could be trusted," they passively ignored several of my requests for a briefing on the possible CIA suspects. In desperation, I finally called them to my office and reminded them that they worked under my chain of command, they had an obligation to brief me, and if they could not find a way to do it, I would find a team that would. It felt rather heavy-handed to treat them this strongly, especially since I had some sympathy for their old-school views of counterespionage. But it had to be done. I had a management obligation to make sure everything was being done that could reasonably be expected. They acquiesced, but they probably secretly added me to the "suspect list" immediately afterward.

The unpleasant irony in all this was that the mole was not in the CIA but, rather, in the FBI's own counterintelligence office. Just as we had trouble coming to terms with Ames, it seemed the FBI had trouble accepting the possibility that it had a mole inside its camp. One of my great frustrations when I eventually left the Agency was leaving behind the unfinished business of the second mole, who was later found to be FBI agent Robert Hanssen.

The Ames discovery and the mystery of the second mole seemed to haunt the place. I had lunch one day with senior officers of the KGB in a small, intimate dining area adjacent to the director's office, where the top leaders of the world's foreign intelligence services occasionally dined with the DCI and members of his staff. It was hard to grasp that, just ten years after our violent confrontation in Afghanistan, I was dining with top-level Russian intelligence officers at CIA headquarters. One of the less diplomatic KGB officers tried to needle me by asking about Ames. I tried to pass off Ames's betrayal as just a part of the intelligence game, but he knew it hurt. I reciprocated when a helicopter passed within eyeshot of the director's window and I noted in passing, ever so quickly, that I hadn't felt the same about helicopters since the mid-1980s. The Russian officer got the allusion to the Stingers in Afghanistan: two can play "gotcha," even in a diplomatic setting.

The poisoned atmosphere post-Ames played a role in Woolsey's decision to submit his letter of resignation the day after Christmas in 1994. While he had had nothing to do with our inability to stop Ames's betrayal much sooner, he became a lightning rod for criticism, and his lawyerly reprimands had satisfied no one. For whatever reason, he never had the president's ear, or confidence, and his estrangement only became more paralyzing after he made it clear in September 1993, just eight months into his term, that he agreed with the controversial assessment that Jean-Bertrand Aristide, Haiti's exiled president, was mentally unstable. It was not what the White House wanted to hear. I was sorry to see Woolsey resign so soon after giving me the job as the DO's number two. I got along very well with him. He was a decent and smart person with a good sense of humor. And he thought outside the box. His presence meant stability in my job as ADDO.

Most CIA directors are remembered for a single accomplishment or failure. Woolsey ushered in what could be called the age of drones. His hallmark achievement was forcing the unmanned aerial vehicle (UAV) program on the intelligence community and the military. Frustrated by the inability of spy satellites to give him the intelligence he needed on troop movements in the Balkans in 1993, he turned to an old friend, a legendary Israeli aircraft designer named Abe Karem, who was then in Southern California building prototypes for "long-dwell" drones—so called for their ability to linger over certain areas. By early 1994 the CIA was operating the GNAT 750, a Karem-designed drone built by General Atomics, over Bosnia. A bulked-up version of the GNAT, called Predator, first flew in July of that year. Both the CIA and the military had experimental and low-capability UAVs, but at the end of the day the air force wanted pilots to man its aircraft. After all, what would the air force be without pilots? For its part, the CIA did not want to get saddled with expensive aircraft, and the intelligence community in general could not see then drones' broad application in the future war on terrorism. Notwithstanding this opposition, Woolsey pushed the system and had his way. His decisive leadership left a lasting impression on me. The UAV gradually became a critically important part of the Agency's clandestine operations and paramilitary program abroad, and the air force began to rely more and more on drones' reconnaissance capabilities. Their full impact on the future of war fighting still remains to be seen.

"Credit must be given to Woolsey," Studeman said. "He came in early on and, because of his Israeli connections and other technology interests and proclivities he had in airborne reconnaissance, pushed the

Agency to go in the direction of the GNAT 750, the precursor to the Predator."[6]

Woolsey's accomplishment was little appreciated at the time of his resignation. So many bad things had befallen the Agency on his watch that Washington seemed relieved that he was stepping aside. Having said that, I see that by then, especially after he became crosswise with the White House on Aristide, he had virtually no access to the Clinton administration. After a small propeller plane crash-landed on the White House lawn in September 1994, *The Washington Post* ran a hurtful Herblock cartoon that had Woolsey piloting the plane, with the caption reading that it was the only way he could get in. The clock started ticking after the dustup over Aristide, and it was only a matter of time before Woolsey had to pack it in.

Changes at the top were part of the business. Woolsey's departure was not a particularly emotional one for the workforce; it passed so quickly that it gave me little time to reflect on it, especially given how fast things were moving. In the weeks before and after his departure, we started tracking an Islamic terrorist whose ideology and penchant for high-profile attacks foreshadowed the rise of Osama bin Laden.

On December 11, 1994, a bomb exploded in midair on Philippine Airlines Flight 434 bound for Tokyo. The passenger in the seat where the bomb had been hidden, a twenty-four-year-old Japanese business traveler named Haruki Ikegami, was killed by the blast, but his body absorbed most of the explosion's force and prevented the plane's outer skin from rupturing. The pilot and crew, helped by a U.S. military air traffic controller on the ground, were able to make a heroic emergency landing in Okinawa, saving all the aircraft's other 272 passengers and 20 crew members. As soon as the plane was safely on the ground, the hunt for the bomber began.

The investigation and international manhunt involved close cooperation among the CIA, the FBI, Japanese investigators, local Philippine law enforcement, and a host of others. First, forensics experts in Japan painstakingly collected the onboard wreckage and pieced together the bomb's components. The device had consisted of a liquid nitroglycerin explosive hidden in a cotton-stuffed contact lens solution bottle, a timer made from a rewired Casio wristwatch, a camera flashbulb to provide the heat for the detonation, and for power, a pair of nine-volt batteries sold only in the Philippines. Their work led the investigation back to the flight's point of origin, Manila.

Even before the attack, Philippine law enforcement and intelligence agencies were already on high alert in the lead-up to a planned January 15, 1995, visit by Pope John Paul II to Manila to celebrate World Youth Day. (The Pope ended up delivering an outdoor Mass that day to somewhere between five and seven million people, which may be the largest single gathering in Christian history.) Longtime CIA assets in the Philippines informed us that the Philippine government was looking at a number of Islamists who had recently entered the country and rented apartments in Manila.[7] On the evening of January 6, 1995, a fire broke out as terrorists mixed bomb-making chemicals in one of the apartments. After the blaze was under control, Philippine authorities used the opportunity to search the premises. The search turned up forged identity documents, bomb components of the kind that had been used on Flight 434, and a computer hard drive that, once it was decrypted with the help of FBI experts, yielded assassination plots against the Pope and the U.S. ambassador and plans for the bombing over a two-day period of a dozen or more planes bound for U.S. destinations. The Philippine authorities were able to make several arrests the night of the fire, but the apartment's main resident had fled the scene and slipped away.

That resident, the perpetrator of the Flight 434 bombing, was Ramzi Yousef, who was already on the FBI's Ten Most Wanted list for having set off a truck bomb in the basement of the World Trade Center in 1993. His attack on this plane had been a rehearsal to test the methods he intended to use in the larger plan found on his computer to blow up a dozen other planes. In Manila, Yousef had foiled airport security by putting the innocuous-seeming bomb components in his carry-on luggage and hiding the bomb's wires in a secret compartment in the heel of his shoe, below the area swept by the airport metal detectors. Once on board and airborne, he assembled the bomb in the airplane bathroom, set the timer for a few hours, stuffed the bomb in an underseat life vest pouch, and then disembarked when the plane landed for a stopover in the Philippine resort town of Cebu. Now that we knew the methods used, the race was on to find Yousef before he could carry out his plans.

The major break in the case came shortly thereafter, in Yousef's home country of Pakistan. A man named Istaique Parker had come into the U.S. embassy in Islamabad off the street claiming he had been involved in a plot to blow up an airliner but had gotten cold feet before carrying it out.[8] The intelligence provided by walk-ins to U.S. embassies around the world generally follows a 90/10 rule: 90 percent of it is worthless, but the remaining 10 percent can be extremely valuable. As a result, the Agency takes walk-ins very seriously, and has agents at every station assigned to process them and hear what they have to say. The cable that came back to us at Langley recounted Parker's story: he had been recruited by Yousef, supplied with bomb components, and instructed to board a flight in Bangkok bound for the United States. At the last minute, though, he had balked, choosing instead to tell his story to the CIA and claim the $2 million reward the FBI was offering for Yousef's capture. Information he provided led Pakistani intelligence and U.S. Diplomatic Security Service officials to arrest Yousef shortly thereafter, on February 7, 1995, in an Islamabad motel. The FBI flew him back to New York, where he stood trial for his crimes and was sentenced to 240 years plus a life sentence without the possibility of parole. He is now serving his time in the Florence, Colorado, supermax federal penitentiary.

The incident was significant for a number of reasons. A terrorist was able to defeat airport security and smuggle a bomb onto an aircraft by concealing explosives in a container of seemingly harmless liquid and bomb materials in his shoe. The security measures put into place to foil these techniques have changed air travel for us all. Furthermore, the intelligence taken from the hard drives seized from his apartment included a plan devised by Yousef and his uncle Khalid Sheikh Mohammed to hijack an airliner and fly it into CIA headquarters in Langley. This may have been the first known instance of a terrorist plan to use an airliner as a missile, an ambition that, sadly, al-Qaeda did not abandon. But the arrest of Yousef also showed that coordinated efforts by intelligence and law enforcement agencies around the world could be an effective tool for bringing terrorists to justice and preventing them from carrying out attacks. Building and fostering these liaison relationships with other intelligence services was a big part of my job. The CIA's collaboration with foreign intelligence services is one of its most important force multipliers in collecting intelligence and taking action against our enemies, especially in the age of transnational targets such as terrorism, drug trafficking, and nuclear proliferation.

A good example of the importance of liaison was on public display in May 2012 with the thwarting of an al-Qaeda attempt to make an underwear bomb intended for detonation on a plane headed to the United States. As reported by the press at the time, the CIA was able to pull off an intelligence coup with liaison support. This reportedly was a result of our close collaboration with Saudi intelligence, which had been able to insert one of their sources into the inner circle of al-Qaeda in Yemen.

I spent a great deal of time developing rapport with the senior leadership of foreign intelligence services when they paid official visits to the United States. We gave them tailored, in-depth briefings by top analysts, who provided high-level interpretations of fast-moving worldwide developments. This kind of personal attention enriches our ties with these important leaders and is a way for the CIA to show its appreciation for the substantial support and hospitality these foreign services extend to Agency personnel in their countries.

On a personal level, these duties also enabled me to rekindle old acquaintances and friendships. During my time on the seventh floor, I hosted separate visits from the heads of the British and Australian intelligence services, both of whom happened to have served in Chile as the Santiago station's liaison contacts during my time there in the 1970s. Reminiscing with them was great fun, but it was also somewhat problematic. They were accompanied by staff who held them in high esteem and were not accustomed to thinking of them as the mere mortals they were earlier in their careers. While dining with the chief of Australian liaison and his staff in the private room of a quality Washington restaurant, I recalled the folklore of a rather formal dinner a long time ago in Santiago at which my Australian colleague was able to awe his dinner companions by showing them an old outback trick. This young intelligence officer asked the host to bring him one of her finest wineglasses. To her horror, he then proceeded to chew the goblet, grinding it up bite by bite. To us, the story brought back memories of a less formal and more adventurous time, and the Australian officer smiled and did not deny the feat. Nonetheless, his staff's laughter seemed rather nervous and restrained.

I had a similar experience with Sir David Spedding, a secretive Englishman who had been a junior officer in Santiago in 1972 and was now chief of operations for MI6. Prior to the coup that toppled Chilean president Salvador Allende, the CIA had been very concerned that we would not be able to handle our assets. Spedding, the British representative at the time, was so security conscious that he would not speak on the secure communication system we had provided him. In a move that we felt was playing the game too close to the vest even for us, he was willing to communicate only by clicking with his radio send, once for yes and twice for no.

When I reminded him of his clicking procedures in Santiago, we all had a good laugh. Defending himself, he insisted that he was only concerned that our system would knock out the electronics in the adjoining office, which it didn't. But some old adages apply in the intelligence business as much as they do in life: "He who laughs last, laughs longest"—as I would experience later.

Unfortunately, maintaining those close and healthy partnerships with other intelligence services around the world is not always easy, especially when we are also responsible for spying on them. At the same time that we were dealing with the manhunt for Yousef, an intense dispute with French intelligence rocked our operations there and soured our relationship with the French service for several years.

It started out with an early morning call to our French desk by Rollie Flynn and David Shedd, the executive officers for the seventh floor, who inquired about an "Immediate" cable received early that morning notifying us of the compromise of our Paris operations. Right away we recognized that we had a major problem in front of us, one with extraordinary political and foreign policy implications. There had been a low-burning feud for some time with the French security services because of their aggressive targeting of U.S. businessmen, especially in the aerospace sector. The long-standing feud first became public in 1993 when a document surfaced showing that the French had specifically targeted twenty-one U.S. companies.[9] This did not come as a surprise to us, since for years we were well aware that the French were running black bag operations, breaking into the hotel rooms of American business executives in Paris and copying sensitive business data and strategies.

In response to this, Woolsey made a rare public statement that year to a group of Chicago businessmen, advising them that the United States would be countering the aggressive French behavior of bugging rooms and stealing documents. He went on to memorably comment that there would be "no more Mr. Nice Guy" as far as the French were concerned. True to his word, we aggressively pursued the recruitment of French government sources willing to part with French trade secrets in entertainment rights and telecommunications.[10] It is relatively uncommon for allies to target each other's internal political or economic interests. The vast majority of the intelligence work in allied countries is focused on common enemies residing in the host country—Russians, Cubans, Iranians, terrorists, North Koreans, narcotraffickers. But this ceased to be the case in France, where Woolsey had the field operators endeavoring to recruit French government officials for trade secrets.

By 1995, the French security service was monitoring a few of our officers who were working on developing government sources in the French economic area. In February of that year, they decided to spring their trap. The timing was suspiciously political: it was in the middle of a hotly contested French presidential election, and it looked like an attempt to direct attention away from a French government scandal involving domestic wiretapping of local political figures. The French were also upset because several months earlier we had quietly declared a former senior French official "persona non grata" for operating in the United States against U.S. targets and had had him kicked out of the country, a process known as being PNG'd.

With this as a backdrop, the French minister of the interior, Charles Pasqua, summoned the U.S. ambassador, Pamela Churchill Harriman, that same month. The minister unceremoniously confronted the prominent British-born socialite with evidence of CIA operations directed against French government officials, including photos of clandestine meetings, copies of false identity documents, credit card imprints, and hotel registrations. Harriman reportedly tried to defuse the situation, to no avail. In the end, the French government officially asked that the chief, Dick Holm, and four of his subordinates depart the country. To make matters worse, the French immediately leaked this development to the press. This was quite shocking. Normally a tête-à-tête like this occurred out of public view, allowing liaison cooperation to continue unimpeded.

Once the incident became public, there was no way to put the genie back in the bottle. The U.S. officers in Paris went into an immediate lockdown operationally, and a few top officers had to be called home. There also was concern about the case officers' dependents, especially the possible need for children to be pulled out of school on short notice. We were able to push back the departures for six weeks, which gave some of the families an opportunity to make a relatively orderly exit from Paris. It still was a very heavy task for the officers and their families.

This action by the French was particularly troubling because it had been directed against Holm, a distinguished professional who years earlier had been badly burned and scarred in an airplane crash in the Congo. The heroic story was well-known, and he was widely admired by his colleagues for his bravery.[11] On this flight, his Cuban pilot lost his bearings in a thunderstorm and crash-landed in the jungle. As the right wing was sheared off the airplane, Holm was sprayed with gasoline and was terribly burned from head to foot. Rescued after ten days in the bush, he spent two years at Walter Reed Army Medical Center. He was blind for a year, but when he recovered his sight he went back to the field, serving with high distinction in China and Hong Kong. The Paris incident sadly put an end to Holm's career with the Agency, and he retired shortly after returning to the United States.

No sooner had this crisis passed than another arose when Representative Robert G. Torricelli, a New Jersey Democrat, said in a letter to President Clinton that the CIA had failed to disclose information that one of its paid informants, a Guatemalan military intelligence officer named Colonel Julio Roberto Alpirez, had allegedly witnessed the murders in 1990 of an American expatriate, Michael Devine (no relation), and Efrain Bamaca, a Guatemalan leftist married to the Harvard-educated American lawyer Jennifer Harbury. (Alpirez had denied that he was a CIA informant and that he had knowledge of the murders.) When the Agency formally notified the House and Senate Intelligence Committees of this lapse, I found myself involved in one of the single most difficult issues I had faced in managing relations on Capitol Hill.

Part of the challenge came from our own insular nature. As a former seventh-floor colleague noted, the Directorate of Operations, unlike the Directorate of Intelligence, tended not to rotate many officers out to Congress or other parts of the government. This changed to a degree in subsequent years, but in those days our officers did not have much of a presence around town in Washington. As a result, even within the government there were few who really understood what we did. Without those sorts of social relationships, we did not always have a reservoir of trust and understanding with our counterparts on the Hill or elsewhere in the executive branch. This made misunderstandings more likely and meant that dealing with the aftermath of a flap or problem could be even harder.

The Agency had reported the allegation involving Alpirez to the Department of Justice in 1991, but had not informed the congressional intelligence committees, which it was required to do under the 1980 Intelligence Oversight Act. Agency officials determined that the information had been included in briefing notes in 1991, but for some reason this was never delivered to Congress. Both committees felt they had been deliberately deceived, which wasn't the case, and the Senate committee went so far as to hold a highly unusual public meeting to express its displeasure over what it perceived as CIA stonewalling.

As the committees investigated, Frederick Brugger, who had served as chief of station in Guatemala from 1991 to 1993, was under intense scrutiny. He apparently had not notified the U.S. ambassador that Alpirez was a paid CIA agent. Brugger was a solid citizen and a good operator, but he was rather rigid in his body language during his first presentation to the committee. As a consequence, when he was preparing to go down and testify again and came to my office, he brought along his lawyer, fearing legal vulnerability. The lawyer projected a sense of mild hostility and, in an off-putting way, wanted to know who from the DO would testify with Brugger.

"I'm going down with him," I said curtly, cutting him off. The lawyer backed off. I thought nothing of it at the time, but after the meeting ended I received a call from the General Counsel's Office. "We really don't think it's a good idea for you to go down with Fred," a very senior Agency attorney advised. "Some here think it might not be helpful for your career."

"Look. It doesn't matter to me what they think," I said. "There is no choice here. Even if I were disinclined to go down to the Hill with him, which I am not, I would have to go anyway, since no one in my chair can expect to lead this directorate and not support one of our officers in a crisis."

"That's your choice, but it's not well received down here," the lawyer said.

Equally important, I thought Brugger and his boss, Terry Ward, who had served as chief of the Latin America Division from 1990 to 1992, were innocent of deliberately deceiving Congress. Their failure to inform Congress about the 1991 intelligence report about Colonel Alpirez, I believed, had been inadvertent. But beyond the issue of guilt or innocence, I thought my presence could be helpful up on the Hill, given my experience there and in Latin America. In the end, Brugger handled himself quite well, and we survived the hearing intact.

The Guatemala incident brought into sharp focus, in the context of congressional oversight, the issue of what sort of people the Agency could or should be involved with. Obviously, the world of espionage is full of all kinds of people, some more unsavory than others. During this time, a feeling was emerging within the Agency that some of those responsible for our oversight were pushing us to limit our dealings with undesirable individuals. According to Dick Calder, our chief of plans, "We felt that, if we were only going to be able to deal with choir boys, we were going to be put at a terrible disadvantage. This was not an attempt to pass over what had happened in Guatemala—actually, I believe this incident led to new rules and regulations about our activities—but we felt the pendulum was swinging too far. There was an implication that the people we were dealing with would have to pass a sainthood test before we could deal with them. But if you think about disrupting terrorist attacks or collecting intelligence on other sensitive activities, it would be impossible to operate that way. That is not to say we should accept every agent, and certainly not condone illegal activities, but the idea that people or whole organizations that failed to meet a certain standard could be off-limits would have presented a major problem." This tension still exists today, particularly in the context of the type of people the Agency and others must deal with to penetrate terrorist organizations and foil their plots. It is a core challenge for any intelligence agency, particularly one working on behalf of a democratically elected government. The military and particularly our Special Forces also face this challenge with regard to whom they train and equip in the field. A couple of simple tests can form our best defense: Is there bipartisan support in Congress for what we are doing? Would the American people support it?

Indeed, testifying before the House and Senate Permanent Select Committees on Intelligence became one of my most important responsibilities, both to protect officers such as Brugger and Ward and to shield the CIA from the budget-cutting mentality pervasive in the post–Cold War atmosphere. I ended up using our strategic plan for the Directorate of Operations—which I had more or less laid out in my job interview with Woolsey and Studeman—as a tool to aid us in our relations with Congress. I had to be sure that the people who provided us with financial and political support understood what we were doing and where we were going. America's sense of our role in the world was unclear during the mid-1990s. The Cold War was over, and the sea change after 9/11 was still to come. Some members of Congress and the public at large were asking questions about whether there was even a need for America to maintain robust intelligence capabilities. Having a strategic plan helped me to explain as clearly as possible—both to those who were supportive and those who were not—what we were trying to do, and how that fit into other government priorities.

"The Agency always has a difficult time with the Hill because the Agency has a proclivity for not telling the whole story, under the notion that it is protecting sources and methods," said Studeman, describing the structural challenges inherent in the Agency's relationship with Congress. "This makes the Hill feel like it has to drag the information out of the Agency. Meanwhile, Congress can be difficult to deal with because of its tendency to go public and hold open hearings on sensitive subjects instead of discussing them behind closed doors. It used to be possible to talk to the leadership about the most sensitive matters, on the basis of disclosing only to the Gang of Eight—the majority and minority chairs of the two Intelligence and two Armed Services Committees. As time passed, fewer of the Gang of Eight wanted the sole responsibility for knowing sensitive information, which led to the desire to expose more committee members as insurance against the possibility of information becoming public in the future."[12]

In this environment, leaks are not inevitable, but maintaining operational security gets even harder. Directorate of Operations officers hold sensitive information very closely, and many—even those who believe in and support the idea of Congress having an oversight role—have trouble really warming to what Congress views as our responsibility for putting everything on the table.

Given the inherent challenges in the relationship, there is an art to dealing with Congress, but there are also skills to be learned. Stan Moscowitz, the Agency's head of legislative affairs, took me aside after my first appearance on the Hill. I thought it had gone very well, but he clearly had misgivings. "When you go down there and they ask you a question," he said, "you have to immediately answer yes or no, and then explain the issue in more detail if you wish. Otherwise they think you're obfuscating, as they did today." It was one of the single best pieces of advice I ever got in terms of dealing with Congress.

In addition to communicating with Congress, those who work on the seventh floor are responsible for maintaining the CIA's relationship with the president, our most important customer. In early 1995, to offset blowback from media rumblings that President Clinton was not paying enough attention to the CIA, national security adviser Tony Lake came out to CIA headquarters in Langley for a meeting with senior leaders. He made very positive comments about the importance of intelligence to the White House. Everything was going fine; it was a lovefest. But then a GS-13 note taker on the back bench asked, "Mr. Lake, is there anything we're not doing right?"

"Well," Lake said, "I did run into former NSC director Brent Scowcroft the other day, and he asked, 'Is the Agency still giving you that lousy reporting on Iran?'" Everybody in the room laughed nervously. Then Lake said, "And by the way, you're not doing so hot on North Korea." I was stunned. This was our top consumer, one step removed from the president of the United States, and he had just delivered a devastating critique of our performance on two of the most important targets we had.

I found the exchange extremely disturbing and went back to my office to write a cable to all our field stations. My intention was to be as blunt as Lake had been in his comments. Some people still remember the cable, because it stunned the DO. It was a departure from the sort of staid cables we were all used to. In essence, I told our field officers that according to our biggest and most important customer, we were not cutting it and we needed to do better. The cable had a polarizing, even shocking effect. Though no one came back to me to challenge my observations directly, a number of senior officers did not like the message and let it be known by sending messages out on the underground bongo drums that eventually reached my ears. Their reaction said to me that, from their perspective, it was wrong to highlight shortcomings so starkly. Others took the message in stride as a call to improve. One senior officer, who had been preparing at the time to retire, said that this cable gave him renewed faith and convinced him to stay on.[13] In short, my candor—and Lake's—cut two ways.

What I was getting at in my cable was this: we needed to raise the bar on performance on the tough targets, and the managers had to take the lead on this at every level. We needed to ask: Did we have the right people in the right jobs, and were we hiring and promoting the right mix of people? Did we have enough officers in the DO who were the equivalent of fighter pilots, male and female, using all the creativity and all the guile that the challenge required?

I tried to get at these quality issues in the strategic plan I developed to reform the Directorate of Operations. When I had told Price earlier in my tenure as ADDO that I planned to undertake a new and comprehensive strategic plan, he agreed without hesitation. The feeling in the directorate was that, if reform was to happen, it would have to be led from within. We wanted to modify ourselves before somebody else did it. We were concerned that someone making changes from the outside might make it more difficult for us to do our jobs. I was aided in this work by our chief of plans, Dick Calder, a top-notch officer. My only self-criticism today is that I probably should have stepped out even further, although at the time I thought I was pushing the envelope as much as possible.

It was surprising to me, in a global intelligence service, how little time and energy was actually spent on strategic issues. We hired very bright officers, but a large percentage of them wanted to do only tactical planning. Many would rather have worried about how to arrange a "chance" encounter with a Chinese or North Korean official than think strategically about how best to tackle the Chinese or North Korean regimes. We often spent all day putting out fires without leaving any time to ask the right strategic questions, which was imperative given the times in which we were living. In the mid-1990s we were post-Ames, in the midst of downsizing, and wondering who we were and how we needed to restructure ourselves to remain relevant. "It's common to say that we were the world's second-oldest profession and that profession doesn't change, but things were changing, and we had to take a serious look at ourselves," Calder said. "If we were going to be able to answer our customers' new questions, we had to aggressively develop new resources and assets."[14]

The strategic reform plan we put together in 1995 had as a cornerstone the key judgment that the greatest national security threat facing America was "domestic terrorism." It laid out specific reforms for the clandestine service: increasing focus on transnational issues such as terrorism and narcotics; leveraging the broadest capabilities of the Agency to make our work more relevant; creating multidisciplinary centers to pull together analytical, technical, and support capabilities; attracting and retaining the best talent for the future of the service; implementing new counterintelligence procedures, including policies for screening, clearance, and personnel; increasing technical skills within the service, which had previously focused primarily on source-running skills; and maximizing our "tooth-to-tail ratio," which has to do with how many people are carrying out missions versus how many are required to support those missions.

While we never completely executed all the parts of the strategic plan, we did make progress on multiple fronts, including bringing the Directorate of Operations and the Directorate of Intelligence closer together. With the construction of a new headquarters building at Langley, a major reorganization of office space took place. The DO officers all wanted to remain huddled together, totally separated from their analyst colleagues. Dave Cohen, my counterpart in the DI, and I decided to knock down the wall, literally, that separated the DDI's suite of offices from the DDO's. Somewhere in the archives there is a photo of both us in hard hats, hammers in hand. It was symbolic of the change that needed to come about.

The integration was substantive as well as organizational. When we co-located the regional analytical and operational divisions, it put more analytical input into our intelligence collection and got DI officers involved in the direct assignment of priorities, collection targets, and analysis. Like anything bureaucratic, there were some pro forma steps to it, but it was a serious effort that had a positive impact.[15] It was amazing how easy it was to dictate this change. I simply brought in the DO's chief of support and told him to make it happen. God knows what chaos that produced, but I was determined to break down the walls.

During this period, there were also several misguided reforms that I was able to redirect and prevent. Most stemmed from the need to draw down our budget as part of the post–Cold War "peace dividend." One such reform was a proposal to combine the Africa and Latin America Divisions. The DO program managers at the time apparently wanted to merge the two divisions to appease the budgeters. But that was a fool's errand. At a joint meeting of senior officers from both divisions, I simply announced it was not going to happen, and that was the end of it. Area expertise is a highly valued commodity in the intelligence business and should not be tampered with lightly. Every division has its own unique culture and operating style, and we needed to have dedicated officers in each who knew they could make their careers there. Furthermore, it cannot be overlooked that the United States has vastly different national security interests in those regions. As many before me have noted, nobody in the U.S. government seems to be too concerned about Africa until a crisis strikes there. And one always does, as we can see from the unrest and growth of terrorism in the continent. For example, nobody cared about Somalia until Delta Force showed up there in 1993 looking for Mohammed Farah Aidid and desperately needed intelligence support. And today, Africa is a hotbed of Islamic terrorism.

•

President Clinton's pick to replace Woolsey as CIA director at the beginning of 1995 was Michael P. C. Carns, a retired air force general. But on March 10, after withdrawing the nomination in light of alleged immigration violations by Carns involving a Filipino household employee, he tapped John M. Deutch, an MIT chemistry professor serving as deputy secretary of defense, to run the Agency. He selected George J. Tenet, a former Senate Intelligence Committee staffer then serving on Clinton's National Security Council, to be deputy director. Almost no one at the CIA had a good feel for Deutch at the time, but it seemed that his nomination would be good for the Agency, given his close access to the White House and his prominent role at the Pentagon.

The arrival of a new director at Langley is always met with trepidation. Although for the most part it does not create sleepless nights for the rank and file, for many employees it is still a moment to consider what direction their work may take in the months and years ahead. For the most senior officers, the stakes are higher. For us, a new director could mean reassignment or early departure from the service. As such, we approached our new director with a great deal of caution.

The head of the Directorate of Operations at the time was Ted Price, an experienced China hand who spoke Mandarin and who had taken a nontraditional path to the top. He and I had been friends over our long careers and worked well together, albeit with different styles and backgrounds. Price already had a positive relationship with Deutch, who at the time was his neighbor. After Clinton tapped Deutch to head the CIA, they had met at Deutch's home, and Price came away from the meeting believing he had reached an "understanding" with Deutch that he would stay on as head of the DO. Around that time, Price also brought Tenet down to the Farm in Virginia, where new recruits receive their spy training. Price thought he and Tenet shared a view about the future, and that they would be working together in the years ahead. Shortly thereafter, however, at his Senate confirmation hearings, Deutch announced that, in the wake of the Ames case, the Guatemala scandal involving Colonel Alpirez, and various other small scandals and controversies, he would replace the DO's senior leadership as he moved to rid the Agency of its Cold War spy mentality. Supposedly, there had been a private meeting of the new leadership at which members of the Deutch team decided, unanimously, that Ted Price had to go.

Soon after seeing Deutch's statements to Congress on television, Price turned in his badge and left, leaving a long and distinguished career behind him.

Before the confirmation hearings, I had been more relaxed about Deutch than I should have been, because Price had shared with me his impression that he had an arrangement with the new director. The minute Price walked out the door, I was left to pick up the pieces and run the DO, but with a very uncertain future myself. Deutch's announcement to the world that there would be a shakeup at the top of the Directorate of Operations looked like it would mark the beginning of the end of my tenure there, and because of this concern, I put the job of station chief in a major European country in my inside pocket as insurance. But I was not about to quit cold turkey. Price and I could not both leave, and I did not feel like quitting, especially since I had seen the bureaucratic ball bounce around in strange and unexpected ways in the past.

With my position considerably more precarious than normal, I wasn't sure what I would face when I met the new DCI once he moved into his office at headquarters. Fortunately, I got a lucky break the first time I met him officially, which made it much easier to deal with him than I had anticipated.

Early in Deutch's tenure, his secretary called to notify me that he would like to chat. The staff had prepared me well for this briefing, and I had all the key data at my fingertips. But Deutch had a quick and fertile mind, and his questions could be quite penetrating and detail-oriented. A great deal was riding on this meeting, and I knew that first impressions were critical in such situations.

In recent years, I had been in the director's office numerous times and felt at home. The DCI's office is well-appointed but far from opulent when compared to those of other department heads and cabinet members. It has a broad window spanning its length and looking out, from its seventh-floor perch, onto a densely wooded area. It is not much larger or more decorative than my office, just fifty feet away, and we shared essentially the same panoramic view. My office, however, had a regular visitor, a large hawk that perched on the windowsill for hours on end and added a little mystery.

Despite my comfort being in the DCI's office, I was thrown off balance when I was escorted into the room by the secretary only to find Director Deutch sitting in his underwear in a leather chair with his leg propped up and a huge ice pack pressed against an injured knee. In a split second he went from Mr. Director to a mortal human being. We laughed about it before getting down to business. From that point on, I always had a very comfortable relationship with Deutch, one in which I felt I could be candid and open with him. We often kidded each other good-naturedly. He was self-confident and very smart, and did not feel insecure dealing in frank discourse; in fact, he valued it. Not all directors did.

In the small dining room just off his office, Deutch had hung a painting of former director James Schlesinger. I wondered if he realized that Schlesinger was held in low esteem at Langley because of his handling of a reduction in force during the Carter years. He oversaw the unseemly firing of a few hundred experienced officers. He also had a bird-watching hobby that left him wandering around the wooded areas near the Agency; it did not go over well. Tenet later had the portrait replaced with a picture of Richard Helms.

In early May, once he had officially taken over, Deutch had a town hall meeting with Agency employees in which he said he had formed a committee to recommend candidates to replace Price. "That process will take some time," he said. "During that time, I intend to rely on Jack Devine as the acting deputy director for operations, and to work very closely with every individual in the DO at a time when I know there is a lot of lack of knowledge—and a lot of unjust criticism—about what that group has done."

I was interviewed for the DDO job by John McMahon, the former CIA deputy director who was ostensibly heading Deutch's search committee, but in fact Nora Slatkin, the executive director, was calling the shots at the DCI's behest. Of course, I wanted to stay on to finish the job I had started, and I was committed to doing so if at all possible, but the odds were very slim that the DCI could back away from his public pronouncements about seeking a new DDO. Nevertheless, I was somewhat surprised that Deutch and I developed a positive relationship. He seemed to value my opinion as he and his administration tried to get their sea legs and eventually pursued their own agenda.

From where I sat, I had two tasks in front of me: one was to preserve the integrity of the directorate from any whimsical actions; the other was to help the new DCI become grounded in the DO. It was a balancing act. He clearly saw that I was trying to be helpful, which in fact is the responsibility of all deputy directors. He did not see as clearly my efforts to protect the directorate, but it truly was in everyone's interest to ensure that there weren't any missteps in the early days of his administration. Trust between the new DCI and the DDO had to be built before new initiatives could be pressed on the directorate, no matter how worthwhile. Deutch instinctively seemed to understand this, and gave me free rein during my stint as acting DDO.

Once, during this leadership transition, I was over at the Pentagon with Deutch for a briefing when a secretary came huffing and puffing into the room. "Senator Warner wants to speak with Mr. Devine immediately," she said. Deutch was on my right, and everyone else in the room, all military flag-rank officers, were looking at me in dismay. Despite the senator's gentlemanly manners, they were fearful of the Virginia Republican and former navy secretary who had served on both the Intelligence and the Armed Services Committees. They thought that I might have a particularly close relationship with him, and I was not eager to dispel this notion. I quickly got up and followed the secretary to the phone. The Pentagon being what it is, I must have walked for five minutes. Finally, we got back to the secretary's office and I picked up the phone while she got the senator on the line.

A few days earlier, I had briefed the Senate Intelligence Committee on our ongoing covert actions. During my testimony, Warner, who normally was very genteel in his demeanor, started needling me. It became so obvious that eventually the majority chairman, Senator DeConcini, leaned over and whispered to Warner, "He's a good guy. Go light." DeConcini remembered me from the trip we had taken together to Latin America several years earlier. The microphone was still on, and it was easy to ascertain what was being said. When the hearing was over, Warner came quickly around the table to me and said, "You know, I had you confused with a person I didn't like."

"Senator," I said, "no problem. Ask away."

"Sir, what can I do for you?" I asked when Senator Warner eventually joined me on the phone in the Pentagon. In a most pleasant manner, he said, "I'm just checking to see if you're okay." I quickly assured him I was doing just fine and thanked him for his concern. And that was the end of the discussion. The consummate southern gentleman, he apparently was still feeling bad about having needled me during the hearing a few days before.

I deliberately took my time walking back to the meeting. It seemed as though I had been gone about a half hour by the time I sat back down in the briefing room. Nobody asked me why Warner had called, since it would have appeared to be intruding on a possibly sensitive topic, so I let it just sit in the air. I'm sure Deutch was wondering what the senator had wanted to talk to me about, but he couldn't bring himself to ask. On purpose, I didn't comment about it and let the mystery of the call linger to my advantage, partly for fun and partly for ulterior motives.

I learned quickly that Deutch's decisiveness could pose challenges for me. Not long after he took over as director, President Clinton and the First Lady paid a call to Langley. This was not a regular event for sure. Presidents rarely visit CIA headquarters. In fact, it seldom occurs more than once or twice in each administration. But Deutch knew the president well and pressed him to make a visit, which is always a morale boost for the troops. A full program was put together for the president and First Lady, along with several briefings on key topics, including one on terrorism that was particularly well done.

The DCI and I sat across from the president and Mrs. Clinton while the briefing was conducted. Near the end of it, the DCI slipped me a note asking about the briefer: "What grade is she?" I took a stab at it and responded, "Probably a GS-13." His note came back saying, "Promote her." I sent back a note, "Can't do it. It would circumvent the process and raise hell with her peers." One terrific briefing does not warrant a promotion at the CIA. The bar is set high for promotions, and the competition is stiff. It was an impressive and high-quality briefing, but most of us expect to see that kind of performance from our top briefers on a regular basis. It would have been a disappointment to many analysts to have one of their peers leapfrog the review process on the strength of a single briefing, no matter how good it was. It likely also would have caused problems for her with the employees in her own office, who undoubtedly would have seen the promotion as favoritism and resented her for it. Deutch didn't like my response but did not press the matter further. I often wondered if the president saw the exchange of notes. If so, he probably assumed it was related to a serious operational or intelligence issue rather than a personnel matter.

Deutch's strongest hour came after a European service shared with us an explosive report about an Iranian terrorist threat. When they sent the report over, Deutch made it clear that he needed to know the source before he would take the report to the White House, which the content required in this case. When informed that he was insisting they identify their agent, the service exploded. They refused to give up his name, even to the director of the CIA and the president of the United States. After Deutch was told of their adamant refusal, he picked up a secure direct line to the head of the service who had been installed at headquarters at their insistence, and made it clear that he needed the name of the source—and this wasn't negotiable. Whatever he said to make his case, in the end they relented. This incident did not go down well in the service, and it certainly did not help Deutch's relationship with them. However, it was an important point. When top secret intelligence required significant policy action, the director has to be willing to say, "You have to verify this and put it on the table."

As time marched on and as I developed a closer working relationship with Deutch, I suspected he was becoming uneasy about how long I could continue to operate in an "acting" capacity before he would have to bite the bullet and cut me loose, even though, by then, he realized how well I understood the culture and the DO's capability and appreciated the need for reform. In July 1995, after a detailed briefing on the DO strategic plan, it became clear that we had reached the Rubicon, and he asked that we chat following the briefing. I understood what was coming.

"I have to make the changes I promised," he said.

"John, I understood that when you came in," I responded.

Referring to my next assignment, he said, "You can have anything you want." Then he proceeded to organize a bittersweet seventh-floor farewell event for me in an upscale Georgetown restaurant with the Agency's top officers. Pat, loyal as ever, could not forgive Deutch for denying me the opportunity to continue running the DO. She refused to meet or even speak to him.

A few days after the farewell dinner, I started to prepare myself to depart the seventh floor and begin my new assignment, which would require me to begin spending a considerable amount of time abroad. Despite the hectic pace of the office, moments of peace crept into my last days that allowed me to reflect on my long career and the unique view I had had from the top of the Clandestine Service. This produced a mixture of emotions, which I'm sure many of my predecessors also experienced.

On the one hand, I felt an overwhelming sense of pride and good fortune in having served at the highest level of the CIA, where I had daily influence over world events, oftentimes over issues of life and death. In that context, I had looked forward every day I walked into my office to the high-stakes challenges that came from working on America's key foreign policy issues with the best and most important players in Washington. The environment forced us all to adapt constantly to the subtlest shifts in the political and operational landscape, which made for exhilarating and intense mental gymnastics. And above all, I was honored to have been given the opportunity to lead a very special and elite group of professionals in a highly complex mission in defense of America's national security interests.

But by the same token, as I headed out the door to serve abroad once again, I experienced an unsettling feeling of frustration. So much still needed to be done—operations half-completed, personnel problems unresolved, professional relationships underdeveloped. Under these conditions, I had a deep-seated desire to continue indefinitely in this unique job. But everyone has to move on, and so did I.

In the following days, I wrapped up my work on the seventh floor and left, savoring the joy of personal accomplishment and the sadness of unfulfilled goals.

TWELVE

Undisclosed

1995–98

Tom Polgar, the legendary Saigon station chief, told me early in my career that when I got to be a senior-level Agency official, I would have to speak up and be counted. I couldn't imagine, as a young case officer, that I would ever run the Directorate of Operations. But I never forgot Polgar's counsel. For that reason, I felt compelled to speak candidly to Woolsey, Deutch, and Tenet when they headed the Agency. I tried consistently to speak truth to power, although not all directors wanted that.

Deutch was among the most receptive to this candor, and whenever we met I told him what I thought. Deutch also delivered on his promise—he had given me "whatever you want." The job I chose was a traditional Agency career capstone. It was prestigious and, in its own way, highly sensitive, the equivalent of a combat general serving a final tour at NATO. I would encounter one amazing figure after another, some of them secret intelligence officers, others conspicuously on the world stage. I would get a glimpse of what was coming in Iraq. And I continued to share my views regularly with Deutch, giving me input at the highest level of the U.S. intelligence community.

Because the Agency views information about this assignment and my activities there as potentially causing "serious damage to the national security," I cannot write about it. So be it.

Early on, from this new perch, I'd had a chat with Fred Hitz, the Agency's inspector general, when I bumped into him in the basement executive parking lot. I had just finishing reading a draft of his report on the Guatemala controversy involving Terry Ward and Frederick

Brugger. I asked what he thought of the review. "There's no hanging offense," he said. Hitz was a pretty tough inspector general, but his assessment agreed with what I had thought all along. Whatever Ward and Brugger had not told Congress was inadvertent. There indeed was no hanging offense; there was no firing offense; there was not even a major disciplinary offense. Ward and Brugger seemed to be out of the woods, but that certainly did not turn out to be the last word on the incident, as I would learn soon enough.

I was taken completely by surprise when Deutch fired Ward and Brugger for failing to brief Congress on the intelligence report about Colonel Alpirez in Guatemala. Leo Hazlewood, who was then the Agency's executive director, reportedly told a group of station chiefs that it was "a political firing," which greatly upset the employees of the Directorate of Operations and lost the director a tremendous amount of support among the rank and file. Word of all this spread like wildfire through the building and eventually overseas. I explained all of this to Deutch. He was accompanied by his aide, Marine major general Mike Hagee, who later became the commandant of the Marine Corps. Hagee likely hadn't expected such a frank discussion. It was an emotional issue for me because Ward, a longtime colleague, had been devoted to his work and had accumulated a very impressive track record. Even though we had never served together, he represented the best of the service and had put his career on the line in support of our country abroad.

In a voice that was probably too loud, I told Deutch that his decision to fire Terry and Fred could cost him the directorate's support. I have always felt in the intelligence business that there should be no room for a political firing. The CIA simply cannot put people on the line, risking their lives and their families, and then have the Agency say, "It's politically necessary: you're fired." It breaks the fundamental social contract between the institution and its people—namely, if you take the risks, we will stand behind you. It's the wrong business for politically based personnel decisions. Most important, there wasn't anything in the inspector general's report, in my opinion, that warranted a firing, as the IG himself had remarked weeks earlier to me in the CIA garage.

To his credit, Deutch took my comments in stride—he allowed me to speak my mind. Hagee, who looked visibly pained, did not say a word; a strained disagreement between the DCI and a senior Agency officer was not what he had bargained for. We eventually moved on to other subjects and the meeting ended without rancor.

Pat, on the other hand, was still refusing to speak to Deutch for cutting short my stay as deputy director for operations and for the treatment of Terry Ward.

"I'd like to see Pat," Deutch said that evening.

"She won't talk to you," I said. "I understand why you did what you did, but she still thinks you were wrong."

Deutch sent her a gift of a small Agency clock, but Pat did not budge. Not long after that, Deutch and his wife, Pat, invited us to dinner. I told my Pat that it was her call. "It's great that you stood up for me, but I have a job to do, so don't you think enough is enough?" I said. In the end, she acquiesced, and the four of us went out and had an excellent dinner, including, unlike 007, "stirred but not shaken" martinis. Everyone had more than a few laughs—as I remember, at my expense.

As Clinton's first term came to a close in 1996, Deutch had hoped to become secretary of defense. He resigned when Clinton appointed William Cohen instead, leaving Deutch out in the cold. Clinton nominated Tony Lake, his national security adviser, to take Deutch's place. Deutch had made the White House unhappy for telling Congress that Saddam Hussein had not only survived the 1991 Gulf War but also had gained strength in the five years since. His judgment was both true and unwelcome. When Senate Republicans made it clear they would not confirm Lake, he withdrew in March 1997, and Tenet soon became Clinton's nominee, running the Agency as acting director.

Even before he was finally confirmed by the Senate in July, Tenet told me he wanted me to be his deputy director for operations and to start thinking about whom I wanted to be my deputy. But by the time I had traveled back to Washington and we had lunch several weeks later, I sensed something had changed. Indeed, Tenet confided to me that he was under pressure to consider Jack Downing, an experienced officer who had recently retired after holding the distinction of being the only person ever to have served as chief in both Moscow and another denied area. The day before the official announcement, Tenet called me and said he had decided to go in a "different direction"—with Downing.

Soon after being installed as director of the DO, Downing pulled me aside and asked if I would remain in my new position for another year. Downing did not know me well, so I assumed this was Tenet's idea. Ultimately, I told Tenet that it might be time for me to leave the Agency, but I would return and run the Directorate of Science and Technology if it were available. Tenet seemed surprised by my interest, but it became clear in time that he preferred a scientist in the position.

Game-changing technological breakthroughs—the U-2, spy satellites, drones, the Glomar Explorer—had been a big part of the CIA's history of covert action and espionage. I thought technology was moving so fast that it would be exciting to be part of the effort to try to harness it for intelligence purposes. There was a real opportunity to bring technology into the intelligence business. Woolsey, as director, had recognized the intelligence potential of unmanned aerial vehicles (UAVs) and had pushed for the Predator, in the face of what was essentially disinterest at the Pentagon. Tom Twetten, as deputy director for operations, brought the directorate together with the National Security Agency and pioneered special intelligence-collection efforts that fused human intelligence (HUMINT) and signals intelligence (SIGINT).

From the perspective of the Agency, Tenet would become one of the better-liked directors. But he and I had a fundamental disagreement that I assume directly affected his choice. Tenet's view was that the directorate needed to heal after Deutch's tenure, the lingering problems associated with Iran-Contra, the Ames betrayal, and other smaller headaches. I felt we needed to move forward with robust change and not worry so much about healing. A strong intelligence program in and of itself will take care of the healing. We agreed to disagree. I was disappointed he had changed his mind about picking me as DO director, but like so many disappointments in life, this one turned out in time to be good fortune. I really could not have gone down the path with Tenet on "enhanced interrogations" after the September 11, 2001, terror attacks. Nor could I have abided the way intelligence on weapons of mass destruction was handled in the run-up to the Iraq War in 2003. He made the right choice for both of us.

As it happened, I saw the disastrous Iraq War coming. Since the 1991 Gulf War, the Agency had been reaching out to Iraqi exiles all over the world, to size up their contacts and capabilities. I considered it a good thing, in the mid-1990s, that the Agency was just ending its relationship with the well-known Iraqi exile Ahmed Chalabi, who headed an umbrella organization called the Iraqi National Congress. He was an American-educated Iraqi from a prominent Shi'a family whose ambition was to topple Saddam Hussein, ending his rule in Iraq. Chalabi had support in Washington and had gained the backing of the Agency for a time. He seemed to be uniquely capable of lobbying Washington, and indeed, he would say anything that we needed to hear to bolster arguments for intervention. But he represented only one of many Iraqi dissident networks with which the Agency engaged to determine if we had or could develop a robust network inside Iraq.

Chalabi fell out of favor with the CIA and the White House in 1995, after he allegedly plotted an uprising from the Kurdish-controlled areas in northern Iraq that was aimed at triggering a rolling coup inside Saddam Hussein's military. The Clinton administration gave the plan no chance at succeeding and explicitly told Chalabi not to proceed with it. Chalabi reportedly undertook the initiative anyway, only to have the plan upended when the Kurdish leader Masoud Barzani refused to support it. The United States soured on Chalabi, who seemed to have little support and few assets inside the country and was spending his time and money on propaganda efforts to enhance his image in the United States. Ultimately, it was clear that we were paying Chalabi too much for his modest capability. If there were any dissenters on this in the Agency, they were among a few midlevel officers who apparently liked working with Chalabi and found him useful.

Iyad Allawi, another Iraqi exile, by contrast, looked like a more serious player. After the U.S. invasion in 2003, he became prime minister of Iraq. Dave Manners was an experienced and effective officer who worked with Allawi. Manners describes Allawi as a true Iraqi patriot and "the only Iraqi I have ever met who was completely unafraid of Saddam Hussein." This was a significant assessment, considering that Allawi and his wife had been attacked in their Surrey, England, home in 1978 by ax-wielding assassins believed to have been sent by Saddam. Allawi spent almost a year in the hospital recuperating before resuming his resistance activities.[1]

Allawi's role in the operation was to recruit senior Iraqi military leaders and inspire them to defect to Jordan to organize an opposition force in exile. When Manners met with these senior officers, he understood why we had easily defeated them in the first Gulf War. They were not an impressive lot. However, one Iraqi general, Mohammed Abdullah al-Shahwani, was a different story. According to Manners, al-Shahwani was a courageous, hands-on special operations commander who was well respected inside Iraq and inspired devotion in his troops. As a result, he represented a threat to Saddam, and he eventually had to flee to Jordan for fear of assassination. Because special operations units tended to be of a high caliber in Iraq and loyal to their commanders, and because of al-Shahwani's contacts throughout Iraq, he had some promise.

The Allawi/al-Shahwani operation produced a large volume of credible intelligence for the Clinton administration in the mid-1990s, but the Agency leadership remained uncertain as to the reliability and capability of the network they were trying to organize inside Iraq.[2]

One way to establish that network's reliability was to ask its members to follow an instruction that could be verified. Our Iraqi partners wanted us to provide explosives that they could use to take down some of the regime's communications towers. This act would serve multiple purposes: it would demonstrate the network's reliability to Washington, start to degrade the regime's internal security apparatus, and at the same time send a message to the Iraqi army that Saddam was vulnerable. The administration policy makers were not prepared to take the step of using explosives, so with some misgivings, al-Shahwani was asked instead to smuggle in microwave transmission disruptors to his supporters in Iraq so they could interfere with transmission from specified communications towers at a specified time.

Manners noted that the devices looked like something out of a science-fiction movie, hardly a discreet technology. In the end, al-Shahwani's network was able to smuggle in the devices and carry out their instructions—but their operation was compromised and fell apart, and many Iraqi officers lost their lives.

The Agency was right to be cautious about moving forward with the exiles, but there were critical shortcomings from the get-go. Although there was a desire for regime change in Iraq, the funding allocated was minuscule. This type of regime change cannot be accomplished on budgets of $20 to $30 million. In addition, Manners rightly points out that the network probably did not have the forces necessary to make something significant happen as a follow-on. The regime was crumbling around the edges, but these resistance groups lacked the heft to oust Saddam. Still, there was a feeling that this exile operation could be added to a containment operation designed to isolate Saddam, one that included no-fly zones over northern and southern Iraq, WMD inspections, and humanitarian support to the Kurds and others in the north.

Several people involved in the operation point out that it also went on for too long. All operations are perishable, especially when they are not receiving the high-level financial and policy support required for success. Not surprisingly, the Allawi/al-Shahwani program ended in bloodshed when Saddam arrested and executed several dozen Iraqis working with the exile leaders.

No doubt the administration's limited commitment frustrated both the opposition community and the officers in Amman who were working with the Iraqis. What the Iraqi operation brings to light is the inherent tension in covert operations between the more optimistic field officers, who form deep relationships with our partners in-country and who work to piece together operations in challenging and dangerous circumstances, and the decision makers who must view the larger foreign policy landscape from a more detached perspective. During this period, the Clinton administration had several other priorities vying for its attention. It had undertaken a failed humanitarian experiment in Somalia and a successful intervention in Haiti. The ever-present Bosnia struggle and subsequent Dayton Accord were an overriding focus as well. Rightly or wrongly, it is not altogether surprising that the administration decided to pass on the operation and concentrate most of its resources and focus elsewhere.

However ambivalent we were about Iraq and the threat posed by Saddam Hussein, the CIA clearly saw Osama bin Laden as a global terrorist menace in August 1996 when his first anti-American fatwa, "Declaration of War Against the Americans Occupying the Land of the Two Holy Places," was published in *Al-Quds Al-Arabi*, a London-based newspaper. In it, Bin Laden called on Muslims to drive American soldiers out of Saudi Arabia and praised several attacks on Americans, particularly the 1993 battle of Mogadishu that ended in the death of American soldiers and precipitated the U.S. withdrawal from Somalia.[3] For almost a decade, the Agency had been focused on the threat of Islamic fundamentalism.

As head of the Agency's operations in 1994 and 1995, I had brought the noted political scientist Samuel Huntington to Langley to talk with the division chiefs about his theory detailed in a *Foreign Affairs* article titled "A Clash of Civilizations." He argued that the primary fault lines in the post–Cold War world would be cultural and religious. His views resonated with us.

The Bosnia issue was certainly on the front burner at this point, as well. With the end of the Cold War, Yugoslavia had disintegrated along ethnic lines into several republics dominated by nationalist parties. Bosnia and Herzegovina, which was made up mostly of Serbs, Croats, and Bosnians, had slid into a bloody civil war. Although the United Nations authorized a small peacekeeping force for Bosnia, it proved powerless to stop the fighting characterized by violence against civilians on all sides. Scenes of brutal ethnic cleansing by the Bosnian Serb army—particularly in the UN safe haven of Srebrenica—and its four-year siege of the multiethnic capital, Sarajevo, finally induced the Clinton administration to prod our European partners into providing NATO air support for the newly established Bosnian Muslim–Croat alliance. NATO support and U.S. pressure resulted in the Dayton Accords, negotiated at Wright-Patterson Air Force Base in Dayton, Ohio, in November 1995 and formally signed in Paris in December.

Early on in my new post, Pat and I visited London to see my old friend David Spedding, or "C," the secretive head of MI6 with whom I had served in Chile. Pat and I had the good fortune to be David and his wife's guests at the world-renowned Henley Royal Regatta, an annual rowing race on the Thames in Henley-on-Thames, where Sir David had a house. Even as a kid from Philadelphia, I was familiar with the races. Grace Kelly's father, Jack Kelly, was an Irish immigrant's son and a brick-building magnate from Philadelphia. He was also America's beloved oarsman and a triple Olympic gold medal winner who was famously denied admittance to the Henley regatta because he had worked with his hands and was not a "gentleman." His son, Jack, however, was able to even the score by competing and winning in the Henley races years later.

The opportunity was of particular interest to me because as a college student I had briefly rowed out of the Vesper Boat Club in Philadelphia and for the North Wildwood Beach Patrol. I came to the event prepared to sit in the viewing stands with my binoculars to watch the races. But it soon became clear that this would be a social occasion. Thus, we found ourselves stopping by various tents set up for the team clubs and regularly sipping a Pimm's, a British drink that is reminiscent of a mint julep without the mint. The whole event was great fun, especially watching many of the long-graduated alumni of Cambridge and Oxford sporting their school jackets without first having visited their tailors to have the jackets let out. I doubt if Pat and I saw more than two or three races that day. As I often did at such events, I had brought along a camera to take photos to memorialize the day. Early on it was made clear, however, that taking photos was considered déclassé. I was able, nonetheless, to draw Sir David and Lady Spedding into one snapshot, which I treasure as a memento of them and the day.

I also was offered an opportunity to meet the Queen of England. Complicating matters of high protocol was the question of how I would be described to Her Majesty, in terms of my precise function within the U.S. government, but I wasn't worried. I was prepared to take the entire event in stride. She was a British queen and my relatives had had a tough run with her predecessors, but I was prepared to let bygones be bygones. We were eventually met by a formally dressed protocol officer, who described in detail how each of us would enter the room one by one and be introduced to Her Majesty. The women were expected to curtsey, and they were anxious about getting it right. The protocol officer wisely said don't fuss, have fun, the Queen has seen everything at these events, including people placing themselves prostrate on the ground. I was starting to get into the spirit of the day.

When my turn came, I walked properly up to the Queen, who is quite diminutive. She politely asked, "How are my boys treating you?" I took that to mean she knew exactly what my function was in the U.S. government. I then heard a loud squeaking noise coming out of my mouth, saying, "Wonderful, wonderful!" I couldn't believe it was me, overly excited by the moment. I don't think my relatives would have been impressed.

As the end of my career approached, I felt a deep sadness, mainly for all the things I still felt remained to be done and the Agency friends and dedicated personnel that I would leave behind. But the time had come to go.

THIRTEEN

Splitting a Steak

New York City and Washington, D.C., 1999–Present

I had a couple of months back in Washington in the summer of 1998 to figure out what I would do with the rest of my life. I had had a wonderful run at the Agency, with many fond memories and very few regrets. I felt I had been a good match for the Agency, and the Agency for me. There was no routine for outprocessing a senior CIA official, no debriefing. I chatted up everyone I saw, but strangely, I was not saying goodbye. The idea of separation had not fully set in, and I was working on the assumption that I would see most of these people again. I had a farewell lunch with Tenet in Georgetown, at the Four Seasons. We talked about our families and reminisced. We talked around the issues of the moment that suddenly were no longer my responsibility. On my last day, I stood on the steps and savored the moment and thought just how lucky I had been for the opportunity to serve my country and the Agency, and to have forged relationships with many fascinating and talented people inside and outside the building.

The CIA had been my family, and my family had been shaped by the CIA almost as much as I had been. Pat had coached me on networking and taken part in surveillance operations. My kids had learned all about cover and discretion and how to speak foreign languages. Many of my indelible memories, some terrifying, some hilarious, involved moments when career and family collided. Flying home once from Santiago after three and a half years abroad, Pat dressed all our girls in similar pink dresses for the homecoming. During a layover in the Miami airport, Pat and I split up momentarily and each of us wrongly assumed the other had our seven-year-old, Megan, in tow. When we reconnected, we both instantly realized the mistake and went into crisis mode. We all scurried around looking for her and engaged the airport police as well. They mistakenly thought a few times that they had spotted Megan in her pink dress, when in reality it was one of her sisters, in pursuit of Megan. While this was of low importance under the circumstances, the airline had already started to board our flight, which only added to the crisis. After about ten minutes, we found our sobbing Megan, who to this day believes I let go of her hand. No matter what really happened, I never take my eyes off any of my grandchildren when they're with me.

Then there was the time, on home leave, between assignments, when I decided it would be a good time to discuss my chosen line of work with my middle daughter, Amy, who was next in line to be briefed. It is always tricky deciding when to break cover and tell your children that you are a CIA officer. You want to catch them when they are old enough to handle it responsibly, but not after they have developed hardened misperceptions about the intelligence world. I tried to break the news to them in their early teens and while on assignment in the United States, where they were not likely to spread the news the next day to their schoolmates. One of my favorite techniques was to do it in a one-on-one trip from Washington to the Jersey Shore. I would wait until we crossed the Delaware Memorial Bridge, which would give me about an hour to handle any of their questions but not allow so much time to overwork it. This ploy worked well until I tried it out on Amy, who was almost sixteen at the time, a bit older than I preferred. When I broke the news to her in the car, she let out a shriek: "You are an assassin?" Not the view that most parents would like their children to have of them. The response caught me by surprise and made me wonder what she was being told in high school. In any case, I used the next hour to walk her through her concerns and to set the record straight. By the time we arrived at the shore, she was back to normal and allowed that, in the end, it might be "cool" to be in the spy world. From then on, I tried not to make the same mistake with the others, namely catching them before they hit their late teens.

My daughters' relationships abroad were never uneventful. I'll never forget my oldest daughter's first date in the Caribbean. Christiane (Kee Kee) was invited to the movies by a very polite boy from her swim team.

We thought nothing about it until we received a call from his mother inquiring who would be "chaperoning" them. We tried to explain that in America we no longer chaperoned teenagers. The mother was amazed and immediately volunteered to—or, more precisely, insisted that she—take care of it. Her son's two aunts would accompany the two kids on the date. So, much like the scene in *The Godfather*, the aunts walked a few steps behind them and sat directly behind them in the movie theater. It seemed to be fun for Kee Kee nonetheless, and made us wonder if this tradition might not warrant a resurrection.

•

Leaving these family memories aside, it was time to go. There were people at the Agency whose emotional and family connections to the place were so intense that we literally had to walk them to the door of headquarters on their last day. Leaving the CIA isn't like saying goodbye at a normal workplace, where you can go back for a visit later. Once you leave the Agency, unless you are under contract or have some specific reason to go back inside the building, you're gone. All the people working inside must by necessity become circumspect when talking to you about their activities. It is unprofessional and imprudent to press them about their work. And if you call and you do not have a specific number, the operator will not put you through. In a very real way, when you retire from the Agency you are cut off from the elite team that you had been a part of for so many years. When I walked out the door, I left all my personal materials behind. I took secrecy seriously, and I walked out without a single piece of paper. It was emotional, but I was at peace with it. I felt pride and loss simultaneously. But it felt right.

Initially, I believed that after three or four years I would not feel the same emotional attachment. But as time has gone by, I've remained more psychologically attached than ever to the Agency, and more concerned about it than I realized I would. I now have a thriving, interesting business, but I still feel the pull of the place. The Agency is critically important to our national security, to preserving our way of life and our system of government. And it's very personal.

In the late 1990s, there wasn't the demand for ex-CIA people that there is today. The world was a more peaceful place, and the corporate intelligence business was in its early days. So job hunting was not easy.

Today it is a different ball game. Virtually every large company is now interested in people who are knowledgeable about intelligence and who have a deep understanding of developments around the world. But back then, I was hardly a hot property; headhunters were not knocking down my door. The one thing I did know was what I did *not* want to do. I did not see myself entering a purely security-oriented field, as I wanted to try to put my intelligence expertise to more direct use. I wanted to see if all the years I had spent gathering intelligence and conducting operations could serve corporate clients who, in business deals and lawsuits, often found themselves confronting adversaries but lacked the ability to understand their motivations and tactics. What seemed like a good opportunity just happened to come my way when the former acting FBI director Larry Potts heard from John Deutch that I would be on the job market and asked if I would be interested in joining him at Investigative Group International.

IGI was one of the early firms to enter the risk management market, and a position to run their New York office had just opened up with the departure of Ray Kelly, who later became the New York City police commissioner. Pat and I were quite enthused about going to New York City. We were urbanites at heart, and I wanted to leave Washington to break the circle of worrying about what was going on inside the CIA, or reminiscing with former colleagues on a daily basis about what used to be. I wanted to see if I could carve out a new existence and reinvent myself, which is sometimes easier to do in a new setting. This position would enable me to do that yet at the same time stay close to what I liked and knew best: intelligence.

About a year after I left the Agency, I was back in Washington and had lunch again with Tenet, at an Italian restaurant in Georgetown. We spent much of the lunch talking about the increased Agency presence in Iraq. I told him I had concerns about our engagement there. Afterward, we had just come outside and were standing on the street when I gave him a warning. This is how he recounts the moment in his memoir, *At the Center of the Storm*:

> Jack Devine, a very able clandestine service officer who was acting deputy director of operations during the John Deutch era, once said to me, "George, somebody is going to fire a bullet

today in northern Iraq, and you are going to find out where it landed two years from now." As I was to learn, truer words were seldom spoken. So many things were going on in such disparate venues and coming at me from so many angles that it was impossible to keep track of everything.

I'm not sure he got the quote exactly right, but he was close enough. What I was saying to George was, "You're now in a high-political-risk environment. A bullet's been fired [he got that right] and you didn't hear the shot, but it's headed in your direction, and whether it hits you in the shoulder or the head, it's impossible to say, but it's got your name on it, and I can't tell you exactly how bad that hit is going to be. But Iraq was a good bet on where the shot was fired." I know what I said had stunned him, because he stood there silent for a few seconds. The truth is no matter how close to the mark I was on Iraq, running the CIA is arguably one of the most difficult—and rewarding—jobs in Washington. The chances of getting out of the CIA as director without a hit are slim— look at everybody who has gone into the job in recent years, whether it's Petraeus, Panetta, Hayden, Goss, Deutch, or Woolsey. At the end of lunch, we went our separate ways. As it happened, the bullet had not yet been fired at Tenet in Iraq, but it would be soon enough.

In the private-sector intelligence business, a core service is anticipating where those hits might come from in the corporate arena. One important tool is pretransaction due diligence (searching for red flags associated with an acquisition target or its leadership). Other core areas of business intelligence and risk management include competitive intelligence (providing information on the market and on competitors) and programmatic intelligence (ongoing monitoring of an issue, region, or event). Inevitably, security issues, both physical and technological, enter the mix, as clients travel and work in dangerous places, and increasingly confront cyber threats. Many assignments fit into the category of tailored investigations and intelligence. For example, searching for specific information about an adversary to strengthen a litigation strategy; or verifying a company's stated revenue, distribution network, or regulatory constraints to test an investment thesis. Finally, there is the ever-present catchall of fixing difficult problems—often involving overseas partners.

Not too long after setting up in New York in early 2000, I found myself involved with David Copperfield, the magician. Copperfield had been performing in Moscow in December 1999 when he ran afoul of his local promoters, including the powerful Moscow mayor Yury Luzhkov, resulting in the seizure of his all-important show trucks. After his representatives' efforts at intimidation and persuasion failed to impress the Russians, Copperfield used his ties to the White House, who in turn suggested that we might help him resolve his problem. Knowing how Russian politics works, I arranged to have a retired KGB officer intervene with his former colleagues, who freed the trucks and provided them with a KGB escort to Finland to boot. We did not trust the Russians, and they didn't trust us, but at least we were all part of the intelligence brotherhood and had a common understanding of operations and human behavior. Later, Copperfield invited Pat and me to his show at the MGM in Las Vegas, where we had front-row seats to his amazing performance.

Another case I was involved in dealt with the provenance of seven fifteenth- to seventeenth-century illuminated manuscripts, and required sleuthing skills not foreign to the CIA. The case dealt with the descendants of two Jewish Parisian art collectors, Georges Wildenstein and Alphonse Kann, who had their art collections confiscated by the Nazis during World War II and later petitioned the French government for their return. In 1996, Kann's heirs claimed ownership of manuscripts on display at the Wildenstein Gallery in New York and sued the gallery. The gallery retained Stanley Arkin, the prominent New York criminal defense attorney and litigation strategist who had successfully defended the CIA officer Alan Fiers during the Iran-Contra investigation.

Stanley wanted to find evidence that the disputed manuscripts had never belonged to Alphonse Kann, and he retained us to find records of the Kann family's inventory. Based in part on our findings, Stanley was able to argue that a French statute of limitations applied in this case, and the New York Supreme Court justice Barbara Kapnick ruled that French law precluded a return of the manuscripts to Kann.

Stanley was delighted with the outcome, but he could not keep from ribbing me about our business development skills.

"Your company is so cheap, you never invite even a good client for lunch," he said over the telephone one day.

"Stanley, I'll buy you lunch."

The last thing Stanley needed or wanted was a free lunch, but it set the stage for an extraordinary relationship.

Soon afterward, Stanley and I went to Maloney & Porcelli, the steak house on Fiftieth Street, near St. Patrick's Cathedral. Just as we were about to sit down, Stanley said, "I have an idea I hope you like. Let's go into business together." He certainly caught me by surprise, but it was an intriguing idea to say the least.

I was growing restless at IGI, and the idea of starting a new firm as a full partner had great appeal. Being partners with Stanley represented just the type of opportunity I had been looking for. The waiter brought our menus, and Stanley wanted to split a steak. I don't normally like the idea of splitting a steak, particularly since I had served in Argentina—the land of outstanding beef and huge steaks. But I was magnanimous. "If there's a business opportunity, I'll split a steak with you, Stanley," I said. That's how our corporate intelligence firm, The Arkin Group (TAG), got started in May 2000: nothing more complicated than a handshake over lunch. As it turned out, that shared steak marked the beginning of, in Stanley's words, "a remarkable collaboration and a strong and supportive friendship." In fact, our offices have been next to each other for the past fourteen years.

Arkin's law firm, Arkin Solbakken LLP, specializes in white-collar criminal defense, complex litigation, and problem solving. The firm has a tradition of zealous representation of individuals and companies in intricate cases. Stanley believes that a legal case, like any dispute, is substantially driven by human emotions, motivation, guile, and a self-interest that may not be readily apparent. A case is, in essence, a story. But the litigation process is also a war, and to do it most efficiently, it is necessary to understand what motivates the other side and to know your adversary. While some lawyers rely solely on the litigation discovery process to determine what happened, Stanley also tries where possible to nail down the details methodically, through investigative work. Not surprisingly, he often turned to investigators to aggressively pursue key pieces of information, but found many of them to be uninspiring and unimaginative—more plodding than savvy. In fact, when I joined him in business, almost no one in this field had a genuine international reach or a well-developed network of international sources. There was a real need for a higher-end product more closely resembling the strategic intelligence and rigorous professional investigations that characterize government intelligence at its best.

Unbeknownst to me, Stanley had long tinkered with the idea of starting an intelligence company. He recognized that there were very few people in the private sector with my intelligence experience, and that together we would make a formidable team. We realized that my Agency experience would differentiate us from competitors, making us more credible on the international stage and enhancing our marketability. Together we saw the potential to put together something unique, a corporate intelligence firm that married Stanley's strategic legal advocacy with my three decades running complex CIA intelligence operations all over the globe. Although the use of intelligence to gain a business advantage is a pursuit as old as commerce itself, the world of global corporate intelligence as we know it today was in its formative days in the beginning of 2000, when we started together.

Stanley grew up in Los Angeles and worked his way through Harvard Law School. After apprenticing and then partnering with a distinguished attorney, Harris B. Steinberg, at age twenty-nine he began his own practice. By the 1970s he was already a prominent New York criminal defense attorney. In one of his important early cases, he represented Vincent Chiarella, a financial printer convicted of insider trading after he scoured confidential documents to glean the names of corporate executives targeted in fraud investigations and used the information to trade stocks. Stanley argued Chiarella's case before the U.S. Supreme Court and won. The Court reversed Chiarella's conviction, finding that he lacked either a confidential relationship or a fiduciary duty to anyone else involved in the stocks he traded. Stanley's prominence grew throughout the financial scandals of the early 1980s, fueled by his aggressive and artful representation of Wall Street executives charged by the SEC with insider trading.

Stanley's practice included difficult and sometimes exotic disputes, which reinforced his use of unconventional strategies alongside litigation. His representation of the international banker and philanthropist Edmond Safra was an example. In 1983, Safra sold his Geneva-based Trade Development Bank to American Express, only to split with AMEX the following year. Fearing that Safra was preparing to compete against them, individuals retained by AMEX executives proceeded to orchestrate a smear campaign against him in the press, peddling lies and misinformation to reporters in Europe and the United States.

Safra retained Stanley to find out who was behind the misinformation campaign. Stanley assembled a team of operatives who tracked the media stories back to AMEX executives. Mounting a counterattack in the press, he published an article in the *New York Law Journal* that nailed AMEX. "Spreading false and malicious rumors or flat-out lies . . ." Stanley wrote, "in addition to likely violating the laws of defamation, may well amount to criminal fraud." Within days, American Express was negotiating a settlement that included a public apology from its chairman, James D. Robinson III.

The matter that brought Stanley into my orbit was his representation of Alan Fiers, who led the CIA's Central America Task Force and played a key role in the Iran-Contra scandal. In May 2000, when Stanley and I formed The Arkin Group, I got a call from Clair George.

"You've gone with the enemy!!" George said without an introduction.

His comment caught me off balance momentarily, especially since I had been focused on the future, not the past—and certainly not on Iran-Contra.

"Clair, Stanley had a legal mission: help Alan, a fellow CIA officer," I said. "He's a highly successful and effective lawyer. He did what he had to do to save his client." Clair went on laughingly to say that he understood but couldn't resist pulling my chain, which he had done effectively. He was tough-minded and politically savvy and had no trouble understanding the realities of Washington politics and their legal ramifications.

Stanley and I quickly got to work building our enterprise and developing a high-quality worldwide network of assets appropriate for business purposes. We were inhabiting a relatively new and poorly understood market space. For the most part, our clients had never used the services of an intelligence firm, and they did not fully appreciate the powerful influence that strategic intelligence could have on critical business and legal decisions. Over the past decade, of course, the corporate world has changed in dramatic ways that have created a robust demand for the type of capabilities we have at our disposal. A new concern about terrorist financing resulted in enhanced due diligence in many sectors, particularly financial. In addition, the Bush and Obama administrations have placed an emphasis on enforcement of the Foreign Corrupt Practices Act. More prosecutions have brought greater attention to the issue of corruption for companies doing business internationally. The truth is it's very hard to keep your house in order when operating in many of these far-flung places with likely corrupt business practices.

Our first step was to assemble a staff. From the start we made a decision that would shape the direction of our company and our business model. Rather than hire people with a narrow regional focus or a particular technical expertise, we recruited very smart generalists who had advanced degrees from top universities, understood international dynamics, had traveled and lived abroad, and had a track record of high performance. Many of our staff have served in the U.S. government in various demanding foreign policy and national security capacities. We wanted people who could communicate with business clients at the senior executive level and ride herd over our eclectic network of intelligence contacts all over the globe.

When we started, our network relied for a while on former American intelligence officers. After several months of using these sources, I realized that no matter how much I liked them, it was important, for reasons of substance and economics, to go directly to the sources on the ground. We soon created a leaner organization by working with local contacts who had direct access to the information we needed. We quickly came to understand that there are seasoned in-country intelligence assets and investigative companies of various sizes and shapes all around the world. Many of our sources came from the local intelligence, legal, media, and law enforcement fields. As we worked more closely with these people, we realized that each one of them had his own network of contacts, which created a multiplier effect for us.

Finding the local intelligence collectors, vetting them, and establishing relationships is what in the CIA we used to call "developmental work." Our network has been painstakingly assembled over the past decade with a firm eye on quality and accountability. We have learned where to look for in-country contacts and how to manage them once they are brought on board. Many former senior intelligence and police officials around the world have set up consulting firms that themselves rely on a pool of contacts and reliable sources in the private sector. At TAG, I made it a habit of joining a number of international associations, where I was able to establish lasting relationships and friendships with a wide range of diverse operators. It is probably no overstatement to say that this core group of several hundred contacts represents tens of thousands of sources around the world. Our network also includes all types of specialists, such as forensic accountants, who follow complex money trails, and a corporate psychiatrist, who can analyze the personalities involved in a business dispute and identify which buttons to push and which to avoid. We have used Navy SEAL and Delta Force reservists for global security. Today there isn't a location in the world where we can't put together a tailored network of resources.

Another resource for identifying reliable sources in far-flung places is the Council of International Investigators (CII). Membership requires more than simply paying annual dues, and candidates are vetted carefully.

One additional valuable aspect of CII membership is the council's conferences and events, at which you can make contacts and get to know potential sources. In October 2012, I participated in a CII conference at a game drive lodge in South Africa, not far from the border with Botswana. It provided an excellent opportunity to catch up with a number of investigative and intelligence contacts worldwide. Some of these experienced private investigators, or PIs, work with us on our foreign cases, obtaining detailed due-diligence records and commentary about individuals and companies of interest to us. This trip also allowed me to meet several of our more sensitive sources in Johannesburg and Cape Town outside the confines of the conference. Most of these sources specialize in the African continent and the Middle East and cover highly compartmented and complicated competitive intelligence issues.

One of the fascinating guest speakers at the conference was the renowned game tracker Ian Thomas, who has taken his lifetime of experience hunting lions and has made it a metaphor for the business world. His talk reminded me of certain aspects of the "good hunting" theme, especially his belief that we can learn much from the hunting approach of lions, which is deeply rooted in teamwork. The lioness's pride (social group) is designed for survival in the bush. Each member of the pride has a distinct and crucial role to play in order to ensnare its prey. Teamwork is likewise a key ingredient of good hunting in clandestine operations.

When we reached Cape Town, Pat and I took a side trip to the Mulderbosch Vineyard, which we helped a client evaluate in the run-up to its purchase several years ago. It is located in an amazingly picturesque location in the wine-growing Stellenbosch Valley. The general manager, Chrianto, and his wine expert, Lucinda, treated us to a traditional South African *braai* (barbecue), which included thick ostrich steaks and wildebeest sausages. These delicacies were accompanied by a wine-tasting session under a large oak tree overlooking the estate. The wines were exquisite, especially the Chardonnay. The taste of the wine and food was enhanced by knowing that The Arkin Group had had a role in its acquisition.

On occasion, a new client will wrongly assume I can reach into CIA files and pluck out classified data. I've never gone back to foreign intelligence contacts for information, and I have never contacted people who I know are CIA assets. To the contrary, TAG's network has been built through challenging cases and the development of new foreign sources.

When traveling, and when circumstances permit, I like to pay a call on local friends as a courtesy and to pass on my well wishes. On a trip to Europe, a highly skilled woman operator was most gracious in coming out to meet me despite her hectic schedule. For an hour we chatted about times past and the challenges facing the world today. We also chatted about the Agency flap in Paris in the mid-1990s that placed a strain on the relations between French and American services. It was good to learn that in the aftermath of 9/11 we had returned to our more traditional, close relationship with our French allies.

I wasn't anticipating or looking for surveillance. However, I did sense there was something odd in the environment, but I let it go, since this was not a clandestine meeting or a confidential discussion. Sometime later, when she was back in the United States, she noted that during the Paris meeting she, too, had thought she detected surveillance, by a French couple seated nearby who were intently trying to eavesdrop. We both had a good chuckle about it. I suspect this was not the first time some of my old friends and foes decided to keep an eye on me, even though they know full well my interests nowadays are commercial.

I had had that same sense that I was not alone when Pat and I were passing through London on vacation some years earlier. Pat and I were browsing in a Camden antiques market when it began to rain. Rather than the typical light London drizzle, this was a New York rainstorm, so we quickly ducked into a store with a one-room showroom and wooden chairs hanging along the walls. Sinn Fein leader Martin McGuinness jumped in right behind us, with two bodyguards in tow, although I did not recognize him immediately. There is indeed a sixth sense that gets honed in the spy business, the feeling that something is wrong even if you cannot immediately spot the problem. This was one of those moments. I instinctively stayed clear of him and did not extend any greeting. I soon realized who he was. For his part, he, too, had spent a fair amount of time in the clandestine world and must have felt something was not quite right with his fellow rain dodgers. For a good twenty minutes, he looked at one end of the hanging chairs, and I looked at the other. There were only a few chairs on each wall, but somehow we both knew that we were not going to have a discussion, even if a bolt of lightning hit the front window. The shop owner must have been convinced that surely one of us would buy a chair, given our intense interest in them. To avoid any misunderstanding, I reported the encounter through appropriate channels. The answer I got back was, "We know."

When starting TAG, right away we had two important cases that helped get the operation up and running. One client was a multinational company that had been massively defrauded by local construction firms in Asia. For good reason, the client suspected that it was being undercut by a competitor in collusion with the local government. We uncovered, deciphered, and analyzed a raft of documentation and found evidence of fraud. Then we cultivated local sources who helped us understand the reputation and business practices of the construction firm. Our client filed a lawsuit, which was ultimately resolved in its favor.

The other was a sensitive case for a mining company with an extensive manufacturing operation in Asia. The client's concern was that it had made a significant infrastructure investment in an area that had become embroiled in civil unrest—a local insurgency, labor strife, student revolutionaries, and unpredictable government rulings. Rather than pulling up stakes, the client had us use strategic intelligence to help it stay in front of events and respond quickly to the unexpected. We put together a network of people on the ground to monitor events and anticipate developments, then passed regular briefings through operatives in Manila and London to ensure operational security. The retainer was substantial in both these cases and allowed us to build our staff quickly.

Another early case that mostly featured Stanley's talents involved his representation of the Russian-born banker Natasha Kagalovsky, who headed up the Eastern Europe Division at the Bank of New York and was one of the most prominent Western bankers in Moscow. The bank had placed her on leave on the grounds that the FBI suspected her involvement in a Russian money-laundering scheme. Although Kagalovsky was ultimately cleared of any wrongdoing, Stanley's initial efforts to negotiate with the bank on her behalf were rebuffed. Looking to create some leverage, Stanley flew to Moscow to meet with a Russian human rights lawyer, who agreed to bring a case against the bank there. Once it was filed, Stanley held a press conference in Moscow with more than a hundred Russian journalists and said he was seeking justice for his client, who had been mistreated by the Bank of New York only because she was Russian. The Bank of New York settled with Kagalovsky shortly thereafter.

Less than a year later, in February 2001, I found myself reflecting on Russian counterintelligence yet again after the FBI discovered that one of its own agents, Robert Hanssen, was the second mole. I had known of a second mole during my final years at the Agency, and had carried this troubling secret with me when I walked out of headquarters. I'd felt a deep sense of regret that I hadn't been able to help apprehend the traitor. All this came flooding back when FBI agents apprehended Hanssen at Foxstone Park in Vienna, Virginia, while trying to tape a garbage bag full of classified data to the underside of a footbridge. His only comment was, "What took you so long?"

Robert Hanssen became an FBI agent in 1976. Three years later he contacted the Soviet military service GRU for the first time and offered his services. He spent more than two decades as a spy for the Russians, working under the pseudonym Ramon Garcia. His relationship with Russian intelligence agencies shifted over the years among the GRU, the KGB, and its successor, the Federal Security Service of the Russian Federation (FSB) depending on his sense of a personal threat to his own well-being and his warped mental state. In the mid-1980s he became part of the FBI's sensitive unit designed to identify Russian spies in the United States. It was an ideal spot for a mole.

During his time working with the Russians, Hanssen did immense damage to our national security. His treachery may have exceeded that of Aldrich Ames. He passed on the identities of our most valuable and sensitive Russian agents, including the CIA penetrators Valery Martynov and Sergei Motorin, who were unknown to Ames. All these agents were later executed. Hanssen also compromised sensitive MASINT (electronic intelligence).

One of Hanssen's more aggressive acts was to compromise the FBI investigation into Felix Bloch, a seasoned State Department official who was under suspicion of being a Russian agent. Bloch had been spotted by French intelligence in 1989 passing material to a known KGB operative. Eight days after that pass, Hanssen alerted the KGB that the FBI was onto Bloch. The KGB officer told Bloch, "A contagious disease is suspected," after which Bloch broke off all further contact with the Russians. While Bloch wasn't prosecuted, the State Department fired him and denied him his pension.

Regrettably, by 1998 the FBI had come to believe that one of the CIA's top-notch counterintelligence officers, Brian Kelley, was the Russian mole. Although I was abroad in the late 1990s and had no visibility into this investigation, it is my understanding that the FBI came to the conclusion that Kelley was one of very few people who could possibly have known about Bloch and the KGB meeting witnessed in France, and that therefore he must have been the one who leaked it to the Russians. For whatever reason, they never turned the mirror inward and looked at who at the Bureau might have known about it, even though by then Hanssen had raised a number of security flags that might have attracted suspicion. Kelley had worked for me earlier in his career. He was a stand-up officer and the last person one would have suspected of spying for the enemy. He had none of the security warts that Hanssen and Ames had. Nonetheless, the FBI put him and his family through the ringer during more than two years of surveillance, wiretaps, and interrogations. Kelley said that during one four-hour interrogation session in 1999, he told his FBI questioners, "Your facts are wrong. Your conclusions are wrong. Your underlying hypothesis is wrong"—to no avail. None of his colleagues who knew him well would have ever included Kelley on a suspect list, as officers had done with Ames.

Hanssen was eventually compromised in November of 2000 by one of the CIA's Russian sources. While the file didn't include his name, all the telltale indicators were there, including audio of a voice that the FBI agents were able to recognize as Hanssen's. From that point forward, the Bureau undertook a very careful investigation of Hanssen, placing him under full-time surveillance. It even smartly had one of his FBI subordinates, Eric O'Neill, download information off Hanssen's Palm PDA, which contained damning evidence of his espionage activities.

In July 2001, Hanssen pleaded guilty to fifteen counts of espionage-related charges and was sentenced to life in prison, where he remains today in Florence, Colorado. The supermax federal penitentiary where he serves his time is the most secure prison in the country, which houses the worst of the worst, including serial killers, Mafia and drug cartel heads, al-Qaeda members such as Zacarias Moussaoui and Umar Abdulmutallab, and domestic terrorists Terry Nichols and Ted Kaczynski. It is a fitting home for the perpetrator of the worst counterintelligence disaster in U.S. history.

When Hanssen's life was investigated in great detail, the picture that surfaced was of a true oddball who had many traits similar to those of Ames, including being the son of a difficult father. Hanssen had a split personality that vacillated between religious zealotry and sexual deviation. Despite his professed religiosity, he had a quirky sex life, to say the least. He made it a regular practice to videotape his sexual activities with his wife, Bonnie, and proceeded to share them with his neighbor, eventually even transmitting these sex tapes via closed-circuit TV.

For his lifetime of spying for the Russians, Hanssen received only $1.4 million in blood money. While this is not an insignificant amount of money, its value is diminished considerably when you consider that it was spread out over approximately twenty years by his Russian employers. By all accounts, the money did not fundamentally change Hanssen's middle-class lifestyle. If he had altered his behavior, it could have been a tip-off to his FBI colleagues. The limited role that money played in his actions is important to keep in mind when evaluating his motivation for betrayal. For Ames, deep psychological dysfunction was the real motivating factor. Both Ames and Hanssen had a deep-seated resentment of their superiors for not recognizing their misperceived brilliance and talent. This was the imperative behind Hanssen's aberrant behavior. This powerful psychological issue, along with his distorted sense of self-importance and narcissism, drove him to become a highly damaging Russian mole against his own country. In its simplest form, it provided an opportunity for revenge and for inflating his ego. Interestingly enough, many of these same vulnerabilities are what CIA operatives look for in sizing up potential targets in foreign governments.

•

Seven months after Hanssen's arrest, with the business Stanley and I had created starting to take off, I set up a meeting with Ken Sagat, a talented lawyer and client with whom we had worked on a number of cases. It was September 11, 2001. As I arrived at our downtown meeting location in a taxi, I noticed a long line of Town Cars pulled to the side of the street, with drivers talking frantically on their cell phones. It was clear something troubling was happening. I asked my driver to turn on the radio, where it was reported that a Cessna aircraft had smashed into one of the World Trade Center's Twin Towers. I was saddened by the inevitable loss of life, but I imagined a very different scenario than the one unfolding. If I had known it was a commercial aircraft, I would have drawn a very different conclusion. Sagat and I reflected on the tragedy and then headed to a nearby coffee shop to discuss a commercial matter in Brazil. We sat down next to a large glass window, one of the worst things you can do in a terrorist setting. Over the next hour, we were in an oblivious bubble as the second of the Twin Towers and then the Pentagon were struck by commercial aircraft. The day would end with four planes hijacked and nearly three thousand people killed in New York, Virginia, and Pennsylvania. We were finally shaken from our conversation when the South Tower collapsed in a thunderous cloud. Executives in expensive suits staggered into the coffee shop covered with dust from head to toe. All around were scenes of sheer terror. Then the second tower fell. It immediately was clear that this was a major terrorist event, and my mind went back to the fatwa that Bin Laden had put out in 1996. I couldn't help wonder if this was his doing. I still did not know what specifically had happened, however. I spotted a bank of pay phones and placed a call to Pat, who told me about the horrific scenes she had just seen on TV. As I walked up the FDR Drive with thousands of other New Yorkers, looking over my shoulder to see those two buildings gone, I knew that life would never be the same for any of us. This event would have an enormous effect on the political, economic, and military life of our country. The full impact of September 11, and the actions taken in Iraq and Afghanistan, and all the actions taken here at home, will not be fully understood for generations to come.

At The Arkin Group, 9/11 and the subsequent mysterious anthrax attacks had a significant impact on our business. Up until then, our clients were mostly concerned about the risks they faced doing business overseas. Now these same clients were concerned about the risks to their companies and families right here in New York. Business continuity and emergency planning are typically the orphan children at the bottom of a corporate manager's to-do list. For financial firms in particular, these issues were now front and center. Quickly we recruited a cutting-edge group of WMD and terrorism researchers and medical experts to help us respond to our clients' concerns. Many of our clients, who could afford to hedge any risk, wanted to know what could be done. At their urging, we evaluated military-grade gas masks, hazmat suits, mail sanitizers, escape vehicles, and pop-up WMD shelters. We mapped out safe locations away from likely terrorist targets and put together a team that could detect biological, chemical, and radiation hazards at public events.

Perhaps our most important contribution to the safety of our clients, however, was to help them institute standard operating procedures so that managers were prepared to take control during a crisis. Much of this training was drawn from my Agency experience. When the H1N1 pandemic flu emerged with such rapidity and uncertainty, we had already helped several companies and law firms prepare for just such an eventuality.

In the immediate aftermath of 9/11, Paul Tudor Jones, the billionaire founder of the enormously successful Tudor Investment Corporation, hired us with a proposition that was difficult, to say the least: securing Madison Square Garden before, during, and after a benefit concert sponsored by his Robin Hood Foundation for 9/11 victims, first responders, and their families. The concert was to be held on October 20, and concerns about another terrorist incident were high. In addition to the World Trade Center attack, New Yorkers had been coping with a series of mysterious anthrax attacks starting on September 18. In his trademark take-the-bull-by-the-horns style, Jones asked if we could provide a system for monitoring the Garden for any traces of radiological, chemical, or biological material. A tall order at any time, it was especially so in the fall of 2001, before companies started to specialize in terrorism and WMD preparedness and response options for the private sector. Luckily, we worked with an extremely adept and well-connected British biomedical research scientist and physician with deep ties to government experts in chemical, biological, radiological, and nuclear (CBRN) detection. With his assistance, we brought in a government-level CBRN monitoring team to work with the professional Garden security team to inspect the heating and air-conditioning system and set up and man high-tech monitoring devices throughout the concert.

A year later, Paul Tudor Jones and Mark Dalton invited me to attend their management conference in the Bahamas to talk to their top investment team leaders about the situation in Afghanistan and the unfolding terrorist challenge. The presentation went well, and I was invited to join them in a game designed to test their strategy and risk management skills. As you might imagine, most of the successful people in this field make money for their investors by smartly developing risk management strategies for investments. As in the Agency, managers must decide on a moment-by-moment basis how much risk they can withstand to gain a meaningful reward. Also as in the Agency, they rely heavily on quality information to make this judgment call.

In the game, financial bets were made with different-colored marble-like balls, with each color representing a different value. The lowest value was white and the highest purple. It was fascinating to watch each team develop its own investment strategies to maximize growth potential. As the game unfolded, in a collegial but highly competitive way, it became clear that while those playing the white ball made a steady modest profit, you could not win without playing the high-risk purple ball.

The lesson applies to intelligence (both in government and the private sector) as well as investment: you can't prevail without taking on strategic risk. It is not enough to play it safe. Thinking back to a mid-career course I attended at the Agency in the 1970s, I recalled that one of the occupation tests showed the highest correlation between my intellectual makeup and that of an investment banker! At the time, I had had no idea what an investment banker did for a living and was surprised that I hadn't correlated closer with the legal, military, or educational profession. But dealing with risks is very much a day-to-day experience in the operational world, and something that prepared me well for the private sector.

A month after the Twin Towers' collapse, Abdullah bin Laden, a Harvard Law School alumnus and Osama bin Laden's half brother, sought out Stanley as an adviser in protecting the Bin Laden family, and its $5 billion Saudi-based construction conglomerate, from a public relations onslaught. Even though a large part of the Bin Laden family was involved in legitimate business and had disowned Osama, it would be a hard sell after the tragedy of September 11, which could have tarnished our brand. Stanley and I declined the offer without a second thought, even though it would have been financially lucrative.

We had no shortage of work. In Russia, our skills have always been in high demand, both because of the enormous investment opportunities and the serious potential land mines. When things go wrong there, investors must turn to a legal system that is opaque and not particularly responsive to foreigners. We employ multiple sources to verify trustworthiness and study the information we are given over time to evaluate the Russians' strengths, weaknesses, and reliability. We often start by giving a source a small case and seeing what he or she produces. Over time, these particular Russian assets have gained our confidence by operating with transparency and consistently producing high-quality work. One of our clients was a U.S.-based technology company with a Moscow subsidiary. When the CEO and his Russian partner had a disagreement over strategy, the Russian partner attempted to hijack the subsidiary. His first step was to threaten our client and imply that he had connections to Russian intelligence. The Russian partner even threatened to have our client arrested if he came to Moscow to try to negotiate their differences. His next step was to use the joint venture's workforce to develop software for a different technology company in his name. In order to shed some light on the validity of the threat, we asked one of our Russian contacts to reach out to local security officers to see what kind of connections the partner actually had. We found that the partner was not affiliated with Russian security.

We were also able to make connections with former government officials, who assisted our client in regaining control of the company. The information we provided enabled our client to reassert his ownership of the company and deal more forthrightly with the partner. However, had my contact been inquiring about a national security matter, we could not have relied on our Russian contact.

Another country fraught with difficulties for the foreign investor is China, where we quickly began handling cases relating to fraud or stolen intellectual property. One of our more intriguing cases involved a U.S. financial firm that had the good fortune to detect the theft almost immediately. The firm's investment strategy was governed by quantitative analysis, so when a Chinese-American employee downloaded the proprietary model that governed the firm's trading strategy onto dozens of hard drives and took off to China, the company's executives naturally were very fearful of the potential damage to the company's reputation and profits. Our client thought the employee might try to sell the information to competitors in China, give it to the government, or in some way exploit it for his own benefit. Either way, it would have seriously compromised their bottom line. With our help they eventually were able to make contact with him, negotiate a deal, and recover the hard drives.

I found during my years at the CIA that it was very hard to surveil someone for twenty-four hours without losing him. Putting somebody under surveillance in a denied area, such as in China, presents a significant challenge. But we developed the capability, working with former police and security officials, to put surveillance on someone quickly anywhere in the United States and in virtually any foreign country.

An interesting aspect of the China surveillance matter was that we used a combination of intelligence and investigative work, much as we did at the Agency during my tenure as chief of the CNC, and this would become the hallmark of TAG's evolving methodology. One of our earliest cases using this methodology involved a client that had developed a genetically altered agricultural product and had attempted to bring it to market in Argentina. The company's executives were not familiar with Argentina, and their representatives in Buenos Aires had advised them to go ahead and plant the crop without going through the government approval process. The company was about to learn an important lesson about national sovereignty. Not long after they planted the crop, their representatives were threatened with arrest for violating Argentine agricultural policies and laws. The client turned to Stanley for help, and he told them, "You don't have a legal problem, you have a government relations problem. You need help from people who can walk you through the appropriate process." Argentina is typically rather friendly toward genetically modified products, but it does not like to be treated as a second-rate power whose rules can be ignored. Through our contacts, we enlisted a former minister of agriculture as a consultant, and the minister was able to guide our client through the process properly and get the necessary authorizations.

Our success building The Arkin Group came as the administration of President George W. Bush seemed to be heading inexorably to war in Iraq. I never understood the White House's obsession with Saddam Hussein, which was clearly draining resources and attention from Afghanistan and the hunt for Osama bin Laden. The brilliant takedown of the Taliban in Afghanistan in the fall of 2001 by the CIA, U.S. Special Forces, and air force and navy pilots, leveraging many of the relationships that remained from the covert operation we ran in the late 1980s, was soon to be squandered. Who could have imagined that the Taliban would reemerge in 2007 while we prosecuted a "surge" in Iraq to keep the administration's war of choice from the abyss of defeat.

I knew the invasion of Iraq was a fait accompli when Secretary of State Colin Powell presented a dossier of seeming intelligence gems to the UN Security Council in February 2003 to make the case that weapons inspections had failed to keep Saddam from developing deadly biological and chemical weapons. The administration wanted UN authorization to invade Iraq and seize Saddam's WMD. While the foreign ministers of France, Russia, and China were not swayed and favored stepped-up inspections, the Bush administration was undeterred. I watched Powell's briefing on the television in the office conference room with some of my staff, and I remember Powell's exhortations vividly. I was surprised to see Tenet, who seemed quite tense and uncomfortable, sitting behind Powell. Apparently his presence was required to symbolize intelligence support for what Powell was saying. I was put off by Powell's presentation because it felt more like an attorney's theatrical courtroom argument than an objective, independent intelligence analysis. Powell held up a small vial that could easily hold a teaspoon of anthrax. Less than a teaspoon had thrown the U.S. Postal Service into chaos a week after the September 11 attacks, Powell said, while Saddam had yet to account for 16,500 liters of anthrax. When I returned to my office, I expressed my unhappiness with Powell's presentation to Rob Thomson, a senior staff member. While we were dissecting what Powell had said, a call came in from a former seventh-floor CIA colleague. He thought Powell's performance was terrific. "They will rue the day they made it," I said of those in the Bush White House. My old colleague seemed baffled by my skepticism, which did nothing to dampen his enthusiasm.

At the time, I believed Saddam Hussein had weapons of mass destruction. However, as I had been reminded by some of my UN contacts, weapons inspectors had been to Iraq years earlier and had witnessed the destruction of many weapons. Not all the so-called weapons of mass destruction were accounted for. Consequently, my assumption, like that of my UN contacts, was that some remained, but less than the administration was alleging. In any case, I did not see the immediacy of the WMD threat and felt it had been hyped. We could have addressed Iraq with force at any time, and we should have let the inspectors complete their mission. Then, as now, I believe we should have kept the focus on Bin Laden in Afghanistan and continued to monitor the situation in Iraq until we had a better fix on the amount of weapons and Saddam's intent.

By June 2003, two months after U.S. forces easily toppled the Iraqi regime and sent Saddam into hiding, furious efforts to find Iraq's weapons caches had turned up nothing and the full dimensions of this intelligence failure were beginning to emerge. A year later, Powell was pressing the CIA for an explanation of how the intelligence it had assembled for him had proved so flawed. I don't give Powell a pass on this. He was a sophisticated consumer of intelligence and had spent a great deal of time being briefed on all the CIA material. He was smart enough to know that he was serving as a pitchman that day at the UN Security Council.

In July 2004, portions of a classified review by the Senate Select Committee on Intelligence were released that were critical of the CIA for its prewar intelligence. The committee revealed, as noted earlier, that the Agency's most compelling intelligence, about the existence of mobile biological weapons labs, had come primarily from an Iraqi defector in the hands of German intelligence whose code name was Curveball. It was subsequently revealed that doubts about Curveball had been circulating inside the Agency and that CIA officials supposedly tried to warn Agency leadership and Powell of this on the eve of Powell's UN presentation. When I learned of the Curveball story, I was incredulous. I still cannot believe that the White House went with Curveball's information as its primary intelligence. And if there truly were officials inside the Agency with grave doubts about Curveball, they should have done everything in their power to keep Powell from using that intelligence at the UN, including filing formal written protests, which as far as I know do not exist. I remain baffled by the Agency's action on this, and I'm still not confident that I know the full story.

•

One of TAG's more satisfying domestic cases involved our work in 2004 on behalf of Peter Kalikow, a New York real estate magnate and former owner of the *New York Post*. Kalikow, who was chairman of the Metropolitan Transit Authority at the time, had become the subject of an unusually damaging smear campaign in the New York press. Someone was wrongly portraying him as being in serious financial turmoil by placing phony full-page legal notices in *The New York Times* and the *New York Post* listing all his four-hundred-plus creditors from a decade-old bankruptcy proceeding. The phony notices urged the creditors to call Evergence Capital Advisors to seek further restitution, claiming Kalikow had failed to make full disclosure at the time of the bankruptcy. The claim was false, but that did not stop creditors from hiring lawyers and calling Evergence. Kalikow retained Stanley, and thus TAG. Through meticulous investigative work, we were able to trace the ads back to the New York attorney Marc Dreier, who had placed them on behalf of a

Kalikow rival, Sheldon Solow. Strangely, Solow's gripe was that he had loaned Kalikow $7 million during Kalikow's bankruptcy and Kalikow had paid it back too early! Dreier himself turned out to be a sleazy character who would later be sentenced to twenty years in prison for defrauding hedge funds and other investors—ironically, including Solow—of $400 million by selling them phony promissory notes. In this instance, our evidence was so solid that Stanley and his colleague Randy Mastro of Gibson Dunn persuaded a bankruptcy judge, who called the stunt "tacky, shabby, base, low, malicious, petty, nasty, unsavory," to fine Solow and Dreier $335,000.

Another TAG client, the National Basketball Association, had occassional overseas issues. A particularly delicate matter involved the review of Mikhail Prokhorov, a Russian billionaire bachelor who had agreed to pay $200 million for an 80 percent share of the New Jersey Nets and a 45 percent stake in the team's new arena in Brooklyn. The case proved extremely complex and challenging, beginning with Prokhorov's arrest in January 2007 by French police in Courchevel, an opulent ski resort in the French Alps, reportedly on suspicion of providing his guests with prostitutes. He was released four days later, with no charges filed, but the episode allegedly led the Russian government to pressure Prokhorov to sell his 26 percent share in Norilsk Nickel, the largest nickel producer in the world, to his business partner. Speculation swirled in Moscow that Prokhorov had been set up in Courchevel, though French police said they had been investigating Russian prostitution at the resort for some time. Despite the colorful publicity, extensive research revealed that Prokhorov had no ties to organized crime and that his financials qualified him to become an NBA owner. He took control of the Nets in May 2010.

In the summer of 2007, the NBA asked us to investigate a referee who had been accused by his neighbors of petty harassment. The FBI later discovered through wiretaps that the referee had placed bets on NBA games through a high school buddy, leaving no discoverable signs of his gambling activity. Commissioner David Stern rightfully noted—as the CIA had found with Aldrich Ames and the FBI discovered with Robert Hanssen—that rogue employees can betray their organizations and engage in criminal activity despite the best compliance procedures. As a result of this incident, Stern tasked TAG to develop, along with the

NBA, a robust vetting program for all referees. With the referees' cooperation, we reviewed them annually for red flags that might indicate a vulnerability to gambling.

•

My life in the private sector has been immensely gratifying, but I still find ways to weigh in on issues of concern. As far afield as my new career took me at times, my attention never strayed too far from Iraq, Afghanistan, and the intelligence wars in Washington. I suppose it was force of habit and continued allegiance to the cause. You never really emotionally leave the CIA.

In August 2004, after the 9/11 Commission issued its report roundly criticizing both the FBI and the CIA and calling for the creation of an intelligence czar, the director of national intelligence, to bring the nation's warring intelligence agencies together, I wrote an op-ed piece for *The Washington Post*. I thought the idea was a bad one then, and it's a bad idea now—another costly layer of bureaucracy that has grown so large that its ability to fulfill its original mission is highly suspect. During a follow-on *Washington Post* Web chat in August 2004, I sounded what would become a consistent refrain of mine: focus on killing or capturing Osama bin Laden.

Starting in 2003, I began periodically contributing op-ed pieces to *The Washington Post*, *Financial Times*, and *The Miami Herald* on intelligence reforms. From 2006 to 2008, I served on an advisory panel established by Secretary of the Navy Donald Winter to rethink the capabilities of naval intelligence. Also, because of my role at the Agency Counter Narcotics Center, I was invited in 2012 by the Council on Foreign Relations, of which I'm a member, to serve as the "presider" over a presentation by the director of the Office of National Drug Control Policy, Gil Kerlikowske, entitled "Paradigm Shift: Efforts to Reform Drug Policy."

Earlier, in August 2009, I had served on a panel on private-sector intelligence at the National Press Club with former CIA director Michael Hayden and Michael Chertoff, former homeland security secretary, both of whom were also in the private sector. That morning, *The New York Times* ran an important front-page article on how the CIA had used a contractor, Blackwater USA, to take part in a "lethal" covert action to find and kill al-Qaeda members, which raised questions about accountability in such highly sensitive operations. The issue was obviously relevant to the panel, and I addressed it head-on in my remarks.

I explained that after spending a third of my life and almost all my adult years at the Agency, I had a significant investment in that institution. "I spent thirty-two years in CIA, and when an autopsy is done, you're going to find that part of my heart contains the CIA's stamp." I went on to share my conviction that the *Times* article reflected a huge historical shift that had not—and still has not—been fully appreciated. For the majority of my career, if you mentioned the word *assassination* inside the CIA, you were immediately castigated. An assassination does not necessarily resolve the issue, and in many ways may make the problem worse. I had attended a meeting several years earlier with the DDO at that time, who said he wanted to fire all the contractors because of the sharply increasing outsourcing of traditional DO work. It is my conviction that sensitive HUMINT operations should never be outsourced. As for the assassination program, I told the audience at the National Press Club that day, "It's alien to my experience, and I'll leave it at that."

•

In the fall of 2009, I learned that Charlie Wilson was near death. He had had a major heart operation several years earlier, but now his medical situation had deteriorated. Like many of us who had worked on the Afghan program, I had a soft spot for Wilson and I wanted him to know how I felt as the end approached for him. When I called, I was surprised how chipper and optimistic he was about his health. We made a date for a December dinner at Sparks Steak House, in the East Forties in Manhattan. Charlie loved Sparks. It was where the Mafia don Paul Castellano was shot and killed while leaving the restaurant, and the historical drama associated with the place appealed to Charlie. In late November, I received a call from his wife, Barbara, a lovely former ballerina. They would have to postpone our dinner, she said. I knew what this meant and was deeply saddened. It was the end of an important chapter in my life.

Charlie Wilson died in February 2010 at seventy-six of a chronically bad heart. He had served twelve terms in the House, from 1973 to 1996. The man had such charisma, energy, and passion for life that I could hardly believe he was gone. Not long afterward, I was invited to attend a memorial service for him at the House Appropriations Committee Room in Washington. I welcomed the opportunity to pay tribute to him and his great service to our country. The room was packed when I arrived, but it seemed I was the only one there from the CIA, which was too bad, given Wilson's history with the Agency. Milt Bearden and Frank Anderson would have been there for sure, but they were in Kabul. Charlie's old friend Gust Avrakotos surely would have been there as well, but sadly he had died in 2005.

Many of Wilson's former assistants were there, tearful about their loss. They clearly admired Charlie and were proud to have worked for him. There were several members of the House Appropriations Committee present as well. Each felt compelled to eulogize Wilson, but the best eulogy that day was a video taken of Wilson in 2006, which played on a large flat-screen TV, muted while others spoke. He looked full of life, and he was delivering a great speech, talking about the importance of bipartisan foreign policy and why that had been a key aspect of the successful Afghan program. How right he was.

Back in New York, Stanley and I began negotiating what would become Madison Intelligence. We began the partnership in early 2012 with the former head of Mexican intelligence, Jorge Tello. Several years ago, Tello and I reestablished a friendship when we serendipitously met in a New York City elevator. Madison provides strategic intelligence services to Mexican companies and international firms doing business in Mexico, and its success is another indication of the ever-growing demand in the corporate world for sophisticated intelligence. I had also been serving for several years on an advisory board established by the Mexican secretary of public security, thanks largely to my background as former director of the Counter Narcotics Center and chief of the Latin America Division. The final meeting took place in Mexico City in early June 2012, with heavy police presence everywhere we went. The police clearly did not want to lose any of the foreign guests to an armed attack by drug traffickers. President Felipe Calderón gave the keynote address at the event and took time to have a brief sidebar discussion with the advisory board members. The Mexican government was looking for foreign input on tackling its cartel problem, but more important, it was hoping for international support for its efforts.

Another part of the business that has really begun to flourish is our use of tailored and strategic intelligence to test a trading or investment strategy, particularly in emerging markets. Emerging markets represent a fertile opportunity for TAG because they are an enormously dynamic driver of the global economy while at the same time ranking low on corporate transparency. When firms invest in U.S. publicly traded entities, they implicitly rely on the policing powers of the SEC and the open press to encourage companies to provide accurate disclosures and auditing statements. However, publicly traded companies from developing markets aren't subject to the same scrutiny or policing, which creates a huge incentive for them to lie. Surprisingly, it is only recently that the financial industry has become fully aware of the enormous risk of fraud inherent in developing economies, including the Chinese market. Risk associated with Chinese public companies listed on the U.S., Canadian, and European exchanges was placed in stark relief when the short-selling firm Muddy Waters Research put the Toronto-listed Chinese timber company Sino-Forest Corporation in its crosshairs in the spring of 2011. Muddy Waters accused the company of greatly exaggerating its landholdings and its profits. Sino-Forest filed for bankruptcy in March 2012 and was placed under investigation by the Ontario Securities Commission in May 2012, which inflicted enormous losses on investors such as famed hedge fund manager John Paulson. As of May 2014, the OSC proceedings remain ongoing.

Sino-Forest was able to pull off the fraud because entities that should have conducted rigorous due diligence accepted Sino-Forest's falsified information reportedly without kicking the tires hard enough on the ground. For one client, we took a close look at a publicly traded Chinese green energy technology manufacturer whose ability to sell extremely low-cost solutions seemed too good to be true. What we found was a viable entity with a big factory and many employees. But when we looked at its supply chain, we discovered that it was buying a critical raw material at a significantly discounted below-market rate from a state-run company presumably being kept afloat by government largesse. We also found strong indications that the company was using a series of Hong Kong–registered shell companies to siphon off shareholder value to the benefit of family members. As the client suspected, this was not a commercially viable entity.

In order to protect ourselves and our clients from the threat of inadvertently passing along insider information in these types of cases, TAG pays close attention to our sources of information. As a fail-safe, we filter all our findings through Stanley's law firm, which has considerable familiarity with the relevant rules regarding insider trading and a deep background in financial securities matters. As far as I know, other investigative companies have not developed similar structural safeguards.

Many of our clients are well-known business leaders who have interesting lives. From time to time, we are able to kick back and enjoy social time with them. A few years ago, Stanley and I were invited to the Louisiana bayou for a weekend of fishing and duck hunting at the hunting lodge of our client Jim Bob Moffett, chairman of Freeport McMoRan. On the first morning, long before daybreak, we headed out to the duck blind to await the arrival of the ducks. I wasn't having much luck, and our host gently chided, "I brought along all this ammunition. Use it up." Not to miss the point, the next time a group of birds headed in our direction I got off the quickest round of shots. To my chagrin and the chagrin of the bayou lads, I had blasted out of the sky not ducks but off-season birds, which everyone thereafter assured me were New York teal (ducks)—presumably to fend off the game warden and save me embarrassment. I have no doubt my duck-hunting skills were a subject of great humor around the campfire.

I've always been able to laugh at myself. One of my clients wanted to introduce me to Roger Waters of Pink Floyd because Waters was keenly interested in developments in the Near East. The client asked if I had heard of Pink Floyd. Of course, I responded. My first thought was of a guitar player all dressed in pink. After hanging up, I immediately Googled Waters and realized that I had had him confused with Prince, who was usually dressed up in flashy purple attire. I didn't mention this to Waters when I met him, but my children and staff in the office were incredulous about my lack of hipness. Along these same lines, I was once invited, during Fashion Week in New York, to meet with the famous clothes designer Elie Tahari about a complicated business matter. I fortunately checked him out before the meeting and had a good understanding of his prominence in the fashion industry ahead of time. Pat certainly knew who he was and decided she would make sure I was properly attired for the event; her selection included a French cuff blue shirt with a white collar. I arrived a bit early and refrained from eating any of the breakfast treats set out, for fear of staining my tie. I did, though, try one blackberry from the fruit bowl. And apparently I touched my white collar afterward, leaving two purple fingerprint-size stains on either side. When Tahari entered the room, he immediately spotted the faux pas and had his staff scurrying to repair the damage, which only heightened the embarrassment.

Even back in my CIA days, dealing with foreigners was not always hard work and occasionally you had the opportunity to laugh at yourself. From time to time, you get to socialize with your counterparts under interesting circumstances in special locations. Such was the case one evening when Richard Dearlove and his wife, Roslyn, joined Pat and me for dinner at the popular River Café in London. At that time, the restaurant was a very hot location because it had received a glowing write-up in an upscale New York magazine, and everyone was clamoring to get in. The waiting list was several weeks long. To speed up the process, I invoked the U.S. ambassador's name (with his permission) and was able to get on the three-week list!

Not long after we were seated, none other than James Bond, in the person of Sean Connery, and several companions came into the restaurant and were ushered discreetly to a corner table. Roslyn and Pat, almost like teenyboppers, began making a fuss and insisting that we introduce them to Connery, or at least get an autograph. In a moment of hubris, either Richard or I had the silly notion to point out "that we were the real 007s." This brought loud, derisive cackling from the women: "You have to be kidding. There is only one 007, and he is sitting in the corner with his friends." Appropriately humbled, we beat a retreat and were relieved when the check came.

Years later, I had a chance to tell this story at Lyford Cay in the Bahamas. A friend and client, T. J. Maloney of Lincolnshire Management, asked me to give a talk at his exclusive club, noting that Connery was a member. As a tease, he said he thought Connery would attend and join us at a small dinner table after the talk. True to his word, 007 patiently listened while I regaled the audience with the story of how we had spotted him at the River Café. I'm not sure he found it as ironic as I did, but he was a good sport about it, and we had a delightful dinner together discussing Scottish politics and the making of his movie *From Russia with Love*.

In the spring of 2010, I was invited to the Sixth International Conference of the Paris Forum for Europe, the United States, and the Middle East. I was one of two keynote speakers, along with the former French foreign minister. I also participated in a sharp-edged panel discussion that touched on U.S. efforts in Iraq, Afghanistan, and the Middle East. I was satisfied with my performance, fielding, as diplomatically as possible, questions on potentially explosive issues, especially relating to Israel and the Palestinians.

As I exited the stage, I caught up to Pat, whom I rely on to give me my most constructive feedback. I asked how she thought I had done parrying the tough questions. With a mischievous grin, she responded, "You mean sitting up there with your big Irish legs showing above your socks!" Besides producing a pronounced laugh on my part, it brought me a more grounded view of the event. But she allowed that I had done pretty well carrying the American flag in the back-and-forth with the French and Middle Easterners.

About a month after we returned from that trip, in June 2010, President Obama fired General Stanley McChrystal as commander of the war in Afghanistan for comments he made in *Rolling Stone* magazine, and replaced him with General David H. Petraeus. Around the same time, I wrote a rather controversial op-ed for *The Wall Street Journal* saying the military effort in Afghanistan was flawed and should be replaced with CIA-led covert action. I had seen firsthand the Soviet military fail in Afghanistan, and we were making the same mistakes. Afghanistan is a collection of tribes, not a functioning state, and relationships need to be forged with tribal leaders, not the corrupt and ineffectual government of Hamid Karzai.

A smart covert action program should rest on worst-case scenarios. Afghanistan will likely enter a period of heightened instability leading up to and following our planned departure, so we should figure out now which tribal leaders—and, under specially negotiated arrangements, which Taliban factions—we could establish productive relationships with. We must also consider the possibility that our departure could precipitate the eventual collapse of the Karzai government. Thus we should cultivate relationships with leaders inside and outside the current regime who are most likely to fill the power vacuum.

WHERE IS OSAMA BIN LADEN? was the headline on another op-ed I wrote for *The Washington Post*, in October 2010, in which I argued that finding Bin Laden must remain our number one priority, something that didn't seem pressing at the time.

I also felt that the delicate matter of our relations with Pakistan seemed to underlie our unwillingness to find Bin Laden at all costs.

I had the opportunity to press Pervez Musharraf, the former president of Pakistan, on the issue when he spoke to the Council on Foreign Relations a month later. After listening to him talk for more than an hour, I raised my hand to ask a question. "Mr. President, do you believe Bin Laden is in the North-West Frontier?" I said. "And if so, after nine years, why is he still on the loose?"

"My guess will be as bad as your guess," Musharraf responded on the record. "I don't know, and that's an honest fact . . . Intelligence is doing its best. And when I say intelligence, intelligence is human intelligence, which ISI has in abundance. It is technical intelligence, which you have in abundance there, in that area, in Pakistan. And then it is aerial surveillance, which is—only you have . . . The military, the CIA, all intelligence, is doing their best. And I don't know whether he is dead or alive, and whether he is in Pakistan or in Afghanistan, or maybe he's gone somewhere. I don't know. I can't say." His answer was made up of equal parts "officialspeak" and double-talk.

The world learned six months later, shortly before midnight on May 1, 2011, where al-Qaeda's leader had been hiding, after members of Navy SEAL Team 6 stormed a heavily fortified compound in Abbottabad, Pakistan. They opened fire on four occupants until they found Osama bin Laden, code-named Geronimo. The raid was conducted under Title 50 authority of the U.S Code, which allows the U.S. government to conduct covert actions, or "deniable" missions. The CIA director, Leon Panetta, headed the chain of command, which went from him to the commander of the Joint Special Operations Command. Bin Laden was killed by shots to the chest and the forehead, above his left eye. The raid was the culmination of a CIA operation years in the making.

It began with efforts to penetrate a network of couriers who serviced Bin Laden.

When I heard about the killing, I was delighted. I had been talking, and writing, about the importance of this takedown for ten years. In fact, I and a handful of former DDOs had had lunch with Panetta a year prior and I'd asked him why it was taking so long to get Bin Laden. I'm sure he and his subordinates were equally frustrated. Nevertheless, this is what I thought we should have been doing from the beginning— not nation-building but getting this terrorist.

President Obama addressed the nation on Afghanistan in early June. The Taliban's momentum had been arrested, and our focus was squarely on al-Qaeda. It was time to start bringing the troops home— ten thousand by year's end, and all thirty-three thousand surge forces the president had committed at the end of 2009 by the end of summer 2012. America's mission would change from combat to support. I'd been arguing for years that a large U.S. military presence in Afghanistan would not be successful, as a large Soviet presence had not been. And now President Obama was in effect shifting strategies and turning the mission over to the CIA and U.S. Special Forces.

In August 2011, shortly before General Petraeus retired from the army and officially took over the reins of the CIA, Clair George died at the age of eighty-one. He was a spy's spy, and one of the best of the generation of Cold War officers who joined the Agency in the mid-1950s. It's bitterly ironic that he remains the first high-ranking CIA officer to be found guilty of felony charges committed during the conduct of his official duties. His pardon on Christmas Eve 1992 before his sentencing kept him from ever serving time, which was at least some measure of justice. He always maintained his innocence and never let his conviction diminish his joie de vivre or his loyalty to the CIA. As I told a *Washington Post* reporter writing George's obituary, "If you wanted Paris, he'd send you to Somalia, and when you were done in Somalia, he'd send you to Paris . . . He wanted to know if you were a committed operator, or are you a dandy who wants to be pushing cookies around the diplomatic circuit? That's how he sized people up." I thought it was telling that, in his retirement, George worked as a volunteer suicide prevention counselor, helping man a hotline in his basement. A memorial in October 2012 for him at St. Alban's Parish in Washington was a special moment for me, although bittersweet—the passing of an authentic warrior and leader who regrettably had to end his career when he got caught up in the political morass of Washington. Throughout it all, he kept his positive disposition, his allegiance to his subordinates, and an affection for helping young people.

George's memorial service brought me together with many former bosses, men also now in their seventies and eighties. I couldn't help but reflect on my own place on the actuary charts and think about my own mortality. I left the service that day feeling proud of the CIA and the men and women who had served. I felt fortunate to have been part of its history.

I went back to Langley again in the late summer of 2012 to attend a retirement ceremony for Justin Jackson, a senior officer who had my old job of associate deputy director of operations before he left the Agency.

The headquarters building at one time was almost elegant in the simplicity of its lobby. But now I see some new ornament on display almost every time I visit. To the left of the high-tech turnstile that slides open for cleared visitors, the hallway is adorned with formal portraits of all the directors. I've worked with more than half of them. To the right, toward the special room where they hold retirement ceremonies, hang paintings of auspicious moments in CIA history, including the first Stinger shootdown by the mujahideen in Afghanistan. I felt a twinge of pride that day as I walked past the painting and went inside the room for Jackson's retirement.

In a forty-five-minute ceremony that was warm and rich with fraternity, Jackson received the Distinguished Intelligence Medal. Members of this good hunting club, past and present, don't come together often, and I was in no hurry to leave. Eventually, though, it was time for a meeting with Petraeus, and a woman from protocol came to take me to the seventh floor. We rode up in the director's private elevator, for which I once possessed a key. Petraeus sat at the head of a conference table in his office. We had kept in occasional contact since we had dinner the prior summer, right before he took over. We looked outside at the thick woods that surround the Agency's vast complex and talked for about a half hour.

Three months later, I was stunned when Petraeus abruptly resigned and acknowledged having had an extramarital affair with Paula Broadwell, a West Point graduate and Reserve army officer who had written a book about Petraeus's years in command of the war in Afghanistan. I'd developed a good relationship with him, so it was particularly painful to watch a man of his distinction lose his job and much of the stature he had gained during his career as a four-star general and theater commander over this incident. He had all the qualifications necessary to excel on the seventh floor at Langley, although it wasn't clear to me how he had actually connected with the Agency's senior leaders. I happened to attend a meeting with them a week following his resignation, and it was clear to me that they had already moved on. The CIA is a tough, resilient place after all it has weathered over the years. Obama had just been reelected, names of possible new directors were being floated around town, the Republicans and many others remained in high dudgeon over an attack on the U.S. consulate in Benghazi earlier in the fall that had cost the life of the U.S. ambassador and three aides, as well as contractors, and the Agency needed to reexamine its priorities now that the wars of the past decade were ending.

Following his reelection that fall, Obama named a man I had come to know well, John O. Brennan, to lead the CIA during the president's second term in office. I had worked with Brennan back at Langley when he served as George Tenet's executive officer; he later became a chief of station in the Middle East. I had always considered him to be a smart, serious-minded, dedicated officer who loved the business. Even in an institution that has a culture of putting in very long hours, Brennan stood out as a workhorse. He was one of the few career professionals who rose to the top of the Agency, joining the ranks of Helms, Colby, and Gates. He'd spent twenty-five years at the CIA, serving in both the Intelligence and Operations Directorates. His last post was chief of the National Counterterrorism Center (which is separate from the CIA's Counterterrorism Center) during the administration of George W. Bush. He has stated publicly that he had no role in overseeing the administration's enhanced interrogation techniques—waterboarding and other forms of torture—and commented at the time that he did not agree with such methods. An Arabic-speaking analyst by training, he is an expert in the Near East.

My relationship with Brennan was passing in nature, until he left the government and we worked closely together as board members of a publicly traded defense contractor. We worked together again during Obama's campaign for president in 2008. Brennan served as chairman of Obama's intelligence committee, and I was a committee member. The press referred to us as "spies for Obama," which was hardly the case. Nevertheless, he developed a close relationship with Obama's key campaign staff. In fact, Obama offered Brennan the CIA directorship, but Brennan withdrew his name from consideration because a number of human rights groups opposed him as a result of his role as former head of the National Counterterrorism Center.

I had drinks with Brennan in a Washington area hotel shortly after he withdrew. He was hugely disappointed, but he remained determined to return to the government and serve the Obama administration. We talked about his fallback offer to serve as an assistant to the president for homeland security and counterterrorism. He recognized the heavy burden of such a task for him and his family but decided to accept it nonetheless. For different reasons, I also thought it was a smart move; I had seen the ball bounce before and felt that the job very likely would put him in contention for the DCI spot the next time around. I also had seen how much Bob Gates grew as a result of his time working in the White House as a national security adviser and how effectively he was able to parlay that experience when he became CIA director and, later, secretary of defense. I shared this view with Brennan at the time, and I now feel that history has played out very well for him.

I congratulated Brennan after his confirmation as CIA director in March 2013 and told him that the "fun" would begin immediately. He responded that no one had yet suggested that the top CIA job would be fun. Having served on the seventh floor with a number of DCIs, I understand how gut-wrenching the job can be at times, but there are few places where you can have a significant impact on world events and better serve your country. For me, that is fun. And I'm sure that, in time, Brennan will agree. These are trying times for the CIA, and Brennan's broad experience at the CIA and the White House will serve him, the Agency, and the country very well indeed.

One critical attribute that Brennan and all other CIA leaders possess is the right temperament for intelligence. A spymaster's life is not for everybody. It requires a special psychological makeup that allows him or her to work in the dark world of betrayal and to engage in actions, sometimes lethal, that often irrevocably alter lives, governments, and history. By necessity, it demands a highly compartmentalized mind that can box off multiple conflicting ideas, emotions, and behaviors. On the one hand, the spymaster must hunt for and manipulate potential agents into betraying their country while maintaining a fierce loyalty to his own country and value system. Similarly, the spymaster must undertake foreign-policy-directed covert action operations against our enemies in the uncomfortable gray area of morality and principle while maintaining all the while a rigid black-and-white standard of legal rectitude within the CIA culture. As a result of a mixture of DNA and life experience, I felt that I fit this profile snugly and survived and thrived as a spymaster and covert action operative for many years.

I worried about the CIA for years after I retired. In the aftermath of 9/11 and the harsh criticism that came from the intelligence failure in Iraq and the waterboarding of al-Qaeda terrorists, I found myself despairing. Would the Agency's critics succeed in dismantling the nation's Central Intelligence Agency and fritter away its exquisite capabilities, its unique contribution to statecraft? The new intelligence czar, the director of national intelligence, had usurped both the president's daily brief and what had been the DCI's coordinating role among intelligence agencies. I had come to realize, and publicly stated several years ago, that the Office of the Director of National Intelligence was, for the most part, a redundant bureaucratic overlay. Over time the office has diminished in importance and influence. Because the CIA retained the 1947 charter that authorized "special activities" (covert action), in the end it wasn't much of a contest. With the nation fighting dual wars in Iraq and Afghanistan as part of a global struggle against terrorism, the White House needed the Agency more than ever.

On October 25, 2013, I was honored to receive the Hugh Montgomery Award from the OSS Society at a black-tie gala for eight hundred at the Ritz-Carlton in Washington. It is rare for a former CIA operative to receive any award in a public forum. The main event of the evening was the presentation of the Donovan Award to Admiral William McRaven, head of the Joint Special Operations Command, who directed the raid on the compound in Abbottabad, Pakistan, in which Osama bin Laden was killed. The award is named for General William J.

Donovan, founder of the OSS, forerunner to the CIA, during World War II. In his acceptance remarks, McRaven gave a forceful presentation in support of Special Operation Forces. "Not since World War II has there been such a lethal combination of intelligence officers and special operations warriors," he said. "Not since the fight against Hitler have we had such a talented group of government civilians, intellectuals, businessmen, writers, philosophers, engineers, tinkers, tailors, soldiers, and spies." He delighted his audience by saying, "I'm here tonight to tell you that the OSS is back!"

The night before we had chatted at a smaller dinner about the same thing. McRaven noted that the Joint Special Operations Command had grown significantly and he underscored the military's close working relationship with the intelligence community. When he visited CIA headquarters for the first time, he told me, he was struck by just how many senior officers had worked closely with him in the past. This was a good indication of how much things have changed since 9/11.

In my brief acceptance comments, I noted my good fortune in having met former OSS heroine Virginia Hall when I first joined the Agency. I mentioned Hall earlier for her exploits behind the lines in World War II when she helped organize the French Resistance, eventually becoming the most wanted spy in France. I told the audience that I marveled then and now at her courage, grit, and patriotism. I went on to note with more than a little pleasure that when you walk into CIA headquarters nowadays and look to the right side of the atrium, you will find a portrait of the first Stinger shootdown of a Soviet helicopter in Afghanistan juxtaposed next to a painting of Virginia Hall pumping out clandestine messages from a safehouse somewhere in central France.

In my remarks, I said that "covert action will prove to be the most important tool in our national security arsenal in the complex and unstable world that confronts us today." Finally, I bid farewell to old and new friends with the phrase they knew well: *good hunting*. Since that night, I have reflected often about Admiral McRaven's view that "the OSS is back" and his assertion that Special Operations Forces represent the future. That judgment is far from certain.

First, the OSS was created during World War II as an extension of the U.S. military forces opposing the Axis nation-states of Germany, Japan, and Italy. That's not the national security world we live in today.

After we exit Afghanistan in late 2014, it is most unlikely that we will be involved in another land war in the foreseeable future. Instead, we will continue to face stateless terrorist groups often in insurgency environments where we may or may not be welcome by the local governments. Ideally, we will be able to work with friendly host governments in providing equipment, training, and intelligence to eradicate the insurgents.

Second, despite DOD planning to the contrary, the sixty-six thousand U.S. Special Operations Forces will need to be reduced substantially, since most future paramilitary engagement will be reminiscent of the smaller Cold War covert actions programs. These programs were operated by the CIA with a small agency staff overseeing surrogate forces under its Title 50 authority. In the past, the U.S. military supported these efforts by "seconding" military personnel to the CIA, where they operated under a clandestine civilian umbrella. This practice of "detailing" soldiers to the Agency should be reinstated, especially since our Special Operations Forces have developed such impressive war-fighting skills as a result of their lengthy engagements in Iraq and Afghanistan. This is the covert action world we will live in. Before the decade is out, especially as the U.S. military gradually returns to its more traditional strategy of preparing for potential conflict against hostile nation-states, the CIA should assert its traditional authority and take the lead in conducting political, economic, psychological, and, at times, armed covert action.

Three days later, I found myself on a mixed panel of actors and intelligence practitioners discussing the reality of the popular television show *Homeland*. The panel included Nazanin Boniadi, who costars as the Muslim CIA analyst Fara Sherazi; Navid Negahban, who played the terrorist mastermind Abu Nazir; and John Miller, a former senior official with the FBI and the Office of the Director of National Intelligence who now serves as the NYPD deputy commissioner for intelligence. After a preliminary session with the actors, we were on Showtime's temporary set at the downtown Sheraton Hotel responding to questions from a live audience. Three interested me most: How authentic is the show? How good an actor do you need to be as a CIA officer? And can someone like Carrie Mathison (played by Claire Danes) with bipolar disorder work for the CIA as a top operative?

The high-end technology portrayed in the movies typically exists, but what that technology is capable of accomplishing is often exaggerated, sometimes wildly. But it is surprising to have watched over the years how these over-the-horizon technical capabilities have become part of our real inventory. Edward Snowden's leaks in 2013 exposing the National Security Agency's ability to vacuum up millions, even billions, of e-mails and cell phone calls is a reminder of just how robust American information collection has become. Early in my career, I had disdain for what I thought was Hollywood's trivialization of a deadly serious business. But, with the advantage of time and understanding, I began to appreciate that almost all Hollywood characterization adds to the mystique of the CIA operative and becomes a significant recruiting draw to bring top-level young men and women to the Agency. This seeming omnipotence also makes it much easier to deal with foreign counterparts and agents, as well as potential agents.

The question about the similarities between professional actors and CIA operatives is intriguing. I never considered myself an actor, but as I began to dissect the question I became more and more engrossed in just how much acting skill is required to be a spy or spymaster. The most obvious parallel is that when you are working literally in a false identity and alias background in a foreign setting, you have to become someone else. Also, on the psychological level you must conceal your true feelings when trying to recruit unsavory characters and sometimes upright targets. You are constantly manipulating the environment and the target as if onstage. This is also true in working with counterparts in foreign governments who do not share our values or commitment to civil rights and personal liberties. An operative often must adopt a more cordial and understanding persona than reality would normally warrant. This question even produced a vivid flashback of me telling the Haitian chief of police to get out of his town. On that occasion, I had to conjure up a very stern, no-nonsense personality who oozed sinister traits. I must confess that I enjoyed the role. When you return home you need to cast away the mask and return to your true identity and personality. Acting is very much a part of being an effective operative.

As to whether someone with bipolar disorder could work as a case officer, it is worth remembering that in 2008 bipolar disorder was officially declared to be a disability that would not bar employment in the U.S. government. There are "excepted service" positions in certain high-risk jobs (the Navy SEALs, for example) for which mentally or physically handicapped personnel may not qualify. However, this condition and the associated medicines would have to be declared at the time of employment—something Claire Danes's character, Carrie, does not do in *Homeland*. Nonetheless, I would point out that when I first joined the CIA in the late 1960s, bipolar disorders were not classified as such, and as I think back on the colleagues I worked with through the years, I don't doubt that there were officers at all levels in the Agency who had this disability, and functioned at the top of their game. So while Carrie the rogue operative is out of focus, the concept of bipolar personnel serving in key positions is certainly well within the range of the possible, as it should be. The U.S. intelligence service needs to be a reflection of its people, which includes gender, minority, and disability diversity.

Much has changed in the world since I reported for duty at the CIA years ago. But much has stayed the same. The Agency can still speak truth to power. It can still steal enemies' secrets. It can still run covert operations that Ian Fleming would envy. We have proved we are fallible, to be sure. But we've also proved we are an indispensable force. Riding down from the seventh floor in the DO's elevator after my last meeting with the DCI, its trim still colored with tiny red squares, I felt a surge of pride, confident that the CIA would, to paraphrase William Faulkner, not just endure, but prevail.

FOURTEEN

Good Hunting

New York, 2014–

The role of the CIA and its covert programs in the post-Iraq and -Afghanistan world will be critically important to our national security, and there is no shortage of other seriously troubled countries around the world that will require our attention for years to come. Given the supposition that the United States will not put large numbers of troops on the ground again anytime soon, with the possible exception of Syria and Iraq, and that the defense budget will be cut significantly over time, it is axiomatic that we will need to find a smart way to protect our interests abroad if we wish to stay involved globally and exercise our power for America's benefit and defense. Thus, one of the key strategies by necessity in the future will be an enhanced use of covert power. As we proceed down this path, we must be mindful that these activities are carried out in a responsible and effective manner. I view successful covert action as having six common characteristics. These are principles that decision makers need to keep in mind as they consider whether to commit the United States to a particular covert action.

1. Identify a legitimate enemy. To be successful, covert action must be in the U.S. national interest. This means that it is directed against a legitimate enemy of the United States or an "intrinsically evil" force that should be driven from power or influence. In this regard, it is useful to distinguish the target of the covert operation from the venue in which it takes place. There is no reason the CIA shouldn't conduct covert action in nonenemy territory if it is in the service of action against a legitimate enemy. This will continue to occur across the world, in peacetime and in war. Policymakers tend to forget that almost all covert action eventually comes to light. Thus, there will be hell to pay if a program does not align with our values and interests, as we have seen in the case of the enhanced interrogation program. This is also a reason to be cognizant of the trade-offs between short-term gain and long-term consequences. If something is expedient in the short term but looks like it may turn out to run counter to our interests over time, policy makers should be very wary of making that trade-off, and not only because they may be held accountable later for damage to national security or our global reputation.

2. Determine on-the-ground conditions. We should never undertake any covert action that does not have a reasonable likelihood of success. Thus, our goals must be consistent with reality on the ground. We cannot expect to achieve our objectives in any country where the environment is not suitable for intervention. We must be diligent in avoiding the myth that "all it takes is a spark" to overcome a nasty foreign policy problem. This myth, which essentially states that covert action can instigate change by simply setting the wheels in motion and allowing the United States to step back as history unfolds, has been the source of many blunders in U.S. foreign policy, and still looms large in our government's decision making today. I have provided many examples of such strategies falling flat, beginning with the Nixon administration's premature attempts to overthrow President Allende of Chile in 1970. Without the support of the Chilean military and population, no amount of U.S. covert activity or influence would have convinced Chileans that Allende was not the man for them then. We had to wait for the circumstances to bring the Chileans around, helping out where we could to preserve the opposition. This is exactly what our role should be where the time is not right: we can provide support to a movement, but we can't spark one that isn't there.

3. Ensure adequate funding and staff. Successful covert action requires robust funding and personnel levels that match policy goals. Otherwise, we are not only putting our people at risk and wasting valuable resources but also dabbling in potentially counterproductive activities that could have serious unintended consequences. This shortcoming has been a key reason for many failed covert programs in the past, including the initial attempts to overthrow Saddam Hussein in the 1990s with a vastly inadequate budget. Not only did this program consume significant time and effort and result in lives lost, but it also ultimately empowered a group of exiles who were neither trustworthy nor representative of the on-the-ground reality in Iraq, and who in later years reportedly helped bolster the misinformation campaign that supported the U.S. invasion in 2003.

4. Find legitimate local partners. It is tempting to ignore the need for having viable partners in place. Prominent exiles may have the ear of important political figures and policy makers who believe that exile communities can help them achieve their political goals. However, exiles, by virtue of their distance, are rarely in a position to marshal significant forces within their homeland or provide accurate intelligence on the situation in real time. A base of operations contiguous to the target is critical—London, Paris, or Washington won't do. Moreover, prominent exiles have their own agendas that may not correspond to our own once action gets under way. An effective covert action must have partners within a host nation who share our goals and objectives and are willing to fight and die for their cause. Relying on exiles is a recipe for miscommunication, blunders, and often disaster.

5. Determine proportionality. If the objective of a covert campaign is to eliminate or displace an enemy (for example, to drive the Soviets from Afghanistan), there is a maximum cost in lives and resources that is proportional in the moral and patriotic sense. When covert action is not in concert with American interests and values, whether in purpose or cost, we start to veer into dangerous territory. As mentioned earlier, at some point almost all covert action activities become public, and disproportionate activity that seemed reasonable on the drawing board will be hard to defend in the light of day. History has shown this again and again, so policy makers should never mount an operation that they can't justify to the public.

6. Acquire bipartisan political support. When considering whether to move forward with an initiative, this is among the most important considerations, since all foreign policy, even if it is not public, should support the values of the American people. If elected officials in Congress do not or would not think something is a good idea—Iran-Contra is an obvious example—then it should be abandoned.

Moreover, if the above conditions are met, bipartisan congressional support will be much more likely to follow. Although only very few members of the Senate Select Committee on Intelligence and the House Permanent Select Committee on Intelligence have access to programmatic information about covert action, it is critical that these elected officials specifically charged with authorizing and funding these activities believe our programs are in the national interest and consistent with their constituents' objectives and values.

Returning to the theme of what national security will look like in the years ahead, it is a pretty good bet that there will be a steady pull toward military neo-isolationism in our body politic. The tension between those advocating robust international engagement and others advocating isolationism is as old as the republic itself, appearing as early as George Washington's Farewell Address in 1796. America today is war-weary and wants its troops home and the funding for recent wars redirected to domestic growth. Specifically, when I speak of neo-isolationism, I'm referring to a much-reduced and streamlined military presence abroad and a domestic policy focused on improving our economy, particularly reducing unemployment. If handled properly, this shift could actually enhance our national security. After all, no nation can expect to be taken seriously for long from a weak economic base. Having said this, the United States must remain engaged in this globalized world through the use of its "soft power"—political, economic, and intelligence activities.

Now is the time we need to take a second look at our overarching strategy. The Cold War is long behind us, and our new enemies are less likely to be nation-states, with the possible exception of Iran and North Korea. The new world pits us against threats from asymmetrical special interests, terrorists, and localized interest groups, not to mention economic and political challenges such as the impending bubble burst in China and the fallout from the Arab Awakening. As a consequence, we will need to adjust our foreign policy strategies, our use of the armed forces, and our intelligence community to meet these changing strategic threats and challenges in the years ahead.

The Uneven Tide of Islamic Extremism

Without question, terrorism will remain the key national security threat to the homeland and will have to be dealt with tactically and fiercely. But, compared to the decade following 9/11, terrorism will begin to decline as a driver of U.S. foreign policy and world events, particularly after the Islamic State of Iraq and al-Sham (ISIS) is neutralized, which it surely will be. Unfortunately, achieving ISIS's defeat may take more time and energy than the U.S. would like to exert.

The deadly Jan. 7, 2015, attack on the offices of satirical newspaper *Charlie Hebdo* once again drove home the fact the West cannot expect the violence brewing in the Middle East to stay within the borders of Iraq or Syria. The growing threat from ISIS and affiliated organizations and their stated objectives regionally and toward the West is simply too serious to be ignored.

Thus, the unfolding circumstances in Iraq and Syria, where ISIS controls vast swaths of terrain, will almost certainly delay a badly desired pullback by the U.S. and its allies from engagement in the Middle East until the terroristic force is destroyed or neutralized. Despite their war-weariness and the economic costs, the American people should understand and support this action, and even support putting significant U.S. boots on the ground if needed, a scenario the aggressive nature of ISIS makes increasingly imaginable.

There is little doubt covert action should be the first line of defense in this scenario, as it should be in most conflicts. And a good number of the conditions outlined above are present here. One is to have viable partners in place. However, you are never able to collect the data needed to understand who your real partners are until you roll up your sleeves and jump into the fray.

In the case of the Syrian rebels, we have a group reportedly willing to fight and die for the ouster of Bashar al-Assad, in addition to defeating ISIS, but our unwillingness to forcefully target Assad has compromised our ability to ally with enough of them. Once we demonstrate this policy more clearly, the number of rebels with which we can potentially partner will substantially exceed the 5,000 the U.S. is committed to training for their fight against ISIS. If we are to succeed in the administration's plan to use the rebels as a proxy, we must be willing to take the fight to Assad, not just ISIS.

Another part of having viable partners in place in an undertaking of this magnitude is to have the help of regional allies. Taking the fight to Assad will also enable the U.S. to better solidify the vital support of two critical allies, Turkey and Saudi Arabia. The Saudis, playing a long game to battle Iran's influence in the region, have also been pushing for the U.S. to do more to bring down Assad, a key Iranian ally.

It is also important we meet the condition of committing adequate resources. As of early 2015, our air attacks against ISIS have been too limited. And American efforts to recruit and train 5,000 rebel fighters from the Free Syrian Army is unlikely to produce a game-changing force, which should be at least three times that number. To unseat ISIS we will need a force at least equal to its strength—reportedly between 15,000 to 30,000 combatants. It will only be possible to recruit such a force if we fly under the anti-Assad flag.

Finally, as discussed above, in order to have a reasonable prospect of success, policymakers must have a clear objective and believe that accomplishing it is possible. The administration is trying to thread the needle of beating back ISIS in Iraq and preventing further gains in Syria without taking the fight to Assad. This defensive strategy in Syria amounts to an ongoing bloody stalemate and is unlikely to sustain the support of the public, Congress, allies, or the fighters on the ground.

If this robust effort fails and we are unable to mobilize an effective force to destroy ISIS, and particularly if it follows through on its threat to take the fight to our homeland, then the administration must ready a backup plan of putting a major U.S. and hopefully allied force on the ground to finish off ISIS. This is unwelcome news for a war-weary nation and beleaguered U.S. military, but it is the reality that our country and our leaders face.

If these recommendations are heeded, by the end of this decade, ISIS, al-Qaeda, and their cohorts will be neither the strategic threat we once feared nor comparable to the threat of the Soviet Union during the Cold War that jeopardized our existence, government, way of life, or economic prosperity. That said, weapons of mass destruction in the hands of even relatively small enemies could have a devastating impact on America's sense of security. Similarly, these groups would represent a renewed challenge to our national security if they were able to mount a campaign of ongoing low-grade terrorist events such as bombings, shootings, and cyberattacks against the U.S. and its allies, which so far they have proved incapable of doing or unwilling to do.

A strong case could be made that al-Qaeda and Osama bin Laden reached their high-water mark on 9/11, since they have not been able to pull off a major terrorist event in over a decade and have not carried out even a minor attack against the U.S. homeland. Since 9/11, large-scale international terrorism has actually been a remarkably unsuccessful tool for terrorist groups and their political affiliates. It has brought military and covert action upon their safe havens, restricted their access to assets and finances, led governments to hunt and kill their leaders and adherents, and generally decimated their ranks. So, while al-Qaeda and its spawn will continue to disturb our security for the foreseeable future, they need not be the overwhelming focus of our national security policy as we go forward.

Rather, a long view suggests that terrorism, as an instrument of power, will continue its decline and become a much less serious strategic threat to the West as we reduce our presence abroad. Much of the credit for this can be given to U.S. and allied militaries, intelligence agencies, and law enforcement, which have greatly improved our defenses and abilities to detect terrorist planning. Al-Qaeda itself is also responsible, due to its propensity to slaughter Muslim civilians, for undermining its own ability to garner deep support in the Muslim world.

The Graveyard of Empires Endures

The Middle East and South Asia, the regions with which terrorism has been most closely associated, will continue to be critical for the United States. Afghanistan, Pakistan, Iraq, and Syria in particular will continue to be important battlegrounds for a struggle that will continue for many years. But the context will not be the one that Harvard professor Samuel P. Huntington anticipated almost twenty years ago in his *Foreign Affairs* article "The Clash of Civilizations." Huntington believed that the diversity of peoples, culture, and values would be the leading cause of conflict in this century, and suggested that the West would almost certainly confront the Muslim world as our most serious adversary. After the 9/11 terrorist attacks, Huntington seemed to many to be right on target. However, today this inevitable "clash" seems far from certain. Rather, just as the United States will increasingly isolate itself from broad international conflicts, the nations of the Middle East and elsewhere will increasingly focus on their own internal problems. U.S. engagement with them will become a much more subtle prospect—and one that is better suited to covert action than overt military activities.

With that in mind, there is little doubt that a major withdrawal of Western powers from Afghanistan will lead to instability and possibly even civil war. As Whitney Kassel and I wrote in the *World Policy Journal* in September 2013, the NATO drawdown is "likely to be followed by a civil war between a predominantly non-Pashtun security apparatus and Pakistan-backed Taliban forces."[1] It is clear that the Taliban and other Islamist groups, such as the Quetta Shura and the Haqqani network, will gain ground and sow unrest as U.S. and NATO forces subside. The government of Afghanistan is on the whole far too weak to stand up to these groups or their Pakistani sponsors, although international pressure will likely ensure that, in the near term, Karzai and his successor, Ashraf Ghani, maintain some level of control over at least Kabul, if not the major urban centers of the country.

It is unclear to what extent the future government will allow or prevent elements like al-Qaeda to reestablish safe havens in Afghanistan. Most of the leadership of al-Qaeda and other major international terrorist networks already resides in Pakistan, so until Pakistan becomes less hospitable, they are likely to remain in place. But an Afghanistan in which the United States has little influence or visibility will remain a haven for extremist groups that can threaten the United States and our allies, much as in the 1990s after the Soviet withdrawal. This is why it is critical that we maintain a residual presence, albeit covert, for as long as it is feasible—including some military advisers, a limited counterterrorism capability, and, most important, a robust covert action and intelligence infrastructure—to ensure we do not lose track of what is happening in this important and dangerous country.

As noted earlier, I argued in *The Wall Street Journal* in July 2010 that "we should figure out now which tribal leaders—and, under specially negotiated arrangements, which Taliban factions—we could establish productive relationships with" and that "we should cultivate leaders inside and outside the current regime who are most likely to fill the power vacuum."[2] I can only assume and hope that we are doing this in some form, and that we have put ourselves in a position to ramp up covert activities with tribal leaders should it appear the Taliban is overwhelming other factions or liaising with al-Qaeda after our withdrawal.

Pakistan's role in Afghanistan will soon be the least of Americans' concerns in the broader context of our relations with Pakistan, which poses perhaps the most imminent threat to U.S. national security. Frayed relations between the United States and Pakistan have very dangerous implications, including decreased U.S. counterterrorism options and the increased potential for conflict between India and Pakistan, including a nuclear exchange. This makes Pakistan one of our most immediate challenges and one that has more significant long-term strategic importance than the outcome in Afghanistan. While international terrorism will likely continue to decline gradually, armed groups in Pakistan remain one of the most likely sources of an international attack against Western interests. Our declining ability to conduct robust counterterrorism operations inside Pakistan as a result of deteriorating bilateral relations could prove devastating if even one major attack is successful.

Thus, we need to remain focused on maintaining good relations with the government of Pakistan and attempting to keep that country from falling into greater disrepair than it has already found itself, even after our withdrawal from Afghanistan. Like it or not, we need the Pakistanis if we are to protect our interests across the region, including counterterrorism and nuclear security.

Unfinished Business in Iraq

Like Afghanistan, Iraq will remain high on our list of priorities. Less than five years after our last troops withdrew, we are sending in hundreds of advisors to help fight against ISIS, along with a barrage of air strikes. The Shi'ite leadership, though less divisive than under Prime Minister Maliki, now holds little to no legitimacy in the eyes of its Sunni majority, a reality that has fueled the dramatic rise of ISIS and its seizing of vast amounts of territory since mid-2014. It is clear the Iraqi Army will not be able to defend much of its territory against these terrorists, even with the assistance of various militias and international air support and training. Whether the international community will see fit to further engage on the side of Baghdad and Erbil to reestablish Iraq as a viable state remains to be seen.

Tied to the outcome with ISIS is the extent to which Iraq aligns with Iran, which will also bear strongly on the regional balance of power, as will the outcome of American and European nuclear negotiations with Tehran. The potential for a Western-Shi'a alliance against Sunni extremists like ISIS, while appealing, could easily lead to growing discontent on the part of the Sunni world at large, an extremely dangerous and unpredictable outcome for everyone.

In any scenario, I do not anticipate a democratic state of the sort originally envisioned by President Bush and his advisers. Tragically, nearly forty-five hundred American casualties and more than a million service tours were unable to secure that result for the Iraqi people. Instead, the best we can hope for in Iraq in the next several decades is decreased violence and enough stability to foster economic growth.

Key to America's understanding and ability to influence the Iraqi government's balancing act will be maintaining a robust intelligence infrastructure. This is all the more important now that our overt presence has been vastly reduced, at least for the forseeable future. Overall U.S. influence in Iraq is going to continue to decline, regardless of our boldest attempts to preserve ties with subsequent governments there or of our current assistance to help them oust ISIS. But that does not mean all is lost. While the details of any intelligence infrastructure in Iraq will of course remain classified, it is safe to assume that we will continue to maintain a presence there to monitor the worrisome rise in Iranian influence, ISIS and al-Qaeda activities, and an unstable political situation that is further inflamed by divisions over the disposition of natural resources.

Gambling with the Ayatollah

Iran is another country that could further destabilize the region if we're not careful, though for very different reasons. The situation there is quite unlike what we are leaving behind in Afghanistan, and the strategic game being played goes beyond the subtle tribal and political issues that will dominate U.S. engagements in many other parts of the world. Even with a more liberal president in Hassan Rouhani, the Islamic government of Iran will continue to wage a rhetorical war, making the United States, Israel, and our allies extraordinarily nervous. And if an Iranian nuclear capability is our chief concern, then we absolutely should be worried, because in spite of U.S. and allied efforts to stymie Iran's nuclear program, the Iranian regime will eventually obtain a nuclear weapons capability, even if it isn't fully weaponized. And while the current efforts to negotiate a deal are worth a try, the stakes are high, and in the case of failure, the risks of escalation will shoot up dramatically.

Estimates vary as to when Iran will actually succeed in obtaining a nuclear weapon, but overall most experts agree it is likely to have capability to produce the bomb within the next few years, assuming the current accord to freeze enrichment in exchange for temporarily reduced sanctions does not significantly impact the pace of the program.[3] While Iran has borne serious economic and political costs for its unwillingness to cooperate, it is clear the regime is intent on eventually developing a nuclear weapon capability. The Iranians probably see little chance that anyone will launch a large-scale attack to stop it as long as it keeps such a bomb disassembled. The unwillingness of the United States and, to a lesser degree, Israel to initiate steps toward a preemptive strike surely underscores this assessment, and I happen to agree that an attack is ill-advised. At the same time, nonmilitary efforts, such as sanctions, have not arrested Iran's overall enrichment program, although the argument could be made that such efforts have delayed weaponization, and kept Iran at or near the negotiating table.

There is nevertheless a dangerous potential for miscalculation—an attack by Israel or, worse, the United States. Given Iran's continued antagonization of the international community, the threat of an attack against it is unlikely to deter the program sufficiently as to stop its progress. In the event of an attack, Iran would likely decentralize even further its program and further disperse its facilities and scientists, which would only delay the creation of a nuclear weapon. Such an attack would also have profound negative consequences, including instigating a decision by Iran's leadership to weaponize (or accelerate weaponization), legitimizing Iran's narrative in the eyes of the international community, and bringing regional players further onto the side of Iran. Thus, any efforts to deter Iran from pursuing nuclear weapons are unlikely to succeed in the long run.

The Iranian regime has used demonstrations of foreign aggression to garner internal political support and justify its bellicosity toward Israel, the United States, and the West in general. Thus, it is almost certain that overt action against Iran would amplify the regime's message and reduce the potential for actual political change. Covert action and sustained, robust intelligence collection therefore remain the preferred tools to delay the development of an Iranian nuclear capability.

But again, Iran will almost certainly, at some point, achieve some version of that capability, despite what may appear to be a temporary lull. Fortunately, the reality of an Iranian nuclear capability may be less cataclysmic than many observers predict, as it could create a Cold War–like stalemate in the Middle East based on mutual deterrence. Of course, an ascendant Iran would be problematic for other reasons, including its ability to influence the domestic political balance in neighboring states such as Syria and Lebanon. We are already seeing both Iran and Hezbollah play a significant, destabilizing role in the Syrian and Iraqi civil wars, additional conflicts that call for substantially enhanced U.S. covert action, for all the reasons outlined in this book. In the long term, continued Iranian support to groups such as Hezbollah could prove a more enduring and sophisticated threat than an Iranian nuclear capability.

This is not to say the United States should not seek to do everything possible short of war to prevent or slow Iran's nuclear program. We should continue to gather information on and interfere with the program covertly while using overt means such as sanctions and diplomatic pressure to raise the cost to Iran of its weapons program. But we should be under no illusion that these actions will have a decisive effect, and thus should focus our efforts in such a way that when Iran achieves its goal, we have the greatest possible influence in the region and can encourage regime change in Iran.

We should position ourselves now to encourage and take advantage of trends toward liberalization within Iran. This includes robust intelligence collection, the establishment of a flexible and responsive network of sources within the political opposition, and the cultivation of potential leaders within the Iranian diaspora who could help govern Iran if and when the current regime collapses.

Putin's Miscalculation

From South Asia to Iran, the Middle East to China and Russia, the United States faces a range of challenges that, while resembling past problems in certain important ways, will test our ability to understand our adversaries' intentions and react to them. Understanding intentions will be a critical piece of this fight, as will the robust use of covert action to influence and affect events abroad while staying lean and "under the radar."

The United States is stretched so thin militarily that we will refrain from projecting sufficient military might to prevent Russia from broadening its influence in Ukraine. Moreover, economic threats are unlikely to significantly alter Putin's position on that country.

This is especially true because Putin and the Russian people believe their national security interests are at risk and are willing to use force to preserve them. Ukraine is important to the United States, but it is not vital and has not been seen as such by the American people. Putin understands this and will stay the course, working to lessen the impact of our political and economic actions while striving to survive dramatic fluctuations in oil prices.

In addition, the Russians will continue to use overt and covert muscle to undermine the government in Kiev and likely those of other states in its former sphere of influence. We should be alert to this and try to check them, including via covert action, but short of using force.

One sign that despite his protestations, Putin is very much on the wrong side of history, is the recent restoration of U.S.-Cuba relations. A last vestige of the communist ideology, Cuba is finally being brought into the Western/free market fold, ironically setting an example for

Putin himself. As I wrote in *Politico* in January 2015,[4] the dramatic shift in U.S.-Cuba policy is a long overdue development on its own terms, but it also has implications that go well beyond this hemisphere.

With this opening in Cuba, Latin America can turn its back on the stale communist ideas and socialist arguments of the past, and the U.S. can finally free itself of an unpleasant leftover from the Cold War. But it is also a message to Putin, who as an old KGB officer knows well what it means to lose Moscow's old Havana listening station in the Americas. Nostalgic for the past and Russia's place in it, the Russian president spent the last year trying to reposition Russia as the counterweight to the United States and the West.

The contrast between President Obama's agreement and Putin's behavior could not be greater. Putin may have thought he had a strong hand, but the devastating impact of economic sanctions and dramatically falling oil prices are taking its toll. His popularity will eventually have to bear the cost of a spiraling economic recession at home. The Cuba opening is sending a clear signal to the Russian leader that he is only losing friends in faraway places, not gaining them. We should take advantage of Putin's current weakness to negotiate a reasonable settlement to the Ukraine dispute, which at the time of this writing is only worsening.

The Structure of the Intelligence Community

On the organizational side, there have been several efforts to improve the structure of the intelligence community over the last several years. The most significant of these was the creation of the Office of the Director of National Intelligence (ODNI) in 2005, a recommendation of the 9/11 Commission. In its account of the terrorist attacks, the commission faulted the CIA, the FBI, the military, and other agencies with a lack of information sharing. To ostensibly remedy this situation, the commission proposed the ODNI.

Despite the 9/11 Commission's best efforts and generally accurate findings, the reforms recommended in its report were driven more by political expediency than a clear understanding of the conditions leading up to the attacks of September 11. They were also partially driven by the wars in Iraq and Afghanistan, in which the U.S. military assumed the major role. It was thus unsurprising that the military's purview and power over its own intelligence activities were relatively undisturbed. The CIA's role, on the other hand, was diminished, most clearly in the loss of its long-standing role as the coordinating—indeed, the *central*—agency in the broader intelligence community. Among members of Congress, it was distrust of the CIA, its perceived culpability for 9/11, and its failure to find WMD in Iraq that also helped propel creation of the new director of national intelligence, who assumed the role traditionally played by the DCI as the community's titular head.

The result of the post-9/11 intelligence reforms has been, in my view, a diminished CIA in its traditional role, a muddled new intelligence bureaucracy with less coherence, and more fractured leadership. While it is extremely difficult to roll back any agency once erected by Congress, especially now that the DNI has been running for more than ten years, Congress should revisit its utility and perhaps curtail its staffing and tasking.

Centralization of the intelligence community is a worthy cause, but it should have been done under the CIA, not with an external bureaucracy such as the DNI. When it was created in 1947, the CIA was envisioned as the *central* intelligence agency, and was given a preeminent role within the American intelligence community. Lieutenant General Ken Minihan, who served as the director of both the NSA and the Defense Intelligence Agency in the late 1990s, explains it quite simply: "The C in DCI matters, and the C in CIA matters."[5] I could not agree more. The thinking in 1947 was that the nation needed one agency that would bring together the central disciplines of the intelligence business— espionage and covert action (operations), analysis, and technology— under one guiding hand. Previously, the disparate intelligence functions were dispersed primarily among the various military services, with some additional functions being the responsibility of the Department of State and the Federal Bureau of Investigation.

I continue to believe that the Agency's founding fathers got it right in the aftermath of World War II: the nation needed a strong, central intelligence agency that would bring together core missions so each could influence and enhance the others. Over the intervening decades, however, this vision slowly gave way again to a more dispersed intelligence community. New agencies were added, many of them inside the Department of Defense. This expanded the community and diluted the centrality of the CIA. Many of these agencies specialized in one particular aspect of intelligence collection, such as signals intelligence or satellites or human intelligence for military customers, and this made it somewhat harder to keep all the core missions of intelligence under the guidance of a single authority. The majority of the intelligence budget and personnel was allocated not to the CIA but to the Department of Defense. It is worth pondering that more than half the seventeen agencies that make up the intelligence community are part of the Pentagon.

Authorities and Interagency Coordination

The execution of covert action has and should remain firmly in the domain of the CIA, with the military playing a supporting though often key role—and vice versa in a war zone. A variety of factors—including legal authorities, intelligence community mandates, and personal relationships—influence who controls such covert actions.

The interplay between the CIA and the Defense Department's intelligence agencies is often described in terms of the authorities under which each agency typically operates. Title 50 of the U.S. Code governs the execution of war and national defense and defines and describes how the government conducts covert action. Covert action, according to Title 50, is "an activity or activities of the United States Government to influence political, economic, or military conditions abroad, where it is intended that the role of the United States Government will not be apparent or acknowledged publicly in a country while deliberately obscuring the hand of the US government."[6] To execute covert action, the president must issue a "finding" authorizing the activity. Once this is accomplished, the implementing agency—to date, this has always been the CIA—and the executive branch must follow a strict set of guidelines for keeping the relevant members of Congress informed. There are specific reasons for these stipulations, the most important being that the president is on record as having explicitly authorized the operation.

Others include maintaining clear oversight of covert action by the intelligence committees of the House and Senate.

The Pentagon has undertaken more covert-style activities through what is known within Washington as "clandestine military activities." These activities, generally authorized by Title 10 of the U.S. Code, look like covert action and are often intended to achieve similar results, but are conducted under different budgetary and oversight requirements. Under Title 10, the Defense Department must report all activities to the House and Senate Armed Services Committees. With a larger number of CIA operations being conducted by Special Operations Forces and other military elements that have been seconded to the Agency, the acts themselves are rarely dramatically different. But issues of authority and oversight leave room for confusion and a tendency to zealously guard and not share information, neither of which is conducive to good policy.

The key to cutting through potential confusion and bureaucratic competition due to overlapping authorities is concerted and clear-eyed leadership. Former CIA director Mike Hayden said of the debate over Title 50 versus Title 10 authority: "It is *only* about congressional oversight; it's not about what happens on the ground. I was the director of central intelligence for thirty-one months and I never argued with anyone about this." Hayden, the only man to head both the CIA (from 2006 to 2009) and the National Security Agency (from 1999 to 2005), added, "It was always, 'How do you want to work this?' I never felt like I was being wronged."[7] Even so, there is little doubt among those responsible for running operations on the ground that the roles and responsibilities of different agencies need to be streamlined and clearly defined.

Outside active war zones, where deniability is paramount and the means and ends are more related to politics and economics than military objectives, the CIA is better positioned to oversee operations. Even outside war zones, the Defense Department has a serious and important role to play, but we need to better integrate these operations to prevent mishaps and ensure that all the instruments of U.S. power are working toward the same ends. The CIA-directed raid by U.S. Special Operations Forces that killed Osama bin Laden on May 1, 2011, is an excellent example of how military capabilities—and Special Operations Forces in particular—can be used to conduct surgical operations with the potential for deniability outside active war zones.

On the ground overseas, the lead on intelligence activities in a foreign country should be the CIA chief of station, who typically represents both the Agency and the director of national intelligence. The chief of station is essential to coordinating the intelligence activities of all agencies, including the National Security Agency, the Defense Intelligence Agency, and others within the Defense Department. Ambassador Frank Wisner, a senior retired diplomat and former ambassador to Egypt and India, describes the confusion often present in U.S. embassies and the ways in which we might be able to improve intelligence operations and oversight: "It is absolutely essential that there be a senior intelligence officer in countries of importance and that they have responsibility over and an ability to deconflict all intelligence activities. If the chief of station believes an operation will endanger the U.S., he or she needs to go to the ambassador or to policy channels and appeal. It is important the chief of station is fully empowered."[8] I have to agree that while the Defense Department brings very important collection and operational capabilities to the table, someone needs to oversee all intelligence operations in a given country, and the CIA chief of station is best positioned to execute those duties.

Flying Under the Radar

Covert action is a large umbrella, covering everything from the kind of political action I was involved with in Chile to the proxy war I helped stage and manage in Afghanistan. The ability to make things happen in secret is something that presidents will always need, and when you are talking about achieving objectives outside war zones, covert action is almost always a highly effective tool. As we draw down in Iraq and Afghanistan, we will need to go back to covert action, with surrogates on our payroll—warlords in Afghanistan and tribal leaders in Iraq—and we may be better off. When you are operating under the radar, you are freer to do things such as hire tribesmen—even those who do not get along with each other—as long as their enemies are our enemies. Many past successes in Iraq and Afghanistan have had as much to do with our buying support from these local leaders as with a large military presence.

There is no military unit in Iraq, Afghanistan, or frankly the world that can ever defeat U.S. forces going head to head. But we were not going to win our most recent two wars on a conventional military battlefield.

Consistent manpower, secrecy, and a workforce groomed over time to excel at clandestine operations are essential to running effective covert operations. Retired admiral Bill Studeman, who served as deputy director of the CIA in the mid-1990s and as director of the NSA from 1988 to 1992, said that covert action depends upon a covert workforce of highly trained individuals "who are recruited and trained for their ability to recruit a foreigner to become a traitor and spy for our country against theirs. The Agency has always had the ability to attract top talent, and it's one of the best workforces in the federal government."[9] The CIA has built an extraordinarily stable system with the necessary infrastructure and organizational experience to efficiently and discreetly execute its duties. U.S. Special Operations Forces and other parts of the military have adopted similar skills, in many cases attending CIA training courses and spending many years in the intelligence branches (as opposed to rotating in and out, as is typical in the military system). Nevertheless, the military system overall maintains a larger tail, which makes it more cumbersome to operate in secret over protracted periods of time. Of course, covert action is not historically what the military was built to do; it was built to fight overt wars against declared enemies.

Certainly the CIA has paramilitary needs, and Special Operations Forces and other military assets should be called in or detailed to the Agency when necessary. The size of our Special Operations Forces, at least once ISIS has been destroyed, should and will likely shrink considerably in the coming years as we pull back from engagements in Iraq and Afghanistan and move back toward greater clandestine activities. Special Operations Forces actually began as an offshoot of the OSS and CIA's Special Operations Division in the post–World War II environment. The "seconding" of military personnel and assets has almost always worked well. In fact, I would argue that when it comes to paramilitary activities outside war zones, this is the primary way the military should be operating on the ground. In places such as Afghanistan, Pakistan, Somalia, and Yemen, we are moving toward a model in which discreet counterterrorism operations will be paired with efforts to co-opt and arm local tribes and other indigenous forces. Thus, to be effective, we will need to continue to integrate the military's capabilities with the CIA's tradecraft and deniability under CIA authorities. The military will continue to have a range of duties assigned to it under its own mandate, including traditional military-to-military advisory activities such as training and equipping foreign security forces. But when it comes to activities we do not want the world to know about, we should do it under CIA authorities and CIA command and control. That, along with intelligence collection and analysis, is what the CIA was built for in the first place. We need to keep those lines clear and distinct.

The next few years in Afghanistan will be an important test case, because soon it will no longer be an active war zone but rather a country in simmering conflict with a vastly reduced U.S. and foreign presence. Because we will no longer be fighting an active ground war there, we should place the remaining limited Special Operations Forces military personnel under the CIA umbrella. This would allow the forces remaining in-country to operate under the radar and work with their partners to keep the situation under control, as well as to report through one single chain of command.

If this model is successfully implemented, there is no reason the CIA and the Defense Department should be at odds with one another in the field. Indeed, in this era of increasing interdependence, there is every reason to think that productive cooperation is ongoing and will increase, albeit more efficiently with clearly delineated roles both within and outside the war zones.

Unmanned Vehicles, Innovation, and Espionage

I remain a strong supporter of the use of drones, given their lethality, accuracy, and stealth, which has leveled the playing field against terrorism. In fact, in many ways we have trumped what was long described as the terrorists' "asymmetrical advantage" through drone technology, which from their perspective is a terrifying and unpredictable capability. They now live in constant fear of being hit by surprise in the false safety of their environs.

For this reason, a great deal of news is dedicated to the use of drones as weapons of attack. But drones can do other things as well, such as conduct aerial location and surveillance on a target and provide guidance to ground troops conducting a mission. Some of these are traditional intelligence missions, while others are clearly in the realm of the war fighter. At the same time, field personnel can find themselves in confusing situations, and redundancies can easily become silos if coordination is poor. If a target is identified and located, the process for approving a strike can be unnecessarily time-consuming and complex without clear lines of authority.

As we think about the varying future uses of drones, clear lines of authority should be delineated, based on how and where the unmanned aircraft are used. The authority for deploying and using drones in war zones against enemy forces is different from that needed to oversee and conduct drone operations for surveillance purposes, or strikes against terrorist targets in areas where stealth and deniability are necessary. There are signs that the Obama administration is attempting to stream-line these procedures, although unfortunately it appears to be doing so in the opposite direction—namely, putting the majority of drone operations under the auspices of the Defense Department. That does not enable such activities to be carried out below the radar and in ways that preserve some level of plausible deniability. We saw this in the case of the CIA program in Afghanistan in the 1980s. The Russians knew the United States was supporting the mujahideen, but because our support involved using surrogates, not U.S. forces, our assistance did not provoke a direct Soviet military response. The drone program has a similar re-quirement for nonattribution. There are benefits to being able to act without forcing a confrontation by deploying U.S. military assets on an-other nation's sovereign territory.

By dividing the responsibilities this way, we can have the best possibil-ity of the military using drones to excel at what they do best, while the CIA can use them to maximum effect in intelligence and covert action mis-sions. One warning with regard to using drones as weapons: intelligence is lost when we kill rather than capture and interrogate suspects. This intel-ligence is often critical to the capture of additional suspects and/or the thwarting of potential attacks. When possible, as recognized by most intel-ligence experts, we should always aim to capture rather than kill.

The official who deserves much of the credit for the decision to invest heavily in drone research and development was James Woolsey during his tenure as DCI from 1993 to 1995. Woolsey himself, when interviewed for this book, described the circumstances under which the program began, which is particularly instructive today as we move into leaner fiscal and budgetary times.

"If times had been flush I might have done what the Pentagon wanted to do, which was implement a several-year, multimillion-dollar research program," he said. "But since I knew we would never get the money, instead we did the research with a very small budget and on an accelerated timeline. So, in a way, the financial problems of the early 1990s were an incentive to move very quickly at very low cost with something that we already had an airframe for."[10]

There are important lessons to be drawn from this story, not only in terms of investing in new technologies, but with regard to how organizations—and the intelligence community in particular—innovate and operate in lean times. "We in the intelligence community actually make our best decisions when we are restricted in our intention with regard to what we're trying to do and as well as in our funding," said Ken Minihan, who oversaw massive chunks of the intelligence community during the very lean late 1990s. "Many people think we see the most progress when funding increases, but actually we see more developments when it's not."[11] There is certainly a danger that decreased budgets will lead to important programs being downsized or eliminated, but there is something to be said for the notion that necessity is the mother of invention.

One way we can avoid letting impending budget cuts lead to stagnation and increased risk is to aggressively take advantage of new technologies, including those being generated in the private sector. As we saw with the Arab Awakening, we will be forced to address the impact of social media and social networking. This technology may only be in its infancy, but its impact cannot be denied, and the ability to mobilize people on short notice around important issues is something we must harness to be effective in the future.

Social networks such as Facebook, and even Internet search engines such as Google, have profoundly changed not only the way the CIA does business but also the very meaning of that business. Part of the CIA's traditional role has been to collect basic facts from the far corners of the globe about all the people, places, and things that matter. Now, however, a great deal of this basic information is being collected for commercial purposes, and that means that what qualifies as "intelligence" worthy of CIA collection is rapidly changing. Randall Forte, who served as assistant secretary of state for intelligence and research from 2006 to 2009, put it this way: "The rise of information searches and data aggregators like Google has led to a world where 90 percent or more of information out there is available from open sources. This dramatically restricts the areas in which clandestinely acquired intelligence is actually value-added and places the intelligence community in competition with open-sourced information. Why spend a billion dollars on a collection program that may deliver the same information as can be had for free on the Internet, only slower and with greater risks?"[12]

I found during my career at the CIA that my enthusiasm for new technology was not always shared by many of my colleagues. But times have changed, and now the CIA has several very large components that focus on data aggregation, exploitation, and analysis, including finding ways to pull pertinent intelligence out of the immense volume of information collected by our rapidly expanding repertoire of platforms. Of course, this type of collection has come under significant scrutiny since Edward Snowden's leak of sensitive NSA memos describing various surveillance platforms in the United States and abroad. With regard to collecting telephonic and Internet data abroad, this type of collection is as old as spying itself; while former Secretary of State Henry Stimson may have said that a gentleman doesn't read another man's mail, the truth is people have been reading one another's mail since the beginning of time. In fact, that is a large part of what the spy business is about, and our allies, despite their objections, are well aware of this fact and engage in it to the fullest extent as well.

I do agree it is a very different matter when it comes to collecting data on U.S. citizens, as I take civil liberties very seriously, whether in matters of privacy or even "targeted killings" of U.S. citizens abroad. And while the type of data collection that Snowden exposed—namely, the collection of origins and end points of phone calls and e-mails (as opposed to content)—is far less invasive than many critics allege, the government needs to be extra careful when collecting it on Americans.

The reality is that "big data" is here to stay, and in order to make sure the government has the information it needs to track terrorists, it needs to sweep up a vast amount of data. But if and when the government believes it needs to retain, organize, or act on such data with regard to a U.S. citizen, it must bring the case to a Foreign Intelligence Surveillance Act (FISA) court and make its case. A worrisome fact that has emerged from the Snowdwn debacle is that of the thousands of such cases that have been brought to a FISA court in recent years, almost none have been turned down. This should lead us to closely reexamine our procedures for granting warrants to collect information on Americans, including considering some kind of ombudsman role to argue the "counter" side of the government's case. *"Quis custodiet ipsos custodes?"*— "Who will guard the guards?"

There is a separate issue related to Snowden that harkens back to my experience with the traitor Aldrich Ames, which is the need to prosecute and punish those who commit acts of espionage to the fullest extent of the law. Whatever Snowden's feelings about the legality or morality of the NSA programs, it is absolutely outside the bounds of our government system to take it upon oneself to publicly expose classified information. Our system is built upon the contracts its employees sign in which they agree to respect the legal bounds by which they are hired, including their duty to protect our nation's secrets. If Snowden felt strongly that he was working on programs with which he disagreed, he had every right, perhaps obligation, to stand up and be heard within his organization, or to resign in protest. But each government employee cannot on his or her own determine whether the information to which he or she is exposed deserves to be made public knowledge or we will face persistent governmental crises.

Snowden's disclosures have done a vast disservice to our government's ability to detect terrorist threats abroad and to collect foreign intelligence on critical national security issues. For this he should be duly punished. Unfortunately, at the moment he is in a jurisdiction in which this is not possible. Should he remain outside the United States, we should take all prudent and available steps to ensure his return so he is adequately addressed by a U.S. civilian court. Not only would this allow the U.S. government to set an example for other employees with access to classified data, but it would also allow the programs that

Snowden exposed to be assessed in an organized, and ideally apolitical, space, as opposed to in the media, where the realities of the operational data lost appear to be largely overshadowed by partisanship and obscured by misinformation.

Snowden aside, from manned and unmanned aerial vehicles to new ways of collecting electronic and telephonic data, it is an enormous challenge simply to glean what is usable from what we collect. Some may argue that Forte's point about the amount of available open-source information does not change the nuts and bolts of their work that much. The lesson here, however, is not that the CIA will be replaced by Google but that the CIA needs to be, and is becoming, smarter about how it does its business so it can continue to provide policy makers with information and insights that no one else can produce. This means embracing technology and evolving with the times so that it can remain a relevant element of U.S. national security in the years to come.

Shifting Missions and Cultures at the CIA

Another impact of impending budget cuts and leaner times ahead is that the government will be forced to operate through less resource-intensive tools. For example, rather than using large-scale military assets to implement policy decisions, we will turn to diplomacy and covert action to protect our interests. Ambassador Wisner described this as a perhaps unintended consequence of a reduced military budget. "As we pull back from direct military engagements and reduce funding for DOD and maintain some degree of diplomatic and intelligence funding, the ship is going to come more into balance," he said. "Not so much by design, but that's the effect."[13]

The recent military focus of U.S. foreign policy to which he refers has had an osmotic effect on the rest of our institutions, including the CIA. Specifically the impact of the two recent wars, and more broadly the war on terror, has been to increasingly construe covert action as paramilitary operations alone. This trend needs to be examined and, hopefully, reset. As previously mentioned, covert action encompasses much more than paramilitary activity and counterterrorism. Political and economic influence was once at the core of what the CIA did, and as this period of active conflict slowly draws down, we should bring our focus back to these critical tools. As former director Hayden has put it, "We need a concerted effort to get back to black," namely, a return to traditional espionage and covert action.

Again, the CIA's necessary focus on paramilitary activity and its shift away from political and economic influence have largely been the result of ten years of war in Iraq and Afghanistan. Wars are all-consuming. This decade of war has created a drift toward militarization of CIA personnel that may make it challenging to get everyone back to the traditional core mission as I have described it. "The increasing emphasis on performing what are essentially military missions may lead to a change in the fundamental ethos of the CIA," said Paul Pillar, a CIA veteran who served as chief of analysis in the Agency's Counterterrorism Center and national intelligence officer for the Near East and South Asia.[14] The CIA has always had an esprit de corps that thrived on innovation, flexibility, and creativity in ambiguous circumstances. It is this ethos that needs to be preserved so that policy makers can use covert action and intelligence as alternatives to outright military intervention or simple diplomacy, rather than merely an echo of one or the other.

Mary Margaret Graham, a twenty-nine-year CIA veteran who served as U.S. deputy director of national intelligence for collection from 2005 to 2008, has also described the effects of the war on how the CIA functions. "War is what it is," she has stated, "but as we get away from the wars, we have to get back to the fundamentals, of spotting, developing, and recruiting. It will take five to ten years after we're done in the war zones, if Vietnam is any model, but current leadership is starting to and will reemphasize the basics."

It is undeniable that we need a clandestine service that can do more than fight shooting wars. Understanding and manipulating the political and economic environment in foreign countries, a core mission of the CIA, is also one of the most powerful ways to protect American interests abroad. And it need not always be geared toward regime change, as many wrongly believe. For example, the operations we undertook in Latin America while I was there were focused on influencing and monitoring government officials for signs that they were moving toward the Communist camp, rather than on fomenting any kind of active opposition. This type of covert action would be—and I hope is right now—very effective in places such as Egypt and Libya, where, in the aftermath of popular revolutions, a complicated political, and, in the case of Libya, military game is under way. The United States should be using covert influence and action to monitor these situations for signs of trouble as well as to subtly promote the interests of our allies and counter the efforts of our adversaries.

In a similar vein, and in part in response to the changes that have occurred since 9/11, another set of reforms, this time inside the CIA, has been contemplated by Director John Brennan based on the success of a new breed of integrated "centers" designed to confront specific threats like terrorism and narcotics. Entities like the Counterterrorism Center (CTC) bring together analytic, operational, and technical expertise to ensure the best that the Agency and the government have to offer is being applied to the most urgent issues in a coordinated and holistic way. The CTC has had enormous success in this regard, and it is a model that can certainly work for particular cases.

Brennan's reported consideration of reorganizing the entire CIA along these lines, however, comes with a series of potentially damaging consequences, the most important being the loss of the CIA's most precious asset: its sophisticated, regional expertise. Current operations need an enormous amount of support, including that of talented analysts and operators who know the country in question inside and out and can engage with it in the most effective way possible. But the CIA also needs to continue to provide long-term, in-depth forecasting and relationship-building with every country around the world.

There is also a cultural component to this shift that could be very challenging indeed. As at any organization, professionals at the CIA have built their careers around a certain structure. That structure should of course be adjusted to be as effective as possible, but you risk a crisis in morale and functionality if the people who make up the Agency feel manipulated or misguided. Changes are frequently required, but they must be taken carefully, and with an eye on the fact that cultural change in any organization is painful and often costly.

More important, if everyone is constantly being thrown at the issue du jour, it makes it difficult to build the right kind of expertise on less pressing areas, and often it is these very areas that turn out to contain the next threat to the nation. Capitalizing on the success of the CTC and other integrated centers is a wise decision, but only if the deep regional expertise among both analysts and operators is simultaneously preserved.

Cultivating Strategies in the War of Ideas

Finally, there is the issue of strategy and how we actually determine what is in our best interest at large. In order to properly direct the CIA as a tool, with covert action as one of its mechanisms, the executive branch needs to be clear-eyed in determining what our country's strategic vision should be in the face of a new set of threats. For too many years we have looked at operations from a tactical standpoint. But what will be more important is looking at how each discrete tactical operation fits into a larger campaign to achieve a specific set of goals. Policy makers will always be forced to respond to the crisis at hand, but simultaneously taking the time to pull together real strategic analysis based on how we reasonably believe the future will look is also critical to any successful foreign policy and the correlated intelligence business. This will become all the more important in the face of the localized political and economic threat environment I've described here.

This applies in particular, but not only, to our current struggle against Islamic extremism, which has been dominated by a tactical response to terrorist acts. It is reminiscent of my experience fighting the drug epidemic in the 1990s, when we vigorously attacked the supply side (production) of the narcotics trade and destroyed many cartels and "kingpins" throughout Latin America. Despite our best efforts and our great success against those producers, we never really stanched the flow of drugs, because it was fundamentally a demand problem. As long as there remained a high-paying demand for drugs, the market would always find entrepreneurial risk takers who would meet that demand for the right price. This cycle could be changed only by our altering narcotic consumption trends in the United States and by lessening the appeal of certain drugs. It is hard to pinpoint why, but in the late

1990s demand started to decrease, especially for cocaine. If I had to put a finger on it, I would attribute the change to the coverage of the theme by mass media, and specifically television and movies, which portrayed drug use as a less "cool" lifestyle, especially for upper- and middle-class Americans. So, essentially, it was the psychological "war of ideas" that portrayed a desperate lifestyle and made drug use a less appealing endeavor. This, rather than our kinetic efforts against the sources of the drugs, eventually changed the trend. This battle continues today, and unfortunately there has been a resurgence among the young in believing that marijuana and other drug use is "cool" again. This belief, and the subsequent increase in demand for drugs, can be deterred only by images to the contrary.

The same dynamic applies today in our fight against terrorism. We have become quite successful and adept at using drones and high-grade technology to kill and dismantle terrorist cells. But much like drug traffickers, the terrorists continue to spawn new recruits because the ideological motivation persists for engaging in violence against the West, its allies, and even other Islamic sects. In order to reverse or at least slow down this trend, we have to face up to the driving force behind Islamist terrorism, which has propelled hundreds of young people to become suicide bombers against targets they consider inimical to their belief system. We are confronting a fundamental difference in a worldview underpinned by political and economic factors, and we must meet it head-on, including using the CIA's covert action capabilities to counter the widely held view that the West is corrupt and bent on destroying Muslims' religious beliefs and culture.

What is required to do this is a robust multiagency program to promote moderate nonviolent leaders, opinion makers, and media outlets in the Muslim world. It is undeniable that the Muslim world itself must take the lead in dismantling dangerous, extremist ideologies, and many moderates from that community speak out loudly against the distortion of their faith these ideologies present. Their efforts should be coupled with an equally robust clandestine program directed by the CIA, drawing on its age-old covert action and influence skills. During the Cold War, the United States and its allies waged a relentless ideological war against the Communists. It was above all a "war of ideas," where selling Western ideas and values played a central and, I would argue, decisive role in the outcome. While the economic failure of the Soviet empire and its retreat from Afghanistan contributed greatly to the Soviet Union's collapse, what inevitably did it in was its failure to win the ideological battle between democratic, free-market economic thought and its authoritative, state-driven economic planning. People across the world were convinced—both through compelling evidence and years of concerted messaging by the West—that communism was a failed system, and they rejected it. With the subsequent loss of zeal and the inability to win over converts to its beliefs, the air was slowly but surely sucked out of the system until it collapsed under its own weight.

Planting the Flag Through Robust Covert Action

Ideas do matter in international struggles as much today as they have in the past. The better ideology almost always prevails, and, to be sure, we hold the stronger ideological hand in dealing with Islamic extremism. It remains my belief, having lived and traveled extensively around the world, that there is an almost universal drive toward freedom, civil liberties, and economic independence. This sentiment flies in the face of today's extremists, who have little regard for any of these values. Their worldview is bankrupt and grossly distorts Islam, one of the world's great religions, which at its core has deeply held tenets about the well-being of families and social structure. It is not a belief system that promotes mindless bloodshed. We should capitalize on this sentiment to the maximum extent possible and push it within the Muslim cultural and religious context using all the tools at our disposal, including covert action.

Some rightfully will point to existing U.S. government programs to promote moderation—the Department of State's International Information and Public Diplomacy programs, Voice of America, USAID funding of foreign media, and even the Department of Defense's strategic communications efforts—to suggest that we are already waging this battle. But even a cursory look will show that it is a very modest effort, and is neither a central element of our strategy to confront terrorism nor even an integrated effort, with different departments promoting different agendas at different times. The funding for these programs is also woefully inadequate. Our strategy instead continues to rest almost exclusively on physically destroying terrorists—a worthwhile goal, to be sure, but not one that will effectively stop the spread of Islamic extremism.

The CIA clandestine mission in this regard should be tasked to "hunt" for and provide support to individuals, groups, social mechanisms, and media outlets that can promote moderate Islamic thought much in the style we did with communism during the Cold War. In that struggle, we promoted many diverse groups who shared a common cause to block communism but who were not expected to sign up to our Bill of Rights or the "American way." Similarly, this effort should target a big tent that incorporates diverse groups with the common goal of neutralizing radical Islam. This program should not and cannot look as though it has a U.S. stamp on it or be made to coincide completely with our belief system; this is precisely why the CIA is the right organization to implement it. It is only on the battlefield of ideas that we will truly be able to reduce the terrorist threat, in turn enhancing our national security and protecting the homeland in the long term.

While I do believe tactical operations have been overemphasized in recent years, it is actually in this very environment, where ideas are supported by subtle, under-the-radar acts, that special operations in the military and the CIA's covert action are really going to come into their own. "While there are some structural things reinforcing a defense strategy based on conventional forces, principally the inertia of having large and highly institutionalized conventional forces," says John Hillen, former assistant secretary of state for political-military affairs, "there is a great attraction to the use of smaller, unconventional forces because of their unique capabilities, and that will likely see an increased reliance on them in the near future." This is no less the case with the CIA and the many options it grants to policy makers. Years ago Ray Warren astutely opined that the strength of the Agency is that "it plants the flag everywhere in the world." I've shared that view unwaveringly for many years, even as its popularity among policy makers has ebbed and flowed. I do believe, though, that we are seeing the beginning of a new period of ascendancy for this approach.

As we march forward in this new century, espionage and "planting our flag" globally will be as important as ever. With limited diplomatic access to places such as Iran, the CIA may provide our best hope if we want to reliably protect global stability. Our ability to run spies inside Iran and other inaccessible countries who can tell us what is happening at the policy levels of the government may end up being the corner-stone for encouraging change in those places. And encouraging change—including regime change where required—is a critical piece of the CIA mission. While regime change is not always the goal of covert action, in cases where large portions of the population are genuinely behind a movement toward revolt, support from the CIA can be the straw that breaks the camel's back, should the right conditions be met.

There is no reason to shy away from support to campaigns of re-gime change. In cases where regime change is a genuine goal of U.S. foreign policy, it must absolutely be in concert with efforts by indige-nous forces. In most cases our activities will look more like support to allied actors, even in nondemocratic states. And if we do not like a government, the worst thing we can do is spark something we cannot finish. This has often led to disaster. We need to be strategic, use our assets as they were designed to be used, and ensure we have a feasible endgame supported by solid collection and analysis before we start stir-ring the hornet's nest.

Even if the pointy end of these endeavors is covert action, we also need espionage, because we should not base our assessments on specula-tion. Drawing general conclusions about a regime's plans and intentions simply isn't good enough. We have to understand what makes the lead-ership tick in order to build effective international action, conduct strong American diplomacy, and create shrewd and prudent covert action plans. We also need to be able to protect our investments and assets abroad. The United States spends billions annually on counternarcotics pro-grams in Mexico and Colombia. Without robust intelligence capabilities, how can we know whether our police and military contacts, which we rely on for information, are on the take and cooperating with our ene-mies? The United States needs to be able to answer these questions in order to smartly act on them.

Indeed, a smarter, leaner, proactive foreign policy with a robust co-vert action program will position the U.S. government best to anticipate and influence major political and security shifts and reduce any major foreign policy surprises. And this gets to the heart of where the intelli-gence enterprise as a whole is going in the future. After all, a smarter, leaner foreign policy rests on a smarter, leaner intelligence community and, more specifically, a robust and empowered CIA covert action strategy. To get to this point, the policy makers and the Agency will need to undertake a series of important initiatives, some of which will mark a return to its past activities, and some of which will break into new territory to keep up with advances in technology and a changing world order.

Postscript

Intelligence is about "hunting"—for information about our enemies as well as for ways to neutralize them. This has been the case in our pursuit of Kansi, Bin Laden, al-Qaeda, the Russians in Afghanistan, and kingpins such as Escobar and the Cali Cartel in Colombia, as well as Russian moles such as Ames and Hanssen within our own national security system. This account points to the CIA's record in bringing these enemies to heel through covert action and in seeking accurate intelligence that protects our country and allows our leaders to make informed policy decisions.

Francis Thompson, the nineteenth-century poet, wrote lyrically in *The Hound of Heaven* about man's seemingly perpetual flight from God. Thompson's language applies to our relentless pursuit of our adversaries in this world: "I fled Him, down the nights and down the days . . . down the labyrinthine ways . . . Across the margent of the world . . ." But in the end, Thompson concludes that man cannot outrun his destiny. So, too, America's enemies cannot outrun the CIA's long reach.

People Consulted

Charles Allen, former assistant secretary for information analysis and chief of intelligence at the Department of Homeland Security

Frank Anderson, former head of the Afghan Task Force

Stanley Arkin, prominent New York attorney

Milton Bearden, former chief, Islamabad

Richard Betts, professor at Columbia University, School of International and Public Affairs

Vinx Blocker, former senior Latin America operations officer

Ed Boring, former senior Latin America operations officer

Brian Bramson, former chief of operations, Counter Narcotics Center

Jay Brant, former senior Latin America operations officer

John Breckenridge, former senior operations officer, Europe

Tim Burton, former chief of logistics for the Afghan Task Force

Morris Busby, former U.S. ambassador to Colombia

Richard Calder, former deputy director for administration

Richard Coffman, former senior CIA officer

Charles Cogan, former chief, Near East and South Asia Division; and associate, Harvard University Belfer Center for Science and International Affairs

David Cohen, former associate deputy director for intelligence

Claude Connelly, former senior Middle East operations officer

Jeffrey Davidow, former U.S. ambassador to Mexico, South Africa, Venezuela, and Zambia

Carol Rollie Flynn, former special assistant to the deputy director of operations

Randall Forte, former assistant secretary of state for intelligence and research

Norm Gardner, former chief of staff to deputy director of operations

Robert Gelbard, former U.S. ambassador to Bolivia and Indonesia and assistant secretary of state for international narcotics and law enforcement affairs

Barry Gibson, former senior Latin America operations officer

Mary Margaret Graham, former deputy director of national intelligence for collection, DNI

Sandra Grimes, former member of the Ames mole hunt team and author

Brad Handley, former senior support officer, Directorate of Administration
Dorothy Hanson, former special assistant to the CIA director
General Michael Hayden, former NSA and CIA director
John Helgerson, former CIA inspector general
John Hillen, former assistant secretary of state for political-military affairs
John Kambourian, former senior Latin America operations officer
Gerald Komisar, former director of Crime and Narcotics Center
Brian Latell, author and former senior CIA Latin America analyst
Kathy Lavinder, founder of Security and Investigative Placement Consultants
Michael Levien, cofounder of LexPro Research
William Luers, Colombia University professor and former U.S. ambassador to Czecho-
    slovakia and Venezuela
David Manners, former senior Middle East operations officer
Lieutenant General Kenneth Minihan, former NSA and DIA director
Hugh Montgomery, former CIA national intelligence officer and former director, Bu-
    reau of Intelligence and Research, Department of State, and ambassador
Paul R. Pillar, Georgetown University professor and former deputy director of the
    CIA's Counterterrorism Center and senior director of intelligence analysis
Thomas Polgar, former chief of station, Saigon
Ted Price, former deputy director of operations
Paul Redmond, former deputy chief of Counterintelligence Center and assistant sec-
    retary for information analysis at Department of Homeland Security
Martin Roeber, former deputy of Counter Narcotics Center and deputy chief of Latin
    America Division
Dr. Marc Sageman, terrorism expert, author, and forensic psychiatrist
Tom Sheridan, former analyst for Afghan imagery, Directorate of Intelligence
Jacqueline Shire, member, United Nations Panel of Experts (Iran)
Admiral William O. Studeman, former NSA director and CIA deputy director
Dr. Kerry Sulkowicz, psychiatrist and founder, Boswell Group LLC
Gerald Svat, former deputy chief, Latin America Division
Robert Thomson, partner, Fortitude Partners
Thomas Twetten, former deputy director of operations
William Wagner, former senior officer, Latin America
Raymond Warren, former chief of station, Santiago
Winston Wiley, former deputy director for intelligence
Robert Williams, former Afghan Task Force military analyst and retired infantry officer
Vice Admiral (Ret.) Thomas Wilson, former director of Defense Intelligence Agency
Joseph Wippl, Boston University professor and former chief of Europe division
Frank Wisner, former U.S. ambassador to Egypt, India, and the Philippines
James Woolsey, former CIA director

Notes

INTRODUCTION
1. Bob Drogin, *Curveball: Spies, Lies, and the Con Man Who Caused a War* (New York: Random House, 2007).

1. INSIDE THE INVISIBLE GOVERNMENT
1. Thomas Powers, *The Man Who Kept the Secrets: Richard Helms and the CIA* (New York: Alfred A. Knopf, 1979), pp. 21–22.
2. "Covert Operations of the United States Government," December 1, 1968, Franklin A. Lindsay et al., Nixon Presidential Library, White House Special Files Collection Box Number 1, Folder 1.

2. MULES, PICKUP TRUCKS, AND STINGER MISSILES
1. Steve Coll, *Ghost Wars: The Secret History of the CIA, Afghanistan, and Bin Laden, from the Soviet Invasion to September 10, 2001* (New York: Penguin, 2004).
2. Endnote in George Crile, *Charlie Wilson's War* (New York: Grove Press, 2003).
3. Interview with Frank Anderson, September 14, 2011.
4. Interview with Bob Williams, August 23, 2011.
5. Clifton Dempsey is a pseudonym. The officer is still serving undercover. He was interviewed on August 27, 2011.
6. Interview with Tim Burton, August 18, 2011.
7. Interview with Tom Twetten, February 13, 2012.

3. "YOUR FRIEND CALLED FROM THE AIRPORT"
1. The declassified documents from this era are collected in Peter Kornbluh, *The Pinochet File* (New York: The New Press, 2003). Kornbluh is director of the National Security Archive's Chile Documentation Project.
2. Ibid., p. 112.
3. Staff Report of the Select Committee to Study Governmental Operations with Respect to Intelligence Activities, United States Senate, Washington, D.C., 1975.

4. Ibid.
5. Thomas Powers, *The Man Who Kept the Secrets*, p. 11.
6. Cables, Santiago Station to CIA headquarters, October 7, 1970.
7. Powers, *The Man Who Kept the Secrets*, p. 237.
8. Nathaniel Davis, *The Last Two Years of Salvador Allende* (Ithaca, NY: Cornell University Press, 1985).
9. David Frost, Robert Melnick, and Richard Milhous Nixon, *"I Gave Them a Sword": Behind the Scenes of the Nixon Interviews* (New York: William Morrow, 1978), p. 84.
10. Kornbluh, *The Pinochet File*, pp. 138–39.
11. Sergio Bitar, *Chile: Experiment in Democracy* (Philadelphia: Institute for the Study of Human Issues, 1986), p. 46.
12. Arturo Valenzuela, *The Breakdown of Democratic Regimes, Chile* (Baltimore: Johns Hopkins University Press, 1978), p. 121.
13. Eden Medina, "Designing Freedom, Regulating a Nation: Socialist Cybernetics in Allende's Chile," *Journal of Latin American Studies* 38 (2006): 571–606.
14. Davis, *The Last Two Years of Salvador Allende*, p. 48.
15. *Time*, December 13, 1971.
16. Peter Winn, *Americas: The Changing Face of Latin America and the Caribbean* (Berkeley: University of California Press, 2006), p. 338.
17. *Time*, October 30, 1972.
18. Davis, *The Last Two Years of Salvador Allende*, pp. 324–25.
19. Interview with Jeffrey Davidow, January 24, 2012.
20. Davis, *The Last Two Years of Salvador Allende*, p. 236.
21. Kornbluh, *The Pinochet Files*, p. 161.

4. "WE NEED TO POLYGRAPH HIM"
1. George Lardner, Jr., "Ex-CIA Official Clarridge Indicted in Iran Arms Case," *The Washington Post*, November 27, 1991.
2. Interview with Charles Allen, September 16, 2011.
3. Pete Earley, *Confessions of a Spy: The Real Story of Aldrich Ames* (New York: G. P. Putnam's Sons, 1997), pp. 173–203.
4. Interview with Charles Allen.
5. Walter Pincus, "CIA Aide Acts to Lift Reprimand; Veteran Officer Was First to Warn of Possible Diversion to Aid Contras," *The Washington Post*, January 1, 1989, p. A6.
6. George Lardner Jr., "Eagleton Says George Hampered Senate Probe; CIA Aide Accused of Lying on Iran-Contra," *The Washington Post*, August 8, 1992, p. A4.

5. "JACK, THIS CHANGES IT ALL, DOESN'T IT?"
1. Interview with Milt Bearden, September 30, 2011.
2. Interview with undercover field officer, August 23, 2011.
3. Interview with Frank Anderson, September 14, 2011.

6. DO I LIE TO THE POPE, OR BREAK COVER?

1. Earley, *Confessions of a Spy*, p. 242.
2. Interview with Hugh Montgomery, August 10, 2011.
3. Earley, *Confessions of a Spy*, p. 213.
4. Ibid., p. 246.
5. Interview with Hugh Montgomery.

7. SELLING THE LINEAR STRATEGY, ONE LUNCH AT A TIME

1. Mark Bowden, *Killing Pablo: The Hunt for the World's Greatest Outlaw* (New York: Penguin Books, 2001), p. 63.
2. Interview with Jerry Svat, January 20, 2012.
3. Interview with Brian Bramson, January 6, 2012.

8. JOUSTING WITH THE SOVIETS: WHEN I KNEW IT WAS OVER

1. Powers, *The Man Who Kept the Secrets*, p. 54.

10. THE ROOSTER AND THE TRAIN

1. Interview with Jeffrey Davidow.
2. Interview with Brian Latell, February 13, 2012.
3. Interview with Ed Boring, February 23, 2012.
4. Interview with Marty Roeber, October 2011.
5. Interview with John Kambourian, February 13, 2012.
6. Interview with Vice Admiral (Ret.) Thomas Wilson, February 27, 2012.
7. Interview with Jay Brant, April 9, 2012.
8. Interview with Jerry Komisar, February 22, 2012.
9. Interview with Robert Gelbard, February 14, 2012.
10. Interview with Jerry Komisar, February 22, 2012.
11. Tim Weiner, "Two Senior C.I.A. Officials Lose Jobs in Spy Case Fallout," *The New York Times*, October 13, 1994, p. 1.

11. RAISING THE BAR

1. Interview with Dick Calder, January 10, 2012.
2. Interview with Carol Rollie Flynn, January 6, 2012.
3. Ibid., February 24, 2012.
4. Ibid., January 6, 2012.
5. Interview with Dick Calder, February 24, 2012.
6. Interview with Admiral Bill Studeman, February 6, 2012.
7. Interview with a former senior Agency official, May 14, 2012.
8. Ibid.
9. Craig R. Whitney, "5 Americans Are Called Spies by France and Told to Leave," *The New York Times*, February 23, 1995.

10. Tim Weiner, "C.I.A. Confirms Blunders During Economic Spying on France," *The New York Times*, March 13, 1996.
11. Gregory L. Vistica and Evan Thomas, "The Man Who Spied Too Long," *Newsweek*, April 29, 1996.
12. Interview with Admiral Bill Studeman.
13. Interview with Dick Calder, January 10, 2012.
14. Ibid.
15. Interview with Dick Coffman, January 11, 2012.

12. UNDISCLOSED
1. David Ignatius, "A Big Man to Watch in Baghdad," *The Washington Post*, February 1, 2004.
2. According to a senior Middle East official.
3. "Bin Laden's Fatwa," PBS *News Hour*, August 23, 1996, www.pbs.org/newshour/terrorism/international/fatwa_1996.html.

14. GOOD HUNTING
1. Jack Devine and Whitney Kassel, "Afghanistan: Withdrawal Lessons," *World Policy Journal*, Fall 2013.
2. Jack Devine, "The CIA Solution for Afghanistan," *The Wall Street Journal*, July 29, 2010.
3. Fredrik Dahl, "Experts Argue over Iran Nuclear Bomb Timeline," December 7, 2001, http://af.reuters.com/article/worldNews/idAFTRE7B620020111207?pageNumber=1&virtualBrandChannel=0.
4. Jack Devine, "Obama's Cuban Message to Moscow," *Politico*, January 12, 2015, http://www.politico.com/magazine/story/2015/01/obamas-cuban-message-to-moscow-114189.html#.VMEILy42Vy8.
5. Interview with Ken Minihan, February 7, 2012.
6. www.fas.org/irp/offdocs/laws/usc50.html.
7. Interview with Mike Hayden, March 23, 2012.
8. Interview with Frank Wisner, March 29, 2012.
9. Interview with Bill Studeman.
10. Interview with James Woolsey.
11. Interview with Ken Minihan.
12. Interview with Randall Forte, December 12, 2011.
13. Interview with Frank Wisner.
14. Interview with Paul Pillar.

Acknowledgments

This is the first book I have written, and I can say without hesitation that it has been a wonderful learning and life experience. That is not to say that there wasn't frustration along the way. While I didn't realize it at the outset, it provided a unique opportunity to reflect profoundly on my professional life and to make sense out of it.

Writing the book also afforded me the unexpected benefit of being able to thank many of my former Agency colleagues and bosses in a more robust way than I had when I worked inside CIA. In that regard, I decided early on to interview many of them and to list them in the book. There were only a very few who couldn't be mentioned because of their cover situation. Sadly, several of these legendary spymasters have passed on since I started this project, three years ago. I'm deeply grateful to all of them for so graciously consenting to participate in the project and for their courageous service to our country.

This project started rather serendipitously. Vernon Loeb, an old friend and journalist with *The Washington Post*, came up with the idea. Several years earlier he had written in his newspaper a Style Section article about me and my time in Chile during the Allende and Pinochet era. I had confidence in him because of his professionalism in handling this story, and consequently was receptive to his suggestion that I expand on this and turn my career experience into a book. He also was aware of my continuing concerns about the CIA mission and the use of covert action as an important tool of statecraft. He also knew that I had been unhappy for some time about what was being written about this subject by non-practitioners.

With that as a backdrop, Vernon introduced me to the Wylie Agency, which worked with us in crafting a book proposal that was circulated among a group of select publishers. Since then Andrew Wylie has been a terrific supporter and promoter of the book.

In response to our proposal, I was delighted when Sarah Crichton at Farrar, Straus and Giroux expressed a strong interest in publishing the book. I can't say enough about her extraordinary encouragement, support, and professional skill in driving the manuscript and the approach behind it—all in a brilliant style. Likewise, it is hard to properly give credit to Vernon, who was the key player in developing the theme and richly editing the manuscript. His editing skills were particularly important when we decided near the end of the drafting to move from a chronological to a thematic approach, which meant manipulating a great deal of information and organizing it into a fluid read. He performed superbly in this challenge.

Stanley Arkin, my partner at The Arkin Group (TAG), and his wife, Suzanne, provided terrific support and contributed many insightful thoughts and suggestions to the text. The TAG staff were amazing in their willingness to give of their time, energy, and intelligence to research data, interview sources, and draft commentary about them and other substantive themes. Whitney Kassel, Amanda Mattingly, Susan Varisco, along with my talented and good-humored assistant, Stephanie Danyi, provided invaluable assistance in whipping this book into shape. Also, Pat Loeb, Mark Christopher, David Segalini, Aaron Springer, and Jorgen Augustenborg played very helpful roles in interviewing, researching, and helping to enhance the text.

I should also note that throughout the project I shared parts of the manuscript with friends and former colleagues as a sounding board about its content and readability. All of them in one form or another offered suggestions, observations, and friendly encouragement. The list is long and I hope I didn't overlook anyone: Marty Roeber, John Hughes, Joseph Grimes, Jami Miscik, Ted Blumberg, Ray Warren, Milton Bearden, Ed Boring, Rachel Beers, Sue Terry, Helima Croft, Jerry Komisar, Carole Corcoran, Gordon Goldstein, Rollie Flynn, Ezra Field, Jim Campbell, and Mary Doran.

Finally, and above all, I wish to express my heartfelt gratitude to my wonderful wife, Pat, for her enthusiastic support of the project and for playing such a key role in molding my career and life. It also is worth underscoring that she was the toughest critic of the manuscript. She studied each word with laser vision to make sure that I "got it right." Her comments were some of the most valuable by far, although delivered in such blunt terms that I had to wince before I laughed. Thank you for everything.

Index